About the Author

Llorens is a physician but, more importantly, a student of individuals who have suffered from obstacles out of their control and excelled in life. He works in a lower socioeconomic community and a student of Stoicism. To center him, he has a lovely family. He exercises frequently, skiing, biking and walking in remote regions. He avoids television and spend his off times reading primarily philosophy. His travels have been to remote regions; Belize, Peru, Costa Rica, Africa and Egypt. He loves exploring and eventually will study more Archaeology.

Vulture's Nest

Llorens Pembrook

Vulture's Nest

Olympia Publishers
London

www.olympiapublishers.com
OLYMPIA PAPERBACK EDITION

Copyright © Llorens Pembrook 2023

The right of Llorens Pembrook to be identified as author of this work has been asserted in accordance with sections 77 and 78 of the Copyright, Designs and Patents Act 1988.

All Rights Reserved

No reproduction, copy or transmission of this publication may be made without written permission.
No paragraph of this publication may be reproduced, copied or transmitted save with the written permission of the publisher, or in accordance with the provisions of the Copyright Act 1956 (as amended).

Any person who commits any unauthorized act in relation to this publication may be liable to criminal prosecution and civil claims for damage.

A CIP catalogue record for this title is available from the British Library.

ISBN: 978-1-80074-584-1

This is a work of fiction.
Names, characters, places and incidents originate from the writer's imagination. Any resemblance to actual persons, living or dead, is purely coincidental.

First Published in 2023

Olympia Publishers
Tallis House
2 Tallis Street
London
EC4Y 0AB

Printed in Great Britain

Acknowledgements

There were many people who were extremely helpful guiding and encouraging me to finish this book. Everyone had to put up with my continuous complaints of rewrites and rewrites, ad nauseum. Special thanks to my lovely family, my wife Frieda, my children Elliot, Devon, Jordan. And my grandchildren, Dominick, Alex and Sarah. Also, thanks to the group of physicians and therapist I have met weekly for three years. They have been supportive, querying, "Where's the book, Llorens?" I have always considered those doctors wonderfully supportive. Thanks to my editor Jennifer Floyd, my proof-writer Joni Wilson and Ghislain Viau at Creative Publishing Book Design who put the final touches on this book and brought it all together. Lastly, I most sincerely wish to thank the veterans who have sacrificed so much for our country. I feel blessed every day knowing those brave men and women are watching our backs.

PROLOGUE

The young boy was startled awake at the sound of his mother's screams and the impact of her body falling hard on the wooden floor. His room was lit from the hallway lights, the dirty gray walls devoid of pictures. The room was caving in on him like so many times before. The walls always did the same thing, and when the terror of the beatings fabricated illusions of the ceiling and walls slowly beginning to crush him, he dared not close his eyes. A succession of screams pierced the air and he could tell the man was dragging her by the hair. Lewis—the man they'd fled from New Orleans to California to escape from and his mother's second violent drunken husband—was back.

The weak floorboards creaked and buckled as he dragged her and slung her body against the wall, causing a horrifying boom as her limp body bounced off the wall. She screamed, the house rocked, and the doors rattled on their hinges. The boy was sure she would crash through the thin corrugated wall at any moment. The man began to strangle her, beat her in the face; she choked and gasped for air. As she fought back, only a faint gurgling noise was audible. The bright red blood the boy had seen many times before was clogging her throat. Lewis had just begun to beat her; the flow of her crimson blood followed more punches to her jaw. The resulting image in the little boy's brain made him nauseated.

As all four walls rocked back and forth, and inched closer again, his head exploded in pain like so many times in the past. His heart pounded as the man screamed.

"Goddamn you, bitch. Come here, come here, you fucking bitch!" His mother screamed with each devastating punch to her face and stomach. Tears streamed down his face and clouded his vision. Another hit and the floor shook, the bed bounced upward. The boy knew the sound that a fist or an open hand created after hearing so many beatings. He could recognize the impact of each part of her body taking the blows. It created horrific and vivid images in his young mind. He now recognized the gruesome noises of bones cracking and lips splitting. His vivid imagination could picture the blood from his mother's mouth bubbling down the sides of her face.

It was all too familiar, too horrible for the boy, and as much as he tried to contain them, soft whimpers crept from his tight lips. *Someone must hear this,* he thought, trembling. How can anyone not hear the screams, the blows, the flying furniture? Where was anyone who could help? Where were the police, where was God?

The boy prayed to make them stop. If he killed her, maybe his pain would stop. Blinding darkness surrounded the boy and he could no longer see the walls or lights from the hallway. For a moment, the blackness seemed to be creeping closer to him. He felt his heart racing, his chest tightened, and he struggled for a breath. Something large crashed in the hallway and pieces of glass exploded in all directions. The light from the hallway lit the tiny slivers of glass on the floor. As before, he felt time in slow motion, but her screams continued and reverberated in his head in haunting echoes.

The ceiling began to lower and the walls crept closer to his bed. He was momentarily startled by a piercing scream, before realizing it had come from within himself. Due to some strange distortion of sound, it seemed to come from someone else.

Another crash soon followed, and a leg from a wooden chair flew into the hallway and ricocheted off the walls into his room. The boy lay perfectly still, frozen; he was terrified to make a sound, the ceiling and walls were even closer. Terror ripped through his tiny frame, and he squeezed his eyes shut, hoping it would end soon. Suddenly it was silent.

He sat up in bed, rubbed the dried tears from his face, and saw slivers of glass all around the room. Soft voices could be heard coming from the hallway along with occasional laughter. He slid off the bed, his urine-soaked pajamas clinging to his legs as he carefully tiptoed past the glass. Beyond the hallway was a small space, which included a compact kitchen and living room.

It was morning now and sunlight began to reflect off the paneled windows. He stood in the hallway, mesmerized at the sight of all the destruction. The floor was spattered with blood, and the walls were smeared with gory handprints. His mind could not comprehend what his eyes perceived.

"Elliot, don't step in the glass, watch out!" his mother startled him. "Come here with me and your brother." She was sitting on the floor. He crisscrossed the room, avoiding the shattered remnants of furniture. His mother's dark brown hair had bloody clumps that matted her skull. He stood in front of her as she held a bloodied towel to the side of her face, barely recognizable. In a muffled voice, she told him to sit down next to her. "Did you just wake up?" she asked.

"Yes," he replied.

She lowered the towel; her tongue was split and hung through swollen lips caked over with dried blood. She blew through her mouth where teeth once were and her flapping lips made a dreadful slapping sound. The left side of her face was swollen and red from the endless volley of blows, and the sockets of her eyes were so puffy that only eggplant-colored slits remained. The boy's vision went black and his head fell to his chest.

She caught him before he passed out, grabbing his hair and arching his neck back in a painful jerk.

CHAPTER ONE

Lumas frequently wrote to his grandparents. It was a comforting act and whenever he did so, he felt safe again. He felt the warmth of their hugs, as well as the glow of their smiles and nurturing presence whenever he spoke with them, pen in hand. But he never sent the letters, both Grandmother and Grandfather died many years ago without ever seeing Lumas after his mother forcefully snatched him. He did not realize until many years later, and an insurmountable number of night terrors, that having lost them so early in life affected his whole perception of himself. A child's brain is nothing more or less than a blank chalkboard, an emotional being that should be caressed into a caring person, loving themselves foremost. Everything else, self-esteem, self-respect, intuitive curiosity, mindfulness, all are the consequences of an affectionate childhood.

Dear Grandparents,
I hope to push the anger off my chest as I write. I am in the fight for my life and I am emotionally shattered. I am now a doctor, but I feel so distraught, lonely, and ashamed, I dare not share my feeling with anyone for fear of being completely ostracized from my colleagues. Whether I am right or wrong, being exposed is what I fear the most. I started medical intern- ship training and I am not doing so well. I think a physician named Jeremy is trying to fire me from the training program and I do not know what to do or how to survive. Being a doctor has meant so much, maybe too much. Please, help me, pray for me, hold

my hand. I need you both so much now. You were all I had to depend upon in life.

I will share all that has happened to me over the years. Life has been so lonely. I had to get a job the day I graduated from grammar school. She made me. Not because we did not have food on the table, I was simply expected to carry my own. So, I bought TV dinners, sliced hot dogs and beans, and ate late in the evening when everyone was asleep. I didn't mind the solitude, at least it was quiet and I didn't have to hear how worthless I was, I am.

She beat me mostly when her anxiety was out of control, which was always. She hit me so hard once I fell into a window and shattered it. I cannot remember one day when we enjoyed a sit-down dinner together, not even at Thanksgiving. I do not feel a bit pitiful for myself, although those early days were very lonely. I realized later in life that I was depressed and still am. But also I realized that everything in life is relative, and I could have been born in an underdeveloped country where people survive on pennies, and mothers struggle to keep their babies from dying from starvation or diseases. I try to think in those terms when I feel sorry for myself.

For the same reason, I avoid the doctors' lounge because the older guys have the stock report on all day, and they bitch about their retirement accounts. It is obnoxious and I have very little in common with them.

I worked odd jobs, doing janitorial work, bussing tables, washing dishes—anything I could get. It was okay, at least I could pay my tuition, bus fare, and had a few bills left over for clothes. Shoes were a bit more difficult; I stretched my budget by having one pair of sneakers. When the soles wore out, I covered my feet with sandwich wrap until I could afford the next pair. At that time, there were not these perfectly shaped plastic bags for sandwiches, so wax paper and tape sufficed. At least that kept my feet dry.

Around age thirteen, I met Juan who lived down the street from me. We became incredibly good friends for years, and one day, graciously, his father gave us a job after school. We cleaned a Chinese restaurant after closing at the farmers' market. That job was fun. We could finish washing the pots in lightning speed, then spend the next hour having a fruit fight with the neighboring crew. By the end of the night, we smelled of oranges and peaches, my favorite choices because their size and symmetry delivered a nice curveball. The introduction of seasonal fruit ignited excitement, and the aerodynamics of fresh cantaloupes stretched the imagination.

I floundered throughout high school and struggled to keep my GPA above 1.9. I cared mostly about getting through the weekdays to party. Mom did not know about my high school debauchery. She probably wouldn't have cared anyway, other than missing opportunities to perfect her blows. I kept my grades to myself and intercepted the mail carrier many times. Mom was not worried about me as long as I had a job and went to school. Occasionally a teacher would reprimand me for not caring about my grades. That went in one ear and out the other. I really did not give a damn.

Toward the end of high school, I thought about joining the Navy and traveling the world, but I knew that with only a high school diploma I'd be indefinitely mopping the deck. I just wanted to get away, except from my friends. What kept me going were parties, work, sports, and books, for which I always had a passion. Books took me away from everything, everything except the ghosts of depression, that is.

Thank God, I had a group of good buddies. We had family similarities, which probably strengthened our friendships. I think it also may have been something very subconscious. We spent Saturday nights partying in South Central Los Angeles. Those times were fun, distracting, and often extremely dangerous. Do not be upset with me, please. I needed friends and they were my only family. I will admit that things did get scary at times. Once we were at a party, a line formed at the front door to leave around two or three in the morning. At that time, we were asking for trouble. The crowd was slow to move till I saw two men with guns ordering the next in line to move up. Just like at McDonald's, the line moved forward, we emptied our pockets and the cycle continued with the next person.

Another night, we were sitting in a car outside (yes, another party, and yes, again at three in the morning). The guy in the back seat finished his cigarette and flicked the butt at an oncoming car. We tore out in laughter as the ashes exploded in all directions. This, we thought, was hilarious until that unmarked police car did a three sixty and ordered us out with our hands up. We sat on the curb while they tore the car apart looking for drugs. They didn't find anything to satisfy their thirst but accomplished scaring the hell out of us.

In that area, the cops were all white and trigger-happy ex-Marines. After three and still partying, we went to the street races. These took place in alleys, usually located in industrial areas. We knew the police were constantly on alert to find the location, so it changed weekly. This night they caught us. However, there was enough room in that alleyway to creep in a corner and hide. That approach was all good till the helicopter flew overhead and flipped on the spotlight.

That night we learned how to dodge, circle, and outrun that light. We sprinted from one dark corner to the next. The pilot was probably really pissed off, because as often as he circled, he couldn't get us in the open. To hell with him, he was probably another white guy who enjoyed scaring the neighborhood thugs, only that time it didn't work. It was easy to avoid the light and hysterically fun.

At his altitude, we could anticipate his turns. When he went forward, we followed his tail, left, right, even circling. We were so fast, he probably wanted to just start shooting randomly at the ground. The fact is we could never outrun him or successfully hide in corners for long, but if he had little room to maneuver his light, such as in the relatively small space of an alley, we were safe.

Our maneuvering was reminiscent of a video of a great white killer shark frantically trying to devour a seal. The seal had a tactic and just grabbed the dorsal fin of the whale and hung on. At other times, it would swim close to the shark and mimic its turns with lightning speed. Eventually, the shark ceased its attack, giving the seal ample time to dive and hide in the rocks below. It's good for me to write. I read the works of a Roman emperor by the name of Marcus Aurelius who wrote prolifically to himself. I will write you often. If an emperor can write to himself, maybe I won't feel so insane.

The truth is that sometimes I want to die. I have had a taste of happiness on only two occasions in my life. With both of you and when I was young running the streets, when friends were family, so I stayed gone from home as much as possible. I loved playing sports, any sports. It kept me and my friends out of trouble, some of the time. Jerome was another best friend and a gifted athlete. He was the strike-out king and terrified batters with a speedy fastball and, if necessary, a beanball. He didn't want to cripple anyone, it just scared the hell out of batters, like having a gun pointed at your face.

He lives in a box somewhere in downtown Los Angeles now. I don't know just where or I'd deliver him food sometimes. His father was a big man and exercised his authority by beating the shit out of Jerome. I saw his anger too many times, usually during one of his countless drinking binges. In spite of this, Jerome never spoke harshly of him. Except one night, when the drunk lunged at me for yelling at him to stop beating the shit out of Jerome. Jerome hit him from behind then screamed, "You muthafucka!" His old man hit the floor with a thud, he was out cold. After that, Jerome spent most of his time at my home although that was not much better.

Anyway, I slept in a converted room in the garage, we shared it together, and at least we were safe with a heavy bolt, which we had nailed to the door. Mama was not much different than Jerome's father although she did not need the alcohol to hit me. It did not take much to unravel her anxiety into verbal and physical assault. So, we locked the garage door. After a while, the run to the door became pathologically humorous, we would laugh and taunt her till she was tired of pushing and screaming. Sports was our out, out of home, out of sight. And baseball was our god. Of course, neither of our parents ever came to the games, but that was okay since their attendance would probably have distracted us. Besides, we had one another—me, Jerome, Juan—and we were the best of friends. Playing sports still centers me to this day, however, the positive effect doesn't last very long. The times we weren't playing sports, we created entertainment for ourselves. Jerome usually initiated the details, generally starting as a humorous prank with the requisite danger factor. Stealing fruit was a favorite; the trees hung over fences in alleyways all through the neighborhood. Picking fruit over a fence was not difficult; the danger factor was climbing over the fence and taking it in the backyard. Our bikes were used as ladders to scale the fences into the yard, but the exit plan was to be determined.

It was becoming too easy, until an old Afro-American woman and her Chihuahua caught us. She sprinted out her back door, swinging a broom and screaming, "You little sons of bitches, you little muthafuckas!" I could not stop laughing as she ran after us. The old woman could move, she was quick, and the odds were definitely in her favor.

It was a small backyard with not much room to maneuver and her Chihuahua bit at our ankles. She was so mad; spit dangled and flew off the sides of her mouth. In desperation, Jerome charged and destroyed her fence, bringing it down into large chunks of wooden planks. We never stole fruit from her again, although that didn't stop us from moving on to other fertile territory.

We advanced to near-death experiences when Jerome got a driver's license and created "Egg Night." An hour without mischief was pushing our collective impatience. So, we "borrowed" a station wagon and loaded it up with twelve dozen eggs. We created a two-phase plan: first do the deed, and second escape. Timing was crucial.

Our first targets were two military personnel, uniformed guys walking out of a liquor store. Jerome slowly closed in, careful not to attract too much attention. As far as anyone was concerned, we were just a bunch of kids in a junky old station wagon. About twenty feet was the preferred distance; we were excellent baseball players and within that range we could decapitate butterflies. Jerome shouted, "Now!" and twelve eggs flew out the windows with precision and deadly accuracy, hitting both men in their chests. By the time the targets ran to their car, we had pulled into an empty alleyway and hit the floor.

Afterward, we drove down dark streets, headlights off, looking for Good Samaritans. We were rather treacherous and intentionally exploited their benevolence. One gentleman leaped off his porch and yelled out, "Hey, your fronts light are not working." He was toast. The guy probably never walked the neighborhood at night again. We considered excellent timing, teamwork, commitment, focus, precision, and accuracy a matter of both pride and stature.

South Central Los Angeles was, and still is, in a constant state of war. I worked at a local drive-through roach trap and learned how to flip burgers and throw hot grease in self-defense. And on top of that, we almost got killed many times. We had no business walking down those dark streets, in that neighborhood, after partying and looking for open liquor stores. Once, a clerk mistook us for being with three guys who just robbed him. He took out a gun. We panicked and ran, in the wrong direction, the same direction as the robbers.

I zigzagged, trying to keep my sides in sight rather than my back. I was much thinner in those days, which made for a more difficult target. Bullets skimmed the concrete underneath my feet and pinged as they ricocheted off concrete walls. I ran past a man who looked at me as if to ask, "Why are you running, kid?" Then I heard the thud. I have never forgotten that sound, it was horribly similar to a boxer slugging a punching bag, it was terrifying then and now. When I finally stopped running, my clothes were covered with blood.

Grandparents, that was the most terrifying night of my life. I think I grew up that night. Right or wrong, I think a man lost his life because of my irresponsible behavior. And yet, at the same time, I know I was only in the wrong place at the wrong time. But I will never forget that night.

Fast forward, Jerome's ghosts led him to using cocaine, then he just disappeared one day, gone. He was here one day, my best friend, and gone the next. I dared not go to his home, his father would kill me. And no one knew anything more than me.

Eventually, many years later, I received a call from an emergency room asking if I knew a, "Jerome." He had used my name as next of kin and was being treated for an altercation. The emergency room physician described him as haggard and homeless as well as stoned. That was the last time I heard anything. That was over thirty years ago.

His father was shot dead during a hold-up, drunk. Like the fool he was, he refused to give up his wallet. Unfortunately, they did not decapitate him first.

I'll write again soon.

Elliot.

CHAPTER TWO

The VA Medical Center was one of the largest in the country and built close to the downtown area. The outside of the hospital was well-maintained, with one towering main building and five smaller ones built perpendicular to the center structure. The grounds were beautifully designed and manicured. But the aesthetics ended there. The main entrance was littered with a mass of veterans parked haphazardly in wheelchairs blocking the doorway. Others sat on the ground or on two rows of large planters on both sides leading to the foyer.

The air was heavy with clouds of smoke, and discarded cigarette butts cluttered the pavement. Inside the lobby was not much different, except the vets were not allowed to smoke there. Their age group was a decade older and they appeared exponentially sicker than the younger homeless men outside, most of them waiting for the free noon lunch. A few men were having indignant rows with a tree or a signpost. For the most part, the other vets ignored them and kept pace with the line that crept forward slower than an undulating snail. Forty-five gray plastic chairs lined the walls of the rectangular waiting area. Another twenty faced the walls, forming the inside rectangular seating arrangement. Some of the men held their heads and arms in tripod positions, their skin ashen, with nasal cannulas inserted in each nostril attached to oxygen tanks in cylindrical metal dollies. A few had nasogastric tubes clamped at the ends pinned to their gowns or shirts.

Photographs of three smiling presidents and unknown administrators hung here and there. The walls were painted glossy light blue. Numerous handprints were visible and multidirectional scuff marks were scattered across the linoleum floors. There was a closed sliding-glass partition above a narrow mantle with pamphlets of attractive men and women in smart military uniforms. Ventilation was poor, and as a result the seated men were clammy and uncomfortable. The smell of urine permeated throughout the entire first floor and janitors stood oblivious to the stench.

Lumas could never understand why the government was indifferent. Military dogs were treated sounder when retired. He surmised the military leadership was either unaware or didn't care about the plight of these men and women who had served their country with distinction. All of the medical staff knew VAs were top heavy with nonmilitary Washington administrators who rarely, if ever, visited the hospitals.

As he made his way into work, past the familiar old scene, he thought once more of how these vets were lost. Some were severely depressed, some suffering from posttraumatic stress disorder (PTSD), some running from their ghosts. All were looking for a hand, not a handout.

CHAPTER THREE

Lumas and Dino were new interns, grunts told to keep their mouths shut. Don't question the attending professors, "the bosses," don't think too much, and especially don't procrastinate. The first year was structured for interns to learn by osmosis, not by analyzing or studying like in medical school. The assumption created by a pathological narcissist—the more demanding the internship year, the more one learns. If the novice survives, of course.

They hit it off well from the beginning of the year, enjoyed working together, and split the patient load evenly. If Dino was behind, Lumas would help and vice versa. At night, they rotated four-hour shifts to cover emergency room admissions, so that at least each would get some rest. They shared similarities, both respected the vets and detested their boss, Jeremy Reddins.

The day Lumas had opened the letter of acceptance from the internal medicine training program, he was terrified. He feared he exhibited incompetence and insecurity at the initial interview. He believed he would never be considered a viable candidate for a program that groomed academicians and researchers. Intellectually, he knew his psychological pathology was a result of a dysfunctional childhood and adolescence. But acknowledging the damage was the easy part, climbing out of the pit of depression was the challenge.

A viciously cruel and powerful subconsciousness is also cunning, deceptive, demeaning, and agile. Given the opportunity, it destroys all semblance of self-respect, and if left unchecked, irreversibly reprograms the brain. The streets were filled with Lumass living in tent cities. He saw them daily on his drive to the hospital and sometimes wondered which corner he would inherit. Maybe he'd finally meet up with Jerome again, he mused, though deep down he knew that Jerome was most likely dead.

On that morning, Lumas stood at the side of a patient's bed and tried to look confident. A farce, he shook inside seeing a man dying. He couldn't and wouldn't make eye contact with anyone, especially not with the patient. He had no knowledge of what to do to palliate the symptoms of this man who was suffering to death. He could feel the man's loneliness and terror and was distinctly aware of the twelve other veterans who stood close and observed their every novice attempt to improve the man's condition. Dino stood next to Lumas; the room was tense as the other vets became agitated by the scene. Lumas felt emotions escalate into anger. He knew that Dino felt the same. Their boss Jeremy, however, seemed entirely indifferent to the horrific scene.

The young Afro-American man had previously been diagnosed with incurable lung cancer and took a turn for the worse that morning. His lungs were already filled with tumors, but overnight the cancer spread to the lining around his heart and squeezed his ventricles, restricting blood flow, which backed up in his lungs.

The vet's eyeballs seemed to protrude from his sockets, another clinical sign his lungs were filling with blood and now overflowing into his brain. The pressure in his arteries and veins was rising, and he began to lose consciousness. His eyes were now popping out of their sockets like a fish pulled from the ocean floor. Beads of sweat formed on his forehead and began streaming down his face. He began to froth at the mouth. The man grasped Lumas's hand and squeezed tightly. Lumas held on.

Jeremy caught the scene through the corner of his eye but did not acknowledge it. He had no clue what could be done, even though he was a boss, and he panicked. Additionally, he was dumber than the president and slower than a slug. Lumas felt the man's hand began to loosen its grip. Dino and Lumas slowly laid him back on the bed. The other vets watched intently, sadly.

Jason, another boss, jogged into the room. He was smart and cool mannered, much more respected by the grunts. Someone had obviously called him. Immediately upon seeing the vet, he lost his temper.

"Dino, take this man's vital signs," he seethed, clearly livid.

"No, I'm in charge here," Jeremy argued.

"He has no pulse or blood pressure," Dino answered.

"C'mon, Jeremy, what the fuck were you doing? This guy needed blood drained from around his heart. That's called the pericardium, if you forgot, dumb shit. What the fuck have you been doing besides playing with your..." Then he stopped.

Jason realized his anger had no significance and would not change the situation. In fact, the last thing the other vets should see were two doctors screaming at each other over the bed of their dead friend and comrade.

Jason was a virtuous man, mostly never losing his calm demeanor and commitment to teach younger physicians. He was a large man of color, an ex-college football running back. Lumas had intense respect for him. He knew in this situation, all possible control, which would have been to palliate the vet's distress at end of life, was lost. Shouting and showing lack of temperament and empathy was a vice, not a virtue. Lumas had seen other professional athletes with a similar demeanor.

Jeremy was the opposite of Jason, with a short stature and Wonder Bread white skin. He was barely respected because he whined all the time. He constantly needed to prove his medical knowledge. Being obnoxious, vicious, and demeaning hid his insecurities, although glaringly obvious with the grunts and patients. Physicians in the program tolerated his behavior, most were too involved in the care of patients, their own research and/or didn't care. Either way, for the professors he served a purpose, less work for them. Every training program has a Jeremy.

Jason spoke softly so as not to upset the vets even more. "He's dead, Jeremy."

"Don't touch my patient. I am in charge here!" He turned and walked out the door. "I am getting Dr. Chow. He'll agree my treatments were correct. Don't touch him."

Jason put his hands in both pockets and took a deep breath. "Lumas, go get a five-inch needle and a twenty-cc syringe."

Lumas took a step back. "Jeremy's going to kill me."

"Yup, that's why I want you to get the stuff and do the procedure.

Get some balls and stand up to that prick. Now go," he barked.

"Oh, shit, I'm dead," Lumas said.

Jason turned to the room of vets. "Officers, gentlemen, we are so sorry for the untimely death of your friend and comrade. We have no excuses for the care given. We all knew, and you all knew, this officer was dying of lung cancer. Although his dying symptoms were poorly treated, he was dying, nonetheless. On behalf of those physicians who respect the service you have done for us. We apologize for this officer's suffering to the end. I promise you that we who care about your health will try in our hearts to do better," he said with sincerity. "Now with someone's permission, I must demonstrate to the younger doctors the procedure that may have lessened his suffering." A voice spoke from the back of the large room behind a cubicle covering a corner bed. "You have our permission, Doc. We'd request Dr. Lumas, please."

With that, the vets returned to their beds.

Dino and Jason turned to Lumas with instruments in hand.

They both stared at him.

"What, what did I do this time?"

"Nothing, you're doing the procedure," Jason informed him softly. Lumas looked perplexed.

"But—" Lumas began to protest.

"No buts," Jason stopped him. "Let's proceed."

The nurses cleaned up. The vets watched as the dead man was lifted on a gurney and taken to the morgue. The ward remained quiet for the rest of the day.

CHAPTER FOUR

Lumas read the major medical journals; he had a natural interest in science and enjoyed dissecting articles. On a roll, he could read five journals daily and complete all his patient rounds before noon.

He had other unhealthy reasons to study at every opportunity, namely fear that he'd fail his internship. He suffered major bouts of depression and anxiety, had difficulty focusing, and generally felt lonely and disconnected. His sleep was disturbed by frequent nightmares, but he rarely, if ever, recalled details. Occasionally, there were good days, but the majority of his existence consisted of long stretches of introspective periods. He found some peace by burying himself in the medical literature, however, when challenged he still struggled.

The next morning, Lumas and Dino sat in the doctors' lounge charting.

"Dino, what do you think of yesterday's fiasco?" Lumas enjoyed edging at Dino, pushing him to the point where he began to rev up his tone and his voice filled with righteous indignation, like a politician without a microphone. "I can't forget the look on his face before he crashed. What do you suppose the vets were thinking?"

Dino looked at him. "Probably that we're a bunch of heartless assholes."

"I think the same. We should apologize to them. They never said a word, never complained."

Dino stopped writing, sighed, and sat back. "These guys see us running around like chickens with our heads cut off. I think they generally feel the grunts do their best under the circumstances. At private hospitals, the staff have ancillary personnel to do the scut work, but these guys see us crawling out of bed at three in the morning. That is not to say they don't have lots to complain about, but the interns aren't one of them. However, that scenario yesterday was insensitive and undignified, maybe one day we will see some changes and not just here. But the vets' hospital is at the far end of the bell curve. The way we are taught to treat dying patients is immoral."

"Educating the public, that is the only way healthcare changes."

"Before we were doing all this techno medicine, families took care of Mom, Dad, or kids at home before they died. But now we isolate them—we have *visiting* hours," Dino said, his lips twisting in sarcasm. "People live longer but not better. I get it that medicine can cure some stuff but not to the extent that people think. It's a cruel lie and it ain't TV," he continued.

"I think a lot of the end-of-life stuff we do is worthless—shocking an octogenarian, or one of those guys in the ICU who's near death already? Give me a break, that's fucked up. We just torture them!" Dino took a breath. "Do you remember that guy who stopped breathing a couple weeks ago, the guy with alcoholic cirrhosis?" he asked.

"Yeah, he was the younger guy who was yellow from head to toe," Lumas recalled.

"Remember the pastor? He nearly knocked me down running to this guy's bedside. He grabbed this guy's hand and said, 'You're not alone. God is with you,' then he prayed, right there. That took some balls."

"I remember a few people laughing about him later," Lumas broke in.

This time Lumas couldn't see Dino's eyes roll back in his head as he flipped his chair around from Lumas.

"See, that's my point. How many good deaths do you remember?" Dino asked. Without waiting for Lumas to answer, he went on. "The majority of the time we beat the hell out of these vets, especially the ones in the ICU. The majority of them are older than dirt, Lumas. That's not just here, it's all over the country. By the time we go into the real world, we're numb, people don't die, they *expire*. We're slave labor, and they don't give us time to grieve. No, grief is strictly verboten, *unacceptable*," Dino emphasized, his voice rising several decibels. "I want to expire with my middle finger up to academicians. If I die prematurely, please glue my finger in the fuck-you position."

Lumas didn't laugh. He was confused and felt guilty. Dino had never raved like this before, never blasted medicine. It unnerved him. "I get it, Dino. I feel like a bozo. I never gave any of this much thought."

"I rest my case, here comes the asshole," Dino muttered under his breath, getting in a last word.

Jeremy walked in, calmly sat, and waited for them to speak first.

"It was a quiet night, no disasters. We didn't have to call you," Lumas began.

It was considered unacceptable to call the attending physician at night except for the most extreme circumstances. Especially Jeremy, who was even more obnoxious if awakened. If he thought he was unduly disturbed, someone would get a mouthful of childlike berating. The interns described his behavior like a baby needing a diaper change.

They knew what to expect next—the offhand, out-of-nowhere question.

"Did you both finish everything as I instructed before crashing?"

Dino knew the best way to answer was with a succinct one-word response, never an open-ended answer.

"Everything," he confirmed.

"Lumas, did you get a syringe yesterday for Jason?"

Lumas took a deep breath and felt a rush of warm blood go to his head. Jeremy knew interns had to follow orders but he felt belittled and disrespected. He needed to punish someone.

"I had no choice," he said, feeling trapped.

"I didn't ask that," Jeremy disapprovingly clucked. "Yes," Lumas said in resignation.

"Why?"

"You were gone. Jason told me to get it."

"Who is your boss? I repeat, who is your boss, who do you work for?"

"What was I supposed to do?"

Jeremy's voice rose as a group of nurses exited the nearby lounge. "Say it. Who do you work for, him or me?" He was careful to refrain from naming Jason. One or more of the nurses were undoubtedly sleeping with him.

Lumas was devastated. He had no special intuition on how to handle an assault other than physically. "You," he said, his voice small. "Don't forget it again," Jeremy said, getting up to leave. His face now a self-satisfied sarcastic smirk.

For the rest of the day, Lumas wanted to hide in a closet. It was impossible to function. He ate lunch alone and plowed through his work, avoiding Dino. He left the medical floor and headed for the front lobby. He always stopped there and sat on the stairs behind a pillar. He felt some temporary peace in that corner. He was lonely, nowhere to go, and no one to be with. Maybe he was hoping someone would suddenly materialize and take away all the hurt, all the years of loneliness, dejection, and abandonment.

He only wanted some peace in his life. Instead, his brain stalked him endlessly, always screaming in his mind that he wasn't worthy of anyone, anything, or any achievements. It was all so cruel, a sick merciless hoax. His mind raced out of control as his subconscious blocked every attempt to logically move to more positive thoughts, but he was unable to control the deception. He was a prisoner of his past, his insecurities, and his ego. The jailer, his subconscious, was too powerful and viciously brutal.

He obsessed on a new life, one without pain, but the escape never materialized. The predator was waiting for an opportunity to lunge and end his life, but not too soon. It was the enjoyment of the hunt, the incessant pleasure of his subconscious, the jailer controlling him, the prisoner, exhausting his energies, until, of course, the chase was no longer enough to entertain it.

He hated his thoughts, the torturer seemed so much stronger than him. Lumas was losing the battle and he knew it. That was the worst, to be an observer of his own conscious destruction. He was still that terrified, abandoned child whom no one loved and who couldn't love. He needed to forgive himself first. But how could he forgive the jailer? At least the jailer was always his constant companion.

CHAPTER FIVE

He was averaging four to five hours of sleep per night and frequently drank one to two martinis and ingested fifty milligrams of Elavil, which he had conned another physician into writing, lying that he had a painful neuropathy. The following day started in a fog—he couldn't concentrate, had little-to-no energy, and hated himself. He struggled through the day, frequently sleeping when he could find an empty room and avoided new admissions to his team. One of the instructors sent an evaluation to the chief of medicine stating his concern that Lumas was stressed and depressed. The chief sent him a copy and wrote, "Take care of this Lumas" in bold print. He expected little else from the chief, who seldom got involved in day-to-day interactions with the staff; he was clueless. Jeremy received a copy of the evaluation as his immediate chief; he thought that simply perfect. More ammunition to fire Lumas eventually. Lumas knew Jeremy didn't respect his clinical skills and took every opportunity to berate him, the larger the group, the louder the criticism.

Despite his insecurities, he did not understand why Jeremy hated him so much. It began from the very first time they met and prior to working together. Everyone could see Lumas was in his crosshairs. Jeremy was relentlessly successful at having new interns fired soon after beginning the grueling first year of internship, often fabricating the extent and severity of a misdiagnosis or treatment plan.

He did not divert attention to gain favoritism. Jeremy enjoyed chaos, believing he alone could save a sinking ship. He needed sacrificial lambs to create an atmosphere of fear and anxiety. Physicians-in-training would follow his preaching or succumb like Lumas. Patients hated him also, but VA patients had no options to choose their doctors. Complaints were ignored. Jeremy was impatient, rude, and a disrespectful, sloppy diagnostician who preferred reviewing studies to using a stethoscope.

"Come on, let's go!" Jeremy barked at them. He was ruder and more caustic than usual, in rare form.

"Did you round this morning, Lumas, or were you late again?" That was an unfair assumption. Despite his nightmares, he always arrived earlier than the other staff. It took him a couple of hours and three cups of coffee but he finished rounds, wrote orders, and prepared for the worst from Jeremy. This time, he didn't care.

Lumas daydreamed of decking him unconscious.

"I'm finished." He closed down the conversation before Jeremy found an in.

"What about the new patient?"

There it was—Jeremy checked the morning schedule and had transferred a vet to Lumas's service without informing him.

"Did you see him or not?"

Jeremy's tactics were not different, just refined over the years. Usually, he would give the intern time to evaluate a new patient, then vociferously disagree with the diagnosis and treatment plan, always in a forum. Now he added irresponsibility to incompetence. Jeremy had to turn up the heat on Lumas, the new doctors were three-quarters closer to finishing. So far, he hadn't been successful in manufacturing the lies needed to get him fired. This group of interns covered each other's asses too well, and it infuriated him.

"We didn't know there was a new admit."

"What do you mean *we*? It's no one else's responsibility but yours."

Dino stepped in. "He wasn't on the schedule this morning. I checked myself."

"Lumas should have checked the schedule himself," Jeremy retorted.

Dino didn't back off. "What difference does that make? There was no new patient on this morning's schedule."

Jeremy did not like to butt heads with Dino. He didn't intimidate easily.

"Can he speak for himself?"

Lumas was enjoying this too much but he was also embarrassed. "He should have checked with the charge nurse this morning, there's no excuse."

"We did, she did not have a report of a new admit."

That was a lie, but Dino knew the nurses would cover them. "Ask her yourself."

Dino's demeanor changed from conciliatory to defiant.

Jeremy had nowhere to go, all his options were blocked. Reporting this altercation would only make him look foolish and lose credibility.

His face was pale as he took a step back, feeling more fearful than embarrassed.

Dino smirked.

Jeremy turned and quickly walked toward the wards. He needed revenge.

He announced his rank as "the chief", entering the twelve-bed ward. Vets were in various areas, sitting beside their beds or milling around with others. There was no privacy or creature comforts like televisions, radios, or even windows. All looked curiously at Jeremy as if he wanted them to stand at attention.

"Who of you is Grossman?"

A vet in the corner raised his hand; he looked not older than twenty-five. He was unkempt, unshaven, oily, and his shirt was inside out and missing buttons.

Jeremy walked toward him. "Stand up."

The vet's face was blank, as though he didn't understand.

"Up," Jeremy repeated louder, his tone now sarcastic and condescending. He jerked two thumbs up.

The vet logrolled and stood. "What's your name?"

Dino and Lumas were confused and uncomfortable, the vet did not understand Jeremy.

Jeremy's voice rose, the other vets looked on, their body language communicated disdain for the spectacle.

He continued. "Look at me. What is your name? How old are you? Where were you born?"

One older vet stood up, balancing himself with a wooden cane.

Jeremy ignored him.

The old guy spoke. "Maybe I can help you, docto—"

Jeremy cut him off. "You can't."

The others could see the old vet was annoyed with the response. Jeremy proceeded, pointing up and down in rapid succession. Grossman's frame shook as he attempted to sit and stand. He fell, clipping the side rail, luckily the two interns caught him before he hit the floor. Lumas heard the cane striking the floor as the vet moved toward them, he knew this was not going to end well.

He spoke with deathly calmness. "Doctor, I would like you

to leave and not ask Sergeant Grossman to do your monkey tricks any longer."

He took one more step toward Jeremy.

"I am in charge of this ward, and I'd like you to go back to your bed right now."

Grossman, supported by the two, had a grotesque look on his face. He began to yell out unintelligibly, his back arched and stiffened, his eyes widened, then he began shaking.

"He's having a seizure," Lumas said calmly.

They held him safely until the clonic seizure stopped. Jeremy stood by, gazed on, and didn't assist.

"You two, clean this up," Jeremy ordered, turning to walk out.

The vet, with cane in hand, moved behind him. Jeremy turned and bounced off his chest.

"That wasn't right, Doctor." He was daunting and Lumas hadn't seen a stone-cold face like the vet's face since his younger adolescent rowdy years, oftentimes a prelude to a fight. He wished the exchange ended with Jeremy just walking away. Jeremy looked up at the vet, stepped back and around the man.

The vet turned his attention to Dino. "Will he be all right?"

"Yes, he's calming down now. Can you please press the call button for the nurse?"

The vet looked at Lumas after having sized up Dino. "Doctor, can you explain why he did that again?" Not so much a question as a demand.

Both looked perplexed. "Again?" Guitano said curiously.

They left the ward after profusely apologizing to the veterans there. It didn't make much difference, they only looked at the two interns in disgust, then proceeded to assist the nurses placing Grossman back on the bed.

Guitano spoke first. "Robbis wants us to stop by his floor."

"Why?" Lumas inquired.

"Dunno."

Anthony Robbis was a character, extremely intelligent and had a vicious wit. It was difficult to sit next to him in conferences because he had something sarcastic to say about all the lecturers. Anyone within four chairs of him was forced to subdue their laughs. One thing Lumas didn't appreciate about him, however, was his lack of respect for the vets. Many of his jokes revolved around veterans and could be very cruel.

The three went to the medical floor and found Robbis doing paperwork at the nurse's desk.

"Good morning, Doctors, follow me," Robbis greeted them.

They walked into one of the dark patient rooms with fluorescent ceiling lights, dingy gray walls, and no windows. It looked like solitary confinement. Anthony stood to the right of an elderly woman in bed and slightly behind. Just then, Jeremy walked in, and the hairs on Lumas's back stood up.

Jeremy spoke first. "What's up, Anthony?"

Anthony began to speak loudly at the woman, though he didn't make eye contact with her. She looked to be pushing seventy or eighty years old.

"You bitch, motherfucker, lazy, no-good whore vet," he began.

Lumas and Guitano were stunned at what was coming out of his mouth.

"Your mother eats cow shit and your father is a lazy asshole," he went on.

The two took a step back, fearing the woman would lunge at Anthony any second.

"She's completely deaf. How do you like that, boss?"

Anthony explained, uncontrollably laughing.

Unbeknownst to the two interns, Jeremy stood behind them. Jeremy laughed loudly and the woman looked at him puzzled.

Guitano and Lumas didn't laugh. Lumas was hungover and short-tempered today. He blew up at Anthony.

"I don't think that's fucking funny at all, Anthony," Lumas startled him.

Dino pulled at Lumas's arm, trying to calm him. "You mother-fucker, how would you like it if someone did that to your mother?" He went on, unable to stop himself. "Did you ever think we would all be dead if it wasn't for her? It's callous and wrong, asshole." Lumas's voice began to stutter and become louder, and he felt the blood rushing to his face.

Anthony was stunned, his face turned beet red. At this point, Dino was forcefully pulling at Lumas, who had turned his indignation toward Jeremy. When Dino saw what was coming, he stepped in front of Lumas and pushed him out the door.

"Jerk, get him out of here," he heard Jeremy shout.

Lumas turned to confront him head-on, but Dino pushed again. A group of nurses, hearing the exchange, quickly walked toward the commotion, closed the door, and stood in front, blocking Lumas from reentering. They trusted him and they detested Jeremy.

Dino spoke empathetically. "Calm down, please, you're going to get in trouble. That asshole can't say anything unless you confront him. He can't tell the chief without getting in trouble himself. Don't give him ammunition. Why don't you go home? I'll cover you downstairs."

Lumas turned and walked away. Two nurses ushered him to the stairway door.

On the way home, he called a woman he'd met at the

hospital. Not surprisingly and without hesitation, she invited him to her apartment for a drink. She was an administrative assistant and not particularly attractive or interesting, but she had a shapely figure and she was the aggressor. That made the casual encounter easier, guilt deferred.

They were in bed before the drink. She was not a good lover and chattered, coughed, and grunted all the while he lay on top of her. He left as soon as he could and used the convenient excuse that he had to get back to work. Making love to her was as unsatisfying as it was with all the other women, although it was a temporary reprieve from his anxiety. A quick sexual encounter left him feeling like dirt.

CHAPTER SIX

Jeremy was sitting in the chief of medicine office with Howard Jennens. Jennens headed up the financial division. He was generally disliked because of his heavy-handed approach to cutting costs, anywhere. Under his watch, each department was responsible for a monthly allocation of funds to cover overhead, office supplies, manuals, information technology (IT) upgrades—everything. Over- time was paid by the department, not the payroll division. Jennens kept costs down and was an upcoming star in the VA.

Consequently, due to lack of personnel, the halls were rarely mopped, and piles of dirt stuck to the lower walls and accumulated in corners. The patient rooms and wards were rarely cleaned properly. Trash cans were emptied once weekly and sheets were changed only when soiled or when the vet was discharged or died. The quality of food was noticeably worse and not much better than what inmates were fed, so said the veterans.

The patients' food was always late and cold. The nursing staff objected up the chain of command, but nothing changed, so they pooled their monies and bought microwaves for each ward. The residents and interns bought pizzas for the vets every other Tuesday and Thursday. Doctors and nurses lost at all attempts to improve the aesthetics, stave off cutbacks, or buy higher quality food for the patients. Dr. Marvin Karlson walked into his office. The house staff considered him a pompous prick. He despised teaching and research but groveled in academic politics. He had no interest in VA Medical Centers and as a result spent very little time there. The majority of his time was instead spent at the main campus politicizing his accolades for a promotion and gunning for a department head position in the university hospital.

He was irritated. "Okay, what is so important?" Karlson asked.

In the VA system, Jennens was administratively equal in rank to division chiefs. He took every opportunity to remind them.

"I am just as busy, Karlson," Jennens barked back.

Karlson dropped his gaze away from Jennens and sat behind his desk.

"Go ahead."

"I want to cut back on lab personnel and other ancillary services, including allied healthcare. I can't think of a VA employee who deserves the amount of money these losers get."

"So, what does this have to do with the residency program? That's your problem."

Jennens stood and leaned over the desk.

"I need your interns to pick up the additional workload. In return, let's say I have a donation or a grant, whatever you want to call it."

Karlson feigned some degree of interest. "I'm listening."

Jennens went on.

"You tell the interns to do more work such as the phlebotomies, running the tests themselves, transporting patients, maybe even doing the chest X-rays, so I can get rid of the tech. And any more overrated jobs to be determined."

Jennens chuckled loudly. "God, I love myself. Karlson, someday I will head up the VA from a posh desk in Washington."

Karlson shrugged. "I'm still waiting, Jennens. What's in this for the department?"

Jennens looked at Karlson with contempt. "Please, don't give me that department crap, Karlson. I know you want out of here as much as I do."

Karlson wasn't accustomed to being spoken to with such disrespect, but he bit his tongue and kept quiet.

"Look, it's so simple, just do it!" Jennens exclaimed, his voice rising in volume. He stopped, rolled his eyes, and furrowed his brows before continuing.

"Oh my god, I apologize and request your consideration. Please accept my offer, Dr. Karlson," he said, his voice dripping in sarcasm. He let out a loud laugh. "You remind me of my father. He was a doctor also and a self-righteous prick," Jennens went on.

Karlson stood.

"Okay, okay, big guy. Zip it up and have a seat again." Jennens's voice lowered. "Look, it's that simple. I'll make a hefty donation, sorry, a *grant* to you directly, not to the division. You can take that money and negotiate a move to the main campus, just as you want. Say it came from a benevolent donor. Your buddies will move you there for a price, everyone has a price, Karlson, everyone. I will throw in an additional chunk of change to take Jeremy with you."

Karlson's brain began to churn, but he kept a poker face. He had very little interest in taking Jeremy anywhere, however, over the years he'd proven useful. Intimidating the house staff and sacking one intern yearly was profitable. The additional salary was left to the division chief to use at his discretion. Karlson funneled the money to his bank account. He knew Lumas was in Jeremy's crosshairs this year.

"This conversation is confidential, correct?" Karlson asked.

"Of course, Dr. Karlson." Jennens spoke both

condescendingly and pejoratively as if he was teaching kindergarten.

Jeremy sat and dared not utter a word, knowing full well he was out of his league. Karlson reclined in his leather desk chair.

"I'm still listening."

Jennens sat, crossed his legs, and deliberately thumped his foot on the bottom of Karlson's desk.

"I see I have your attention now. The US Department of Veterans Affairs in DC allocates extra bucks biyearly to upgrade medical devices, salaries for promotions, etc. Over the last three years, I've collected a healthy war chest. Under my administration, the nonmedical staff do not move up the promotion ladder or salary scale. I control the evaluations, I control the salaries, and I control the amenities for the vets, simple as that. You and the chief of surgery haven't requested anything to improve your divisions. You clearly don't care, and that is perfect for me. You're too busy trying to get the hell out of the VA, and you see we have something very much in common."

Jennens turned to look at Jeremy.

"Dr. Karlson, I like this guy here. He doesn't speak till spoken to."

Jennens considered him nothing more than a pathetic slave. He knew his reputation; if it weren't for Karlson, he'd have been ousted long ago. He thought maybe these two had a special relationship, but he didn't really care unless it would someday prove useful.

Jeremy attempted to protest, but Karlson stepped in. "Shut up, Jeremy."

Jennens continued. "This place is a cesspool. I get the attention of Washington by cutting costs, and no one gives a crap how I do it, they just love me. That's the VA, my friend. Oops, sorry I took that liberty, but you've been a tremendous asset to my career, Dr. Karlson." Karlson knew guys like Jennens loved to boast and beat their chests.

They think they have thought out all the possibilities as if variables don't exist. The main campus was swarming with pathological professors. However, Jennens may have just pulled this one off. Karlson learned early in his academic career to have a withdrawal strategy, a clown-like Jeremy, someone to dump on, if situations backfire.

"So, how will you fund me? How much and how soon?"

Jennens went for the jugular. "Depends on you and your trusty sidekick Tonto here. I want my investment replenished in three months when your interns leave. That means they'll have to pick up the work for ten full-time employees to maximize my returns."

"You're going to fire all those people?" Karlson asked. "Don't get ethical, Dr. Karlson, that's not your business."

Karlson leaned forward in his seat. "Uhh… to answer the rest of your questions, I almost forgot, six figures in three months."

"How do I know I can trust you and how does this so-called grant just materialize?"

Jennens leaned forward. "From the estate of your generous benefactor Marylyn Stanton," Jennens mouthed unobtrusively.

"And who is she?"

"That's my business, but Jesus, Karlson, you don't get it. She doesn't exist, she's paper," Jennens answered slowly and sarcastically. "One hundred thousand tomorrow, the balance of another hundred thousand in three months. The funds can be deposited by wire to the account of your choice."

Karlson was stunned but composed himself.

"Oh, I forgot to show you this." Jennens handed him a copy of a deposit slip for fifty thousand dollars written to the VA Department of Medicine from the main campus.

Karlson sat up straight, his face turned bright red. "How do you know about this account, Jennens?"

Jennens spoke. "I've known for a long time why you and this guy," he pointed at Jeremy, "have been offing an intern per year. Pretty sneaky of you. And I would guess that the deposit account number is not for the Department of Medicine.

Jennens pointed his finger at Karlson and snickered. "Sneaky, sneaky, sneaky."

He went on. "I would bet that account is, how do I put this, fucking embezzlement and fraud. The accounting department on campus must hire a bunch of morons. Or no one would think a department head at a prestigious academic institution would steal money from the center of excellence. You do remind me of my old man; he was a hypocrite also. At least I don't hide behind a façade; I admit to being a thief, a talented one."

Jennens stood, looked at Karlson, then fixed his eyes on Jeremy. A shower of adrenaline coursed through Jeremy's body and made his heart beat fast and erratically. His face started to get warm and his mouth was as dry as cotton. He was in shock and Jennens could smell blood.

"Dr. Karlson, I hope you can trust Tonto."

He turned and left. Karlson had a disgusted look on his face, having been demeaned and embarrassed by an administrator, a layperson. It didn't matter that Jeremy was there, he didn't care what Jeremy thought, but he needed someone to torture right now.

"Why haven't you fired Lumas yet? It's getting close to the

end of his internship."

Jeremy's voice cracked. "He's protected. They are all protecting each other."

"Don't give me that bullshit, Jeremy. Get it done and soon. Change his orders, make it look egregious or incompetent. I don't care, just get it done. No one cares about one more morbid complication of another alcoholic vet, dammit. If they don't die from the booze then it's from the smoking, think of it as assisted suicide. Do you want to move to the main campus with me or rot here?"

Jeremy was shaking. He had corrupted orders in the past, that was easy, but orchestrating a medical catastrophe to a near-death took skill. Unfortunately, Jeremy's physician skills were as lousy as his ethics. He had created numerous medical complications that had easily been blamed on the target intern. The best were the ones that led to patients having prolonged admissions to the intensive care unit and getting put on life support. The cases were presented at grand rounds weekly and often the intern was nailed to the cross, berated by faculty while the other interns sympathized and prayed their colleague would be forgiven. Jeremy was the physician responsible for organizing rounds, therefore he presented cases. These cases were part fabrication, part degradation, and always portrayed himself as the protagonist.

What Jeremy didn't know was firing one intern yearly forced the medical school to reimburse Karlson. It was a sort of apology for accepting an intern who proved unqualified for the program. However, no one suspected he was dipping into the account for himself. The university never audited department heads, figuring they were too ethical to consider embezzlement. Over a two-year period, he and his wife traveled to Paris, London, Amsterdam,

Geneva, Israel, Russia, and South Africa, all the while touring like diplomats. He renovated his home twice and yearly pocketed the remaining money. Karlson figured he deserved the money for time spent in the armpit of the university-affiliated hospitals.

Somehow Jennens knew everything; he had no choice but to cooperate. Maybe later, he would figure some way of getting rid of him. There was always Jeremy.

He turned his back to Jeremy. "Get out," he ordered.

Jeremy's brain was clicking. He knew he had to turn up the pressure on Lumas but needed him to suffer first. After the conversation in the office, it was much more personal now. He vowed that this would be the last time he allowed Lumas to dent his ego. Jeremy walked out of Karlson's office with his brain in overdrive panic mode. As an idea occurred to him, he picked up his pace toward the psych ward.

CHAPTER SEVEN

Tina Moore sat behind her desk as she clicked away at her computer keyboard, feigning to be deep into a project. She had a clerical position with the VA and rotated between Jennens's and Karlson's offices because there wasn't enough salary allocated to justify a full-time assistant in both departments.

Tina knew something important was being discussed, especially when Jennens began to whisper. She eavesdropped whenever these covert meetings sprang up in either office. Then after her shift, she dropped a plain white unsigned envelope on the desk of Jennens's next victim. Sometimes the employee took the information to the union. Other times Jennens's trumped-up lies were presented sooner than she had time to act on. In these cases, the employee was dismissed pending further review, which in the VA system took a minimum of six weeks. Jennens, of course, arranged the review board schedule, so by the time an individual's case was presented, he or she had already been forced to get employment elsewhere.

By VA standards, she was a dinosaur, with twenty-five years of service, ten of those years in the Army Medical Corps. She was widowed and without children, so she spent time off visiting the hospitalized patients and organizing holiday parties. She detested the treatments given to the veterans, as did most of the employees who were veterans themselves.

The VA administrative leadership, by contrast, never served in the military. Most came to the VA for the benefits and the ability to stay under the radar, knowing termination was nearly impossible if you scratched a lot of backs and kissed a lot of asses. The entire upper echelon of administrators was incestuous, friends of friends, children of fathers and mothers on payroll, fishing buddies, and paybacks. As directed by Jennens, business would stay as usual as long as they did as he commanded. Jennens liked it his way, no one ever questioned him, and they loved him. Jennens's staff commandeered higher salaries than all other administrative divisions.

Jennens stopped at Tina's desk after exiting Karlson's office, and gave her a stark look. He leaned forward, bracing his body over her desk, too close for Tina. She had tossed a stack of papers on the floor when she heard Jennens approaching and began pretending frustration and whispering to herself.

"Good morning, Tina. Do you prefer working here or in my office?"

"It's all the same to me, Mr. Jennens," Tina answered. "VA clerical is very repetitious work."

"So, you get bored occasionally?"

"Occasionally." Tina knew where this was going.

"Tell me, Tina, does Karlson have your loyalty? He seems to demand it from everyone in his little world."

Tina looked hard into Jennens's face. "What exactly do you mean, Mr. Jennens?"

"Well, here you sit, right next to the boss, within earshot of everything he speaks about. All the dirty little secrets, the indiscretions, the behind-the-door deals. He must trust you very much, Ms. Moore."

Tina was seething but kept a poker face. "Mr. Jennens, if I did eavesdrop on Dr. Karlson—which I don't—I am sure his conversations would involve how best to ensure the high standards for graduating the new doctors. I am sure you think about the VA healthcare administration in the same way."

Jennens had nowhere to go now. He leaned back, forcing his shoulders back and his chest forward. "Of course. So, Tina, what do you do on your days off? You're an attractive woman; you must get a lot of offers."

That was enough for Tina. "Well, I attend meetings on women's issues at the LGBTQ Institute downtown. They're very interesting if you'd like to attend. I can forward the agenda to your email."

Jennens just stared at Tina. "No, thank you."

Tina waited for him to leave. Then she stood and touched the pause button on her iPhone, perched high on the bookcase shelf behind her desk. She had drilled a small hole between her cubicle and Karlson's office.

Jennens had long suspected that Tina knew too much. Someday he would have to deal with her for good. When he arrived at his office, he picked up the phone and pressed in some numbers. "I want you to keep an eye on Tina Moore. Yeah, that's what I said, Tina Moore, my assistant. I want to know where she goes and who she is sleeping with, starting today."

CHAPTER EIGHT

Lumas woke the next day with a hangover. He was not a heavy drinker and generally knew his limit, but that night he had one too many martinis. After he left the hospital, he drove to the marina. For the second night in a row, he was still deeply depressed after the latest berating from Jeremy. This time it had been for being five minutes late for morning rounds. It was morbidly redundant how his subconsciousness was a participant at the behest of Jeremy. The next day, after an altercation with Jeremy, he would consistently wake up late despite the fact he set his alarm to give him ample time to get to the hospital. This seemed to happen with or without drinking or sleeping meds.

That night, the bars were full of singles, the forties club, and appropriate ages for him. This watering hole, ironically named "The Pit Stop," was the busiest local meat market. Attractive women sat around a huge rectangular bar huddled in small groups, feigning indifference to men trying to capture their attention from a distance. Muscular men in tight sleeveless shirts candidly moved closer as the evening wore on, until within striking distance to begin trivial gibberish.

Lumas humorously thought of how the mating habits of lower life forms were much more interesting. Homo sapiens should dance like Mick Jagger instead, with inflated chests and extended lower jowls, attempting to impress a potential mate. In his opinion, Homo sapiens completely destroyed courtship, what should be a beautiful and poetic ritual was in reality a dull, boring spectacle. He would much rather bring a big shiny rock to his mate, like a penguin. If she liked it, great. If not, on to the next potential mate, without any need for idle bantering.

On this particular evening, while he looked for an open seat, an unattractive slightly obese woman stepped in his way and quickly introduced herself as Jenny. Two hours later, he wondered what excuse he could conjure up to leave her apartment as soon as possible after he rolled off her huge torso. On the way back home, he felt that familiar gnawing pain in his stomach, guilt and shame.

He and Dino began their rotation on the oncology ward that day. Compared to the medical floor, oncology was even more starkly depressing and poorly maintained. Patients were confined to single tiny, barren, windowless rooms. There were no televisions or radios unless families brought them. Oncology patients lived in solitary confinement with little or no social interactions. Most volunteers avoided the ward because the aesthetics were so dispiriting and the nurses tended to be territorial and crusty. Patients rarely left oncology, except on stretchers feet first.

Neither Lumas nor Dino liked the oncologists. In general, they were arrogant, condescending, narcissistic, boring, and always avoided families. The positive aspect, however, was that they didn't have to work with Jeremy. The oncologist in charge insisted he be barred from the ward many years ago. This was right after Jeremy disrupted the chain of command and riled up the nurses to such a degree that some threatened to transfer elsewhere or do more serious political harm to the oncologist.

Karlson avoided the oncologist because the division was his major cash cow, bringing in millions of federal research dollars, part of which had to be shared with the chief, Karlson himself.

Therefore, he turned a blind eye to their frequent out-of-state conferences, lackadaisical three-day-a-week schedules, and the fact that the oncologists-in-training, the fellows, were forced to run the ward daily. With exceptions, this resulted in a trial by fire for the fellows and murder by neglect and incompetence for the patients.

Dino was sitting and speaking with Dr. David Ganz when Lumas arrived. Dr. Ganz was a stocky, unkempt, elderly man with a stubbly beard and a huge abdomen. His shirt buttons were popped below his pannus, and he smelled of stale cigarettes. He spoke with a thick South African accent. The general consensus was that he was the only instructor who took the time to teach and was a true hands-on physician.

Lumas caught the tail end of their conversation. "What is your thesis?" Dr. Ganz asked.

Lumas didn't know Dino was doing a thesis, however, they rarely spoke about either's interest in pursuing fellowships or staying in academia. Getting through the internship was consuming enough.

"I'll probably concentrate on targeted treatments."

"Good luck. I'm sure we will be speaking again at the scientific conferences."

"Good morning, Lumas," Dr. Ganz said as he stood and pleasantly acknowledged him. "Let's get started."

Most of the patients were in bed and barely awake. The day shift had just arrived and food trays were stacked in large carts ready for distribution. Lumas recalled working in a hospital kitchen during high school, washing and stacking the large serving trays after school. It had certainly not been his favorite job, the hours were long, and the trays had to be scraped by hand, leaving gobs of food on any part of his body not covered by a rubber apron. He mistakenly walked into a patient's room who had hepatitis and was jaundiced from head to toe. That experience terrified him so much that it resulted in nightmares the rest of the week and he ultimately quit.

The first patient on their rounds that day had received chemo- therapy overnight. He appeared to be well over seventy years old, but his ID wrist bracelet read, "45, male, Otis, Don" followed by a long identification number. The room smelled of vomit from an overturned emesis basin. Three empty bottles of chemotherapy hung upside down from the dowel with streaks of blood caked inside the intravenous lines. His face was pale with large brown desiccated eyes protruding from retracted orbital sockets, lips dry and cracking, face unshaven, mostly bald, but with dots of thin hair cropping from his forehead to the back of his neck. He no longer had identifiable facial features, and the resemblance to a concentration camp prisoner was startling. He opened his eyes but didn't visually track their movements, remaining silent.

Ganz turned and quietly told Dino to get a nurse, then sat next to Don.

"Mr. Otis, it's Dr. Ganz. Do you feel like you look, sir?"

"Worse," Don harshly replied, his voice so strained Lumas could barely hear him.

"You can't take one more bout of this, Don. You're suffering."

He didn't answer and seemed to disappear in thought for a moment. "Told my son I'd hang on till he got here."

"I didn't know you had a son. Is he here, may I speak with him?"

"Haven't seen him for years."

Ganz turned when Dino and an attractive young nurse

arrived. Lumas's attention turned to her olive skin, long dark hair, and thin curvy body. She caught his glance. She bypassed Ganz and first spoke to Don. "Mr. Otis, I am so sorry, no excuses."

He looked up and smiled. "No problem, Frieda. How's my one hair look today?"

She went on in a quiet dignified tone, they enjoyed each other. "Very handsome, Don. I'll get the CNA and kick out the doctors, we'll clean you up, shave that shadow, and comb that hair."

He chuckled, she turned and left. Lumas resisted the temptation to watch her behind as she left. Dino, however, indulged.

Ganz began again. "Maybe we can have a family conference. When will he be here?"

"Don't know, he didn't say. The last time I called him he said he would call me back. That was two weeks ago."

"What does Elizabeth say about this?"

He took a deep breath struggling for air. "She says she wants me to hang on till the kid gets here. I don't think that will happen, but I promised."

Ganz struggled with the next question. "Why didn't he come?" "He never intended to visit, just said it to hurt us, especially me. My son has been in and out of trouble since he was young. First drugs and alcohol and then trouble with the law. We love him so much but after a while had to put him out and cut off the money. Elizabeth was furious about that, and probably still is. Of course, he hated me too, and we haven't seen him since then."

"Will Elizabeth be here today?"

At this point, Don was clearly exhausted. "She comes every few days," he whispered.

Frieda strode in with a young nursing assistant. "Okay, docs, we have the salon thing to do. Please, excuse us."

Don had a little smile.

Ganz stood on cue. "Okay, gentleman, we are excused."

They visited the next few patients, one with prostate cancer, and the two others with advanced lung cancer. All were stable, receiving chemotherapy, and expected to be discharged the next day and return in a week for the next chemotherapy course.

"Were all three diagnosed with widespread cancer during this admission?" Lumas asked Ganz.

Ganz gave an exasperated answer. "All three were having symptoms and attempted unsuccessfully making an appointment for months. For the vets here every day is D-Day."

Ganz asked Dino and Lumas to see one more patient before they left. He said she was a very interesting and delightful woman. It was rare to have a female patient, so they decided to peruse her chart before visiting her.

Betty McConnell was fifty-one years old and a graduate of the Air Force Academy. She had flown a KC-135 refueling tanker in Libya. Ganz left detailed notes about her medical and social history, which was much more detailed than his usual documentation. Both interns were in awe of Betty's military career. The Air Force Academy first admitted women in 1976. In 1987, Betty was a top graduate and remained in the service for ten years. She flew in Operation Desert

Shield, then abruptly left the service after her second tour of duty. She returned to her home in Southern California and married. At this point, her social history ended, and she refused more probing.

Betty was emaciated, disheveled, and lice-infested when she was forcibly brought to the VA emergency room by a group of homeless vets who she shared a corner of an alley with. She was dehydrated and in severe pain. During prior admissions, she was diagnosed with metastatic colon cancer and refused treatments, only asking for a small supply of pain medication upon discharge, always against medical advice.

According to Ganz's notes, she was approaching her end of life and heavily medicated with morphine. The emergency room physician wrote that Betty wanted to leave and definitely not be admitted to the oncology ward, but the nurses refused to allow her to sign out again. She acquiesced and was showered, shampooed, dressed in a clean gown, and fed.

The oncology nurses gave the doctors permission to speak with her. Although she was somnolent, she opened her eyes as soon as they entered and gave a wide smile, devoid of both upper incisors.

"Ah, good-looking, young doctors for a change. I was getting so tired of Dr. Ganz's big stomach and dirty clothes. He looks worse than me." She laughed loudly and coughed up a thick wad of gunk that instantly caused Lumas to become nauseous.

"Don't think I don't love him, but you docs need to hose him down and donate a new shirt and hide his cigarettes."

Both interns were stunned, charmed, and unabashedly laughed. Lumas was sure the nurses were rolling outside after essentially setting them up for something far more morose. Betty was clearly not fearful of death, in fact, she was laughing to death.

"Okay, good lookings, what are we going to talk about? Or do you both want to just examine my breasts?"

Dino spoke first, trying to suppress his laughter. "Ms. Connell, my name is—"

"Doctors Guitano and Lumas, well respected by the nurses,"

she interjected. "I bet you two didn't know that. Guitano you have a PhD and working on a research project, what's it called... oh yeah, targeted treatments, very commendable. Lumas, you're Mr. Bootstraps, first family member to graduate from college, much less medical school."

"But how do you know all this?" Lumas asked.

"You two seem to be the brunt of a lot of conversations among the nurses. They appreciate you both, otherwise, they'd never let you through that door."

Lumas tensed. Was he that transparent? It made him feel vulnerable and embarrassed. But he went with it because Betty was such a sweetheart and spoke honestly not pejoratively.

She continued. "Okay, guys, what can I tell you that's not on my chart? Please call me Betty and especially not major."

Dino was about to ask the obvious question when Betty moaned and wrapped her arms around her abdomen. Her face turned scarlet red and she barrel rolled trying to consciously distract her brain from the sudden jolt of pain.

"I'll get the nurse, Betty," Dino said, his voice filled with urgency. "No, no, it will pass," Betty repeated twice.

The room intercom squawked. "Betty, you know that's a lie. I'm on the way." The nurses were listening all along. Dino looked at Lumas and grimaced.

"The walls talk in here," Dino said.

Betty laughed, squeezed her abdomen tighter, took a deep breath, and spoke. "I told you, docs, they're keeping an eye out for you two. Covet it, you may need them more than you think someday. Besides, it was my idea."

The nurse with the beautiful olive skin walked in. She passed Lumas and patted his lower back, no one else noticed.

"Betty, I'm going to push this through your IV line," she

announced.

"No, no. I can't go home on IV meds; just give me the pills," Betty complained. The nurse ignored her, attached the syringe, and squirted the pain meds in the line as Betty was protesting. Betty's eyes rolled back in her head and she mumbled. "That was insubordination, young lady, but I love you anyway." She faded away into a deep sleep.

Before they left, Lumas and the olive-skinned nurse Frieda exchanged phone numbers.

CHAPTER NINE

Glenn Evans put the phone down and thought about Tina Moore. Why would Jennens want him to follow an assistant?

He never trusted the jerk and much preferred to snap his neck than function as his caddy.

Evans was in his thirties and had been employed as a security guard at the VA for six months. No one knew much of anything about his prior employments nor did anyone make any attempts to ask. He was neither rude nor friendly, instead, he was rather aloof.

Evans's past was, for all practical purposes, nonexistent. He left home as a young child after a one-night stint in jail when he was thirteen. Angry with his father, he struck him in the head with a two-by-four, then waited patiently, curious how long it would take for his brains to drip out both ears. The blow only put his father in the hospital for one day, but Evans remembered feeling a sense of intense contentment.

He hated his father, who was a drunk and the worst kind. He drank but never passed out and became more violent as the alcohol levels climbed in his bloodstream. Evans and his mother were subjected to his rage until Evans bludgeoned him. Afterwards, Evans had been reprimanded, sent to counselling, and forced to do an overnight stint in juvenile hall. Still, he never forgot the rush that night. So, he found himself, at the age of thirteen, unable to go home ever again. His father would certainly kill him if he did. The streets became home. Alleyways with restaurant trash cans sufficed; he managed to survive on meagre amounts of food.

Occasionally, he found abandoned homes and flopped on the floor. It was painfully cold most of the time, but at least he had a roof over his head. He found out that a newspaper folded properly made an adequate mattress and coverage. When he couldn't find an abandoned house, large trash bins behind markets worked, except for the rats, the fucking rats. Only roach killer would keep them a few feet away, roach killer was in abundant supply in the bins. But he always kept one eye open for the boldest rodent that nipped at his arms or legs.

The most dangerous aspect of living on the streets was the "others." He was beaten numerous times for the pittance of food he scavenged and hid in his pockets. The homeless keep a keen eye on passersby, especially the young ones. They would frequently follow and rob them of anything of value, primarily food.

Evans lived for six violent and terrifying years on the streets. He wondered if his mother ever attempted to find him. But the brunt of her beatings always began about him. His father constantly reminded her that all his financial troubles began with her producing a hungry "pig" for a son.

He would scream at her, "Because of you and that bastard, I have to work two jobs."

The last slap to his face, nearly knocking him unconscious, was the last time he saw either of them.

Evans was by nature harmless, if not provoked. At sixteen, he was nearly six-feet tall and thick-chested with huge arms. At seventeen, he killed three men in self-defense, while attempting to strip him of his tattered clothes. Each was bigger than him, but he was faster, more agile, and ruthless when cornered. He picked up a trash can lid and a broken Coke bottle and stood waiting for their lunges.

The first man threw a punch, but Evans deflected it with the metal lid. He howled and grabbed his wrist. Within a second, the sharp bottle pierced his throat, he fell to the ground with blood gushing down his chest. The two other men stood momentarily shocked, recuperated, and then together sprang toward him. Evans turned sharply left, causing the two men to collide, stumbling as they tried to turn in unison.

The first to trip and fall had his throat cut from ear to ear before he hit the ground. The third crawled backwards and was shocked at the thick gush of blood pumping from his forehead, his face was dripping with the warm ooze. He turned and ran but the glass bottle pierced his right upper back puncturing his lung. Evans pulled down with all his strength until the shard of glass cut horizontally through his spinal cord. Even in his teens, he had street smarts and knew he would have to kill them, or they would return better prepared to kill him next time. The rats had a feast that night. Evans would never have to worry about looking over his shoulder again for these three. As the years passed, he hopped from one mundane job to another. His life would not end up in an alley somewhere with a needle in his vein or a bullet in his brain. He looked for simple jobs that seemed to fit his talent—a gift he learned on the streets to survive. Parks were wide open and generally offered some protection during the day. He chose to sleep during the days and scavenge for food and safe shelter at night.

Most homeless adjusted their nocturnal sleeping patterns to avoid the maniacs, thieves, and drug addicts who perused at sundown and slept throughout the day.

One morning, after waking in a park, Evans noticed a man

paying close attention to a young girl walking toward the toilets. When the child entered the restroom, the man casually walked in behind her. Almost instinctually, Evans ran into the toilet.

The child was pulling away from the man, attempting to scream, but he covered her mouth. Evans casually walked toward him and motioned him to let the child go. He didn't. Evans immediately gripped his throat and squeezed. He pivoted the man in a semicircle to get a good look at his eyes before tossing him into the metal windows above the sinks. It created a huge thud, arousing parents to the danger.

Evans said to the girl, "Lock the stall and don't come out. Don't look out. Scream as loud as you can and stay right there," Evans said to the girl.

"Yes," the child mumbled. She began to cry and screamed for her mommy and daddy.

Evans timed his next move, so the parents knew he was the savior, not the molester. He picked up the pedophile, pivoting him over his head and waited seconds until he heard running and a woman screaming for the child. Three men ran in, just as Evans tossed the pedophile the length of the room and over the top of the last stall.

The men stopped after visualizing the scene, awestruck. The pedophile hit the top of the stall and went over and down headfirst. The men could hear the crushing thud as his head smashed into the toilet. Then a limp arm fell under the stall door. At that point, all movement ceased. The three men gawked at what they had just witnessed. They stared at Evans, part terrified, part perplexed.

From outside the restroom, a voice screamed. "Is my baby okay? John, is Sarah okay? Bring her here to me!"

Not one of the men spoke for a moment. Then, John said,

"Yeah, she's okay. We'll have her out in a second."

Evans was still staring at the limp arm under the stall.

An older Afro-American man on forearm crutches limped into the restroom and scanned it. "You okay, son? Are you hurt?" the man asked Evans.

"No, I'm not hurt."

He spoke again. "John, go get your child. Keep her eyes away from the trash."

"Mark, see if he's dead but don't touch anything."

The man didn't immediately move. The old man was annoyed. "Mark, Mark," he said.

"What?"

"Damn it. Go see if he's dead."

Mark walked past Evans but didn't take his eyes off him. He opened the stall door. "Half the pedophile's brain is in the toilet."

The old man spoke softly to Evans. "Did you mean to kill him, son?"

"No, just cripple him for life."

The old man chuckled. "Well, then, I don't think you have to worry about that. Gotta admit that was impressive."

"His brain is dripping in the toilet," Mark said.

The old man spoke with an air of abject authority. "Let's get out of here. Someone put an out-of-order sign on the door for now. Everybody out. You come with me, kid."

Evans turned his attention to the old man. "Are you a police officer?"

The old man took a long look at the kid. "No, how many times have you seen an old black man in crutches give a bunch of white dudes orders?"

"Never."

"Okay then, let's get out of here before the cops arrive. By now, someone in the park has seen the commotion and called it in. Come with me."

Evans didn't. He was suspicious of everyone.

The old man looked at him again, contemplatively and staring at the kid. "You've been on the street too long. You're dirty, probably hungry, wearing your only pair of shoes and have nowhere to safely sleep. The cops will arrest you for questioning. You want that?"

Evans didn't answer. "Then let's go."

The old man walked Evans to a table of some ten older codgers playing chess. None looked up or introduced themselves.

"Do you play chess?"

Evans looked at the man sarcastically.

"Okay." Looking at his partner across the table, the old man said, "Give the kid room."

"I should go, the police will be here soon," Evans spoke. "Stay here; you'll be safer with us."

Evans was perplexed. "Won't someone point the cops toward me?"

"Nope," the old man replied. "Now look down, do not raise your eyes, and look seriously at the board. Someone give the kid a coat and water. Wash your face, kid."

CHAPTER TEN

On any given day, there was a continuous flow of picnickers, young people throwing Frisbees, kids chasing one another, and couples huddled under the canopies of thick oak trees. Evans slowly acclimated to the comfortable pace and began to settle in and get to know the regulars. He was asked to participate in various sports, especially volleyball matches primarily because of his tall muscular frame. The old Afro-American man had given Evans a small wad of cash for clothes and a hotel room. He refused to answer any question about why he was helping Jennens. His sole request was that Evans show up at the table five days a week. Evans met with the old men. His daily routine was mundane, but he felt protected.

He was invited to dinner by a couple of single women but declined, promising, "Another time," but thanked them profusely.

For the first time in his life, he settled in and took joy in meeting new, friendly, and hospitable people. The women thought he was intelligent, funny, handsome, and coyly mysterious. All in all, Evans enjoyed the park, the people, and the serenity. It gave him a taste of community and family, which he'd never felt before. He was welcomed.

The old guys helped him secure a job at a VA Medical Center, telling him they had contacts in the personnel office. The VA had openings for security guards all the time. No one with any real talent wanted the job; it was mundane and security guards were banned from carrying firearms. But it gave him income and ample time to read and self-educate.

Evans caught Jennens' attention late one night while tossing a drunk disorderly vet into the back of his car with one arm and then driving off. Jennens thought Evans would throw him out on the major boulevard, down the street from the Medical Center. In reality, Evans drove the vet to McDonald's and paid for a meal.

Jennens needed someone like Evans, who he perceived could intimidate anyone. In return, he promised to pay him two hundred dollars in cash weekly under the table. But Jennens only made the offer if Evans agreed to stay for a minimum of one year, which would be enough time for him to conclude his plans.

The old guys seemed to be pleased, even after he told them of Jennens's offer, which he found curious. Evans frequently thanked them. They in turn waved him off and returned to the solitude of their chess game.

"Everyone needs a little help at times, my boy," Ben would tell him.

Evans never knew who hired him. After leaving work, he received a letter left on his car window with instructions to hang an American flag in his rear car window, if he wanted additional work. Within two days, he received another letter instructing him to open a bank account and a mailbox at specific locations and leave the account numbers and duplicate keys under his car seat at home that night. He was instructed to check the mailbox one week after completing a job. The next week, he opened the box and found a letter with the name, address, and profile of a pedophile typed on plain white paper and a check for five thousand dollars. He researched the name that night. The man was a fifty-year-old white guy just released from the California Correctional Institution after serving five years for attempted child abduction. He also served two prior sentences for molesting two girls (both three) and one boy (age five).

Evans's scanners were on alert for the next week. He avoided the park, thinking the police were hiding in cars or infiltrating the picnickers for information about him. No one knew his true history, especially the killings of the three street bums who tried to kill him, or so he thought. Irrespective, he never killed anyone except in self-defense. Why would anyone think he would kill for hire? Why him?

He considered the stupidity of the question when he recalled Ben and the other men who witnessed the carnage he'd inflicted on the child molester at the park. His mind began to play "unhealthy" with his reasoning abilities, it was all perfectly intuitive. He parked his car on the highest level of the hospital's parking structure, a block away from the park, and scanned the park with binoculars. He sat low in his car, looking for new faces in the park, new chess, basketball, or volleyball players. When he saw nobody he didn't recognize, he scanned the faces of the lovers under the trees, as well as people reading the newspapers and any park maintenance staff. No-one new. He continued his surveillance every day for two weeks before he felt assured there was no suspicious activity or new frequent visitors.

Once he was certain he wasn't being stalked, the answer to his next question was easy. Why? Because it was a test. So be it, Evans reasoned, there is no place in society for a man who injures a child or an adult for pleasure. No, there is no reasoning nor purpose in that.

The man was easy to follow, and Evans had no trouble clocking his schedule. He lived across the street from a large park with broad oak trees, park benches, three baseball diamonds, and a fifty-meter lap pool. It was close to a major freeway and a well-to-do community with lots of foot traffic.

Beginning at five-thirty a.m., Evans jogged around the baseball fields. At six-thirty a.m., the man left his home and walked toward Van Nuys Boulevard catching the 233 North and arrived home at three-thirty p.m. He didn't need many more details, although it was daylight saving time and that gave him more flexibility to take time and plan well. Typical for pedophiles, the man was short, scrawny, ugly, and dressed like a bum. He reminded Evans of a timid alley cat nervously looking over his shoulder, dawdling more than walking. He was a pathetic-looking creature.

It became clear that whoever hired him simply wanted to rid the world of this dirt. He drew a map of the park and nearby homes. It was a youngish, working-class family neighborhood and the departure times were relatively consistent. The man's front door faced the park. That wasn't optimal, but the yard was a mess and appeared to have never been maintained. Consequently, overgrown shrubbery offered ample coverage, especially a corner wide enough for him to hide. This would allow Evans to be completely hidden from anyone walking nearby, and from the man's sight when he walked out his door. He planned to kill the man midweek at dawn.

The EVOLUTION 9mm silencer, bought at a pawn shop, was barely audible, especially at dawn when the crows in the park were getting restless and squawking. He hooded and walked casually away after two head shots. Then sauntered around the block to his car. There he took off his sweats and began jogging. It all took less than fifteen minutes. Someone would eventually notice the man's body partially covered behind a thick fern bush in his front yard as planned and call the police.

The following day, Evans decided to spend the morning with

Ben and the other elderly man for chess matches. There were Andy, Bob, Harry, Tim, Ben, and Larry, who were all in their seventies and who reminisced with one another as if they were childhood friends. The jousting banter was on topics that ranged from politics to children and grandchildren. Evans thought it curious they never spoke of their health or complained that the kids didn't visit enough. He knew he would never rely on anyone to bring him happiness. He was content. If it happened, good. If it didn't, so be it. He was comfortable with his emotional intelligence and ego and he was never lonely. He enjoyed life. Despite his violent childhood and years living on the streets, he was never an angry man. He felt everything that happened to him in his past was out of his control and history. This concept he had adopted by reading philosophy—Seneca and Marcus Aurelius, in particular. He was an intelligent man and a prolific reader.

Over the years, he began to look at negativity as an entirely different entity. When his brain began ruminating, he forced his consciousness out and visualized himself walking out a door into reality. It worked well. He practiced and identified triggers that brought him toward that negativity. He began to understand that with exceptions, like Hitler and Stalin and other psychopaths, the difference between right or wrong, good or bad, lovely or ugly, is an illusion. He read about these concepts from Eckhart Tolle, Deepak Chopra, and Richard Green and meditated to think out of the box. He challenged his intuitive comfort zones and reflected against the norm. Evans had a higher-than-average IQ.

A heavyset officer approached them. "Hello, gentleman. I guess you guys have seen the crime scene tape around the house over there. Can I interrupt and ask some questions?"

Ben looked up from his intense gaze at the table. "Larry, that okay with you?"

"Yeh, yeh, yeh, that's okay but not for long. I got to beat this octogenarian son of a bitch."

The cop's tone changed from casual to authoritative. "I'm sure you old guys would notice new people hanging around, isn't that right? Let's say within the last few months."

Ben straightened his back and turned toward the officer, his demeanor was businesslike and firm. He looked into the man's eyes. "Let me enlighten you, Officer Barney Fife. First, we didn't give you permission to denigrate us as old guys, and second, we are here to play chess, not monitor the park."

The officer was embarrassed and dumbfounded. The other men, including Evans, laughed loudly.

"I didn't mean to insult you guys, just wanted to ask a few questions." The officer's tone returned to conciliatory like a chastised child.

"No, we haven't seen anyone new," Larry said. "The same old crowd be a comin' here for years. Occasionally, some new people take up the area there for picnicking but not that often. I think most of the crowd goes to the beach on a sunny day. When you been around this park as long as we OLDER GUYS—ya know, one of us disabled, demented, piddle-pissing OLDER FARTS we be notice." Larry had a PhD in physics and linguistics from Tufts before joining the Navy.

The group chuckled but didn't look up from their chess sets. Ben looked at the man again. "Any other questions, officer?"

He quickly turned his sights on the board and moved Nxf7 to checkmate, then guffawed so loudly that some of the picnickers turned to look. Then Ben looked at Evans directly across from him. "Got you again, Evans. I must have beat you with that move about a hundred times in the last five years. When are you gonna learn, son?" Evans looked at him and faked embarrassment. "Never again, Ben. Next game, you're dead."

Nothing more was discussed and when the officer left, the men resumed their games. On the way home, Evans thought hard about why those men would lie for him. It made him uncomfortable but not threatened. He knew there was something that was not what it seemed with this lot. They never spoke of the murder, the officer, or covering for him. Evans continued to frequent the park and played chess with the men on Sundays more often.

Evans decided to follow up on Jennens's request to check up on Tina. He detested the guy and told him on multiple occasions to correct his tone during their brief encounters. During the day, Evans roamed through the administrative wing every few hours. He made it a point to look bored and irritated, no one paid much attention. Between the rounds and checking the secretarial schedule on the daily schedules board, he was able to get a good handle on Tina's daily routine.

At five, he'd change into street clothes and sit in the lobby until she exited the elevator and walked to her car. She always parked in the corner spot of the back parking lot. Evans found it curious that she exited through the front lobby most of the time until he noticed she'd meet an older man every Tuesday and Thursday. They'd speak for an hour, exit together, and separate. He'd walk to the bus stop and she would round the building to her car.

However, it was the demeanor of the man that caught most of his interest. He appeared disheveled and broke like most of the vets, but he wasn't just any vet. He didn't slouch or stretch his legs but sat like a cadet at graduation, at attention. Tina spoke nonstop for about thirty minutes while the vet listened intently, not once interrupting her. Evans was too far away to eavesdrop but not so far that he couldn't read her lips saying, "Yes, sir."

He carefully searched her desk after hours and found what he had suspected.

CHAPTER ELEVEN

After the meeting with Jennens and Karlson, Jeremy hurried to the psychiatric ward. Karlson wanted the money for canning Lumas, but that would have to be done quickly by firing him with cause, even if that cause consisted of trumped-up facts and overt lies. So far, Jeremy had failed Karlson for the first time and there was much to lose, time was running out. These interns were aware of Jeremy's tactics immediately at the beginning of the year. After a week of daily rounds, Jeremy had shown how vicious he could behave toward the novices. He didn't teach, he embarrassed and demeaned them. They were able to anticipate how sick he was and the extent he would go to wreck a physician's career.

What Jeremy wasn't unaware of was the interns' knowledge of this VA program's reputation for covert unethical practices, especially firing an intern before the end of the year. Some of the interns were terrified when they were matched with the program. Some egotistically assumed they could manipulate Jeremy in their favor. Others reconciled that they would have to work together and watch one another's back. After the first three months, everyone realized they had to work together, anticipate Jeremy's pattern, and constantly remind one another the best defense is a better offense.

Between the pitiable care of the vets, the aesthetics of the facility, Karlson's indifference to research and his all-around despicable reputation, acceptance there was considered to be the bottom of the barrel. All of this in spite of the fact that it was a major university-affiliated program.

What Jeremy and Karlson were not aware of was that Jason, the football prodigy, organized a welcome meeting off campus at the beginning of the year with the new physicians. He made it clear that the healthcare delivery was downright doleful. There was a lack of administrative leadership and one or more instructors were known to fire an intern prior to the end of the year. They had no control over those circumstances, if anyone repeatedly screwed up, none. He was blunt and honest. However, there were good guys also. They could help in some circumstances, but the new guys had to stay focused, compulsive, and under the radar as much as possible.

Jason said, "Do not try to be a star, or you'll find a bullseye on your back. Working together will afford all of you a better chance of getting through the first year." Within their control were virtuous qualities, pursuits, desires, and their own actions. "The first year of training is designed to destroy camaraderie and independent thought. If any new physician thinks too much out of the box, he or she becomes a target and fodder for bush meat."

Jason stated vehemently. "No one can steal your virtues unless you allow them to do so."

Jeremy had sprinted all the way to the psych ward. The huge wooden door had a small rectangular window that the residents used to look inside before opening the door with a large skeleton key. The staff called the psychiatric ward "the cell" and the residents "zombies." Older and younger vets circled up and down the hallways. Most wore only pyjama bottoms and were barefoot, unshaven, and unkempt. A few stared at Jeremy, most spoke to ghosts and incoherently mumbled.

The VA refused to pay the higher costs of new antipsychotic

medications. Consequently, the staff used older drugs with more side effects. Most of the patients walked around with staring faces, slurred speech, and catatonic gaits, causing them to frequently fall. All of them had some form of bruising on their arms, chests, or foreheads. The ward was painted typical depressing VA grey, and was dirty and smudged with brown streaks. Jeremy could hear shouting back in the single rooms. These patients were usually strapped in four-point leather restraints and either paranoid schizophrenics or angry disruptive. Violent patients transferred there were heavily sedated. Once a veteran was marked as disruptive, all further rehospitalizations required a three- day stay in the cell prior to going to the medical wards. Diagnostic workups and procedures were—sometimes indefinitely—delayed.

A muscular Afro-American orderly sat behind the nurses' station and didn't acknowledge Jeremy. Unlike medical floors, there were no ancillary healthcare workers or student nurses; the patients would oftentimes fondle their breasts and butts. Only male orderlies staffed the cell. A psychiatrist came and went, spending the least amount of time as necessary there.

Jeremy tried to muster an authoritative tone. "Where is—"

"Patrick is in room three," the orderly interrupted.

Patrick was in his mid-thirties, a white man from the South. He was lying in bed, smoking, and didn't acknowledge Jeremy entering. His chest was heavily tattooed with a cross from shoulder to shoulder and sternum to the umbilicus. It had long since lost the blackness of the original work and pale white skin spotted through shades of gray. A swastika was drawn at the center of the horizontal and vertical intersections. Red hearts were tattooed below both breasts with stilettos stabbing each and drops of blood dripping off the blades.

His right arm had a machine gun drawn from elbow to wrist. Above that, the stars and bars, the left arm scarred with Jesus in a white robe wearing a storm trooper helmet with bloodied tears dripping down both jowls. Both thighs had poorly drawn Balls and Beauregard flags. Patrick's chest was scrawny, his bony rib spaces especially exaggerated when he drew on the cigarette. "Alabama" was written between his hyoid bone and mid clavicles, the "B" bounced vertically up and down when he spoke.

Patrick enlisted in the Army out of high school. It was either that or face jail. His three brothers were doing time in federal penitentiaries, and he was headed there quickly for car theft, drug use, and assault and battery.

He sat up and smashed his cigarette against the rails of the bed and began to speak.

Jeremy stepped back and closed the door. "Shut up. The orderly will hear us."

Patrick laughed loudly.

Jeremy walked toward him. "Do you want me to up the dose of the Demerol and Xanax, Patrick, or do I find someone else to do a job?"

Patrick sat up. "I'm listening."

CHAPTER TWELVE

Dino and Lumas managed to cajole two other interns into trading three consecutive days off. Lumas asked the lovely, olive-skinned Frieda to join them. He'd taken her out on two prior occasions, and it went well, but deep down, Lumas knew it was a mistake. He was too emotionally fragile, on the verge of creating another relationship that ended in disaster.

Their first date was spent riding down the boardwalk. He enjoyed the beach; it always gave him a respite of peace. He knew from many years of riding that people who barely knew one another shared the most intimate details of their lives. There's something both psychologically and physiologically advantageous about running one's mouth and physical exertion—the walls melt, hearts pour out, and it's difficult to lie. He never understood why.

During those times, he could process and compartmentalize his emotional peaks and troughs to become healthier and forgive himself sooner. Normally he knew his triggers, but not now, not since beginning a medical career. Now he was treading water. He knew he needed to make changes, but distractions worked in the short term. Any competent bipolar could find an abundance of unhealthy distractions at any time, in any place, and with anyone. The anxiety was too much to handle alone. He was suffering and to continue down that road was insanity.

Dino's parents owned a thirty-six-foot Winnebago camper with enough room to comfortably sleep four adults, two separately. At least that's what he told Frieda. It was completely self-contained with a kitchen, shower, generator, and a Cummins diesel engine powerful enough to pull his parents' fifteen-foot MasterCraft ski boat.

The campsite was eighty miles north of the city, surrounded by vegetable fields in a farming community that had once been a dry flat desert. It was well manicured and grassy with an abundance of shady trees, and the boat could be moored directly in front of their site. The water was muddy brown but warm and flat. It would be both Lumas's and Frieda's first attempts at water skiing.

The four launched the boat in the early morning before the younger camping crowd woke from partying the night before. The boat plopped up and down over the flat water at twelve knots, sending a warm mist of water over their faces. Lumas thought this was like how other people lived, people with money. He forced his brain not to go there; it was unhealthy. He liked Dino and his girlfriend Nellie; they were good people, likeable and unpretentious.

Dino spoke over his shoulder while driving. "We'll stop over there at the corner. I'll pull you guys on the float."

Lumas looked at Frieda and smiled. She was an attractive woman with Middle Eastern facial features. Frieda just made five foot three and had defined calf and shoulder muscles from working out three days a week. He loved eyeing her shapely figure and especially now that she was wearing a skimpy two-piece bathing suit that revealed her cleavage.

She caught him staring at her shapely russet legs, reached for his arm, and wrapped it around her waist. Dino stopped the boat and blew up the wave warrior mat, which looked to Lumas like a king-size red mattress. They snapped on life vests and jumped on the "thing," as they called it with trepidation.

"Hold on, guys!" Nellie laughed loudly.

Frieda turned to Lumas and spoke with a crack in her voice. "What the hell are we doing? How is this fun and how fast is this thing going to go? Don't let me drown, hold me tight."

Lumas squeezed her waist.

"That's not tight enough, here. No, here, higher, higher, wrap your legs around me. If I go over, you are going with me, Lumas. Got it?"

Lumas, Nellie, and Dino began to laugh uncontrollably.

She let out a shriek as Dino pushed hard on the throttle. The front of the floating mat lunged up and then crashed down hard, launching their torsos perpendicular to the water. Dino turned and donned a huge Cheshire cat smile and throttled down more. The mat bounced over the wakes as he steered wide right, left, and made jerky S turns. Centripetal forces pushed their bodies back and forth, careening, flopping about, and bashing into one another.

Nellie was holding her stomach and laughing hard, then cupped her hands to her face and shouted. "Hold on, guys."

Lumas looked at Frieda and said, "Oh, no."

Frieda was the first to go overboard. She shrieked and immediately disappeared over his head. Lumas looked back, seeing her arms and legs flailing skyward and skipping along the water's surface like a rock. With the vest strapped on, she looked like an upside-down turtle before she tumbled, smashing into the water face first. For a second, he thought Dino would stop, instead he turned hard, the boat listed, and a huge wave headed straight toward him. He braced, but the crest of the wave shot him up, out, and somersaulting backward till he belly-flopped hard.

Dino and Nellie looked at each other like two guilty children. Dino uttered, "Oops!"

Lumas swallowed a mouthful of putrid muddy water, turned, and looked back for Frieda. She was swimming toward him, laughing through strands of long auburn hair covering her face. When she reached him, she wrapped her arms and legs around him.

"Are you okay, babe?"

"Ow," was all she could utter.

Nellie barbecued steaks as the others sat around the firepit. Frieda sat next to him. He enjoyed her smarts, wittiness, and he loved eyeing her beautiful figure. She was sensual and confident with ease. She possessed all the qualities he wanted in a soul mate, but she was too perfect.

Lumas knew this relationship would end in another disaster like all the rest. He rationalized that he was not prepared for a commitment, especially a monogamous commitment. It was an excuse and his brain nurtured it. Failure became a consistently dependable guest. Slipping out a door at three a.m. lent less guilt, especially with someone he never wanted to see again. He knew he'd find a way to sabotage whatever Frieda was thinking about, if not now, certainly later, and he would hate himself more-so.

Frieda nudged his shoulder. "Hey, stranger, where did that brain of yours go? You're so quiet."

"Sorry. I was off on Mars temporarily."

She looked at his eyes. "I want to share something with you. I came here with you because you're a nice guy. I wanted to have some relaxing down time, that's all. I don't have ulterior motives, expectations, or any of that stuff. So, I really don't want you to worry."

Lumas began to squirm. Unlike him, she could speak freely

and honestly.

"You have a lot of things bouncing around that skull of yours," she continued. "I can see that and, no, we nurses don't sit around and analyze you from a distance. That would be horrible. I do only because I can feel your thoughts, sort of the Tao thing. I know it sounds a little crazy but it's true. You're not at all transparent, exactly the opposite—you're complex and conflicted and very hard to read. But not all the time, like here and now, you're here and now. This place is lovely, fun, and relaxing. Let's decompress and see where it goes, we deserve it. And remember, 'We are all of us calling and calling across the incalculable gulfs which separate us.' A philosopher by the name of David Grayson said that. Mull that over for the rest of the weekend."

The two days were blissful. Lumas's head cleared and nothing seemed as important as before. They spent the mornings attempting to ski but mostly cruised around the lake's periphery ogling the sites and relaxing. Frieda and Lumas shared conversations about prior relationships, crazy families, and insane people they had encountered at the VA.

During their long walks, he spoke candidly and didn't feel threatened or ashamed to share some sensitive and painful past experiences.

It was like the old biking days when everyone knew everything about everybody, and no one felt threatened or belittled. He didn't drink alcohol or sleep with her. He felt at peace for the first time in years.

Dear Grandparents,
I left the church very young and I do not believe in God, but I believe in the universe. My belief—part spiritual, part scientific—is that energy

never disappears. It can't, it just recycles. All thoughts, both conscious and unconscious, are electromechanical in nature and, therefore, all forms of life still communicate after the body or form dies. Therefore, I believe you're always with me in my subconscious and I try to listen, but this life is so difficult and your voices are muffled.

I had a wonderful weekend camping with three very nice people. I took Frieda, a nurse I met at the VA, who is beautiful. I don't know where this may go, but she is like that nebulous dream I have of meeting a soul mate. However, I am both happy and fearful that she may dump me when she knows me better. I will continue to write about her, for now, I am hesitant and cautious. I have a lot of ghosts and I pathologically continue to create more and more. However, for once this was a healthy weekend not filled with drama.

It wasn't the first time I camped, but the first time I camped without getting into trouble. Before, I had friends who were not so healthy, and we partied way too much. I was the oddball without a consistent partner when I met these people. Bill and Kate and Peter and Victoria were two couples who knew each other since high school. These four were hysterically funny. Their pool parties started with margaritas, greasy burgers, and loud sixties music with a twinge of Motown. The jokes were usually sexual in nature and so funny that my stomach muscles hurt. Eventually, the five or six of us, whenever they set me up with a date, ended up butt naked in the Jacuzzi. My date was usually someone, as the joke goes, that I'd prefer to chew off my arm than wake up next to in the morning. However, it was all very cathartic then.

Bill and Kate had a small camper that slept six of us, we called it cramping. Our mornings started with margaritas, beach football, and reading. Afternoons consisted of more margaritas, music, and football. In the evenings, margaritas continued to flow, and we played dominos, cards, and music until near dawn. All in all, those friendships were the nearest I've come to real friends since Jerome and the gang. As the years passed, I consciously isolated myself from close associations by choice.

Anyway, I have a story for you. The two women took a walk along the beach to investigate a seal at the edge of the surf, which hadn't moved for hours, at the edge of the surf. They approached it cautiously, then quickly one woman turned and ran back to the RV, grabbed a bucket and threw ocean water on the seal. It was intended to be a heroic effort to cool the animal from the midday sun. Instead, that seal opened its round startled eyes, arched its body upward, barked viciously, and went after them. That seal was pissed and plopped furiously trying to nab them. They ran in circles trying not to die.

I could not believe the crowd of onlookers pointing and roaring in laughter. Campers were piling out of their vehicles along the entire stretch of beach. All the while, the women kept running but gave up circling and ran in different directions. My date, of course, it had to be my date, ran for the water and that was bright. How could she possibly think she could outswim an angry seal? She was rescued by campers who distracted the seal until dumbshit made a getaway. I didn't see her again after that trip.

I am very tired. Good night.

Elliot.

The room was pitch black when Lumas awoke in a puddle of his own sweat, cold, shivering, disoriented, and terrified. Again, his brain was attacking him for having such a pleasant weekend, subverting the friendship developing with Frieda, even Dino. It was always the same. Three or four days of healthy psychological and physical activities, then payback.

This night terror in particular was crystal clear, terrifying, and historically accurate. His grandfather was away when she knocked at the screen door. Grandmother cautiously walked toward the door but stopped short of putting her hand on the doorknob. She kept the screen door locked and her foot shoved tight at the bottom.

"What do you want, Sarah?"

"I was coming to see you and my baby." His grandmother didn't respond.

"Can I come in, please?"

Grandmother looked over her shoulder but failed to see the dark blue car, three houses down.

"What do you want, girl? You know we don't want you here. The baby don't want to see you either. Now go on," she said assertively.

"I was passing by and just wanted to kiss him, that's all." Sarah said this in a way that sent an empathetic shiver down his grandmother's spine but also made her even more suspicious. Besides Sarah hadn't been around their house to see the baby in months.

"I am going away for a while."

"Say goodbye right there. Whenever you come here you hit him for no reason. Just go."

Sarah pressed her hand against the screen door and looked hard at Lumas's eyes. The boy grabbed his grandmother's skirt. Even as a child, he could feel the tension mounting, his tiny heart began to race, and tears formed in his eyes.

"I can just kiss him right here. I won't come inside. Just unlock the screen door. I won't come inside," she said sympathetically.

"Stay there. You are not welcome in my house." His grandmother unlocked the door. The boy began to cry. "Stay there, Sarah. Lumas, give your mother a kiss goodbye."

Grandmother picked him up, clasping her arms around his

tiny waist. Lumas gripped his grandmother's neck tightly as she clicked the lock open. Within a second, she screamed and fell back slamming to the floor.

Sarah kicked at the door again, swinging it fully open. Pictures and a lamp flew across the small living room, smashing to the floor, and exploding.

Sarah rushed in and kicked his grandmother solidly in the stomach. The thud and rush of air from her lungs terrified Lumas. The old lady screamed and choked. She tried to fend off the second kick with an outstretched arm but took another one to her right eye. Sarah tightly gripped Lumas's neck and turned to leave. She could not see his grandmother as she struggled to her feet, reached out, and clasped a handful of Sarah's hair, pulling her to the floor.

They fell with a terrifying solid thud that shook the house, both squirmed and yelled in pain. Grandmother grabbed her hair with both hands, arched her leg high, and began kicking her face. Lumas was frozen. He had crawled under the couch as fast as his tiny legs would move, and now squatted under the arm of the long sofa and covered his ears.

His mother screamed, arms flailing, trying to unlock the hold on her hair and dodge the blows to her body. Grandmother pulled with all her strength, her face inflamed with anger. Lumas thought her head would pop off and she'd just die. He began to cry loudly. It ended suddenly when a man ran through the front room, dropped to one knee, and gripped his grandmother's neck. He raised his fist and punched her in the face. She crumpled, her eyes became glassy, and a trickle of blood began to drip from her mouth. Her body was limp, and her head tilted toward Lumas.

Lumas looked into her face, she opened one eye and tried to speak, but only garbled sounds emerged amid frothy bubbles of blood. Lumas's frozen hands reached out and touched her mouth, then looked at the spots of blood that remained on his fingertips when he pulled his hands away.

"Stop, stop, stop!" he screamed. He jumped to his knees and began punching chaotically in all directions. The room spun and his heart pounded. He sucked air in so fast it made him dizzy and breathless. Clenching his fists to his temples, he screamed.

"Lumas, Lumas, wake up," a sweet voice urged from beyond the veil of sleep.

Frieda grabbed his arms and straddled his chest until he stopped shivering.

He looked at her, embarrassed and exhausted. Frieda could feel his heart throbbing between her thighs, she didn't loosen her grip.

"I, I am so sorry, Frieda," Lumas said.

She said nothing but helped him to sit up, removed his soaked clothing, turned him on his side, and gently held him. Lumas was embarrassed but said nothing. Frieda tightened her hug.

"You are okay now," she said softly, "I won't leave you." He slept well for the rest of the night.

The next morning the two sat under a big oak. Neither spoke, enjoying the light breeze.

"Ever heard of Epictetus?" Frieda asked. "Vaguely," Lumas replied, gazing at the grass.

"He wrote, 'The struggle is great, the task divine—to gain mastery, freedom, happiness and tranquility.'"

She opened her backpack and pulled out a book, handed it to him, and kissed him on the cheek. "Promise me you will read this, Lumas. Promise me."

Lumas read the title: *Stillness Is the Key.* The author was

Ryan Holiday.

She held his hand tightly. "How about Henry Wadsworth Longfellow?" she asked. "Listen to what he wrote in "A Psalm of Life."

"Trust no Future, howe'er pleasant! Let the dead Past bury its dead!

Act—act in the living Present! Heart within, and God o'erhead!"

CHAPTER THIRTEEN

Lumas and Guitano met early. Ganz wanted all patients evaluated prior to his arrival. This was his norm: they discussed physical exams, any events overnight, and treatment plans for the day. Dino was in rare form.

"Lumas, did you sleep last night? You look like dog shit."

By this time, Lumas had downed eight hundred milligrams of ibuprofen and a liter of Gatorade. After returning from camping, he'd had two full nights of insomnia, ultimately resorting to two martinis and trazodone in desperation. That did it, but left him with a blistering headache to deal with that morning. As the nurses clanged charts across their desks, the noise sent bolts of electricity through his left eye. He barely managed to avoid grimacing in pain.

Only time and massive amounts of strong coffee tempered this degree of pain and cleared his head, somewhat. A student nurse tried to catch his eye, but he pretended to be deeply into charting.

If he succumbed to language, he'd stammer and sound as ridiculous as he looked.

This was the norm for Lumas. A short period of solitude, peace, quiet, and, in this case, companionship and intimacy without sex, and his brain declared war on his emotions. He had a paucity of emotional intelligence.

Brain to Lumas: "You didn't deserve the virtues you tasted. You weren't worthy of the morality, wisdom, courage, or moderation you experienced with Frieda. Lies and cheating are our 'modus operandi.' It's more comfortable; we're experts, you and me. It didn't happen, it wasn't you, you're irresponsible, Lumas. I am your past, your future, and most important, your present. We work together, we are the team, I am your only guardian, your only friend. I'm even your grandparents!"

"That's not true," Lumas hissed at his brain.

"You caused all the pain and suffering, you must pay for all the harm you've inflicted."

Dino did a doubletake, noticing Lumas beginning to shake. Lumas became terrified, realizing he was having auditory hallucinations. He stood and quickly walked out of the lounge.

In the stairwell, he held his head tightly and yelled, "Stop it, stop it, go away. I won't let you destroy my life!"

Dino was seriously concerned for his friend's psychological condition. He knew Lumas was a target. Jeremy made it a point to slaughter his clinical acumen and charting skills. What was worse, he perpetuated lies and accused Lumas of verbally abusing patients. Dino thought that immensely ironic—Jeremy had survived all these years without a vet disemboweling him. The staff knew he was protected by Karlson, it was his job to make the internship as painful as humanly possible.

Karlson and others in academia believed only that the strongest and brightest should survive the one year of internship, that compassion is overrated and clinicians who use stethoscopes are dinosaurs. Consequently, the interns were demeaned, demoralized, and petrified into submission, the desired consequence, conformity. Jeremy was the death dealer. Karlson was—like so many academic department heads, as if by supersonic Darwinian selection—a total fucking asshole.

Lumas sat on the stairs until the demons shut up, at which

point he walked back to the lounge.

Dino was leaning in his chair, legs outstretched on the desk, and pretended to ignore Lumas as he walked in.

"I am getting tired of these oncologists. They are full of themselves and believe their own billboards. Ganz is benign compared to the rest. We lucked out having him this month."

"The oncology division is as secure as the White House," he continued sarcastically. "No one gets in except by invitation. They bring in lots of research bucks, commandeer a separate ward, pick their nurses, and demand loyalty. In return, they badger the nursing supervisor to give them preferential schedules. They run together like a pack of wolves."

"They name those chemotherapy drugs like something out of *Star Trek*," he went on. "They intend it that way because it resonates as *ahead of its time*," he said, exaggerating the words for dramatic effect, "and revolutionary. Pharmaceutical companies must hire ad agencies to come up with those catchy names. What other specialty calls its drugs Gemzar, Caprelsa, Zolinza, Zyclara, and Xalkori?" he asked with an incredulous laugh.

"Captain, the Caprelsa are launching an attack on Zolinza," he mimicked the captain from the TV show.

"Mr. Xalkori, power up the Zyclara crystals. Give it all you've got, man," he went on, imitating the other cast members.

"But captain, the Gemzar can't take any more or she'll tear apart. I've given her all she's got, sir. The men are crapping Herceptin all over my power grids."

"Stop, Dino, you're making my headache worse," Lumas finally interjected. Lumas's face was throbbing but now it was from laughing so forcefully.

When Ganz walked in, they both quickly turned to their

charting. Dr. Ganz looked more unkempt than usual and reeked of sour cigarettes. His eyes were bloodshot, his face unshaven, and he sported oily uncombed hair and a dirty stained lab coat. Lumas smelled alcohol on his breath from two feet away. He looked like a man who hadn't slept in a week.

His voice cracked when he spoke. "Gentlemen, I am not a man who lies. I depend on you to get me through rounds this morning. Obviously, I am not at one hundred percent. I apologize."

It was impossible to be anything other than supportive. They respected Ganz for his honesty and felt empathetic and protective. For the rest of the morning, he sat in the lounge away from the nurses. Guitano took a piece of paper, wrote, "Do Not Disturb! Conference in Progress," and taped it on the door.

The only patient who needed special attention was Don Otis. He was in more pain and needed pain management escalations. Afterward, they quietly slipped Ganz out the back door. Dino drove him home. Later Ganz called Lumas and asked them to check on Mr. Otis. The nurses reported his symptoms were out of control. When they arrived, he was blue, gasping for air, and frothing at the mouth. Lumas called Ganz and uneasily spoke about his findings.

"Do whatever you can to stop his suffering," Ganz replied.

With the charge nurse's help, Lumas and Dino fumbled with multiple different pain medications, but Otis continued to deteriorate. The tips of his fingers turned blue, his skin changed to a cold sickening sallow façade with patches of rigor mortis. They put in a desperate call to the chief resident, but Otis died before he arrived.

The next morning, both interns were criticized for failing to call for help sooner, but the ultimate blame was solely on Ganz.

After the verbal reprimand, Lumas careened into a deep depression. It was less traumatic going through it with Guitano, but, nonetheless, Lumas began catastrophizing.

Even though all three had worked to alleviate Ben's pain and suffering, it wasn't enough. It was a bad death, an undignified death. Lumas's mind spun and he feared he could be fired, that the chiefs were preparing the requisite plans for a replacement. The end of that day, his compulsive brain could not accept consolation or support from his friend.

Dino made a point of reminding Lumas that they were in this together. It was little consolation. Lumas dreaded ever going back to oncology, believing the nurses had lost confidence in him. Dino knew Lumas was at a low point and told him to come in late the next day.

Lumas wrote quickly in bed. He was both physically and psychologically shattered.

Dearest Grandparents,
If I didn't include this before, I worked at Ralph's grocery store at seventeen. It was the first stable job I had and somewhat less dangerous than the others. Prior to that, I quit Jack in the

Box, when a customer pulled a gun on me for a burger at the drive-through. He fell back and resorted to just grabbing my shirt and driving away, ripping me out of the window as he did so. That was the end of fast-food jobs for me.

Everyone carried guns in that neighborhood. There were constant fights and shootings in the parking lots and in the stores. Stealing was so commonplace that people would tell me beforehand. I didn't want to hear it, but the purpose was clear: "Don't tell anyone." I came to kindly ask them to "not tell me," or would just shrug and walk away. I hated the daily violence; there wasn't a day without it.

I saw two men fight—the thud of a fist to a face is terrifying. It's no wonder kids from violent homes are psychologically ruined and struggle throughout life. Yes, I struggle every day to survive the next. I know I've had a rough childhood but lots of kids do, lots worse than me.

I don't feel sorry for myself. I learned how to stay alive back then simply by having good friends. I miss them, God, I hope they are still alive. The pathetic part is that I admit other kids had it worse than me, but I feel my own emptiness much, much more. That's not a recipe for recovery.

Good night,
Elliot.

CHAPTER FOURTEEN

Dino and Lumas were finished with the oncology rotation and reassigned to the emergency room. Lumas took the offer to sleep in and Dino gave the attending doctor an unconvincing excuse for Lumas's absence. Dino enjoyed working with him, they got along well, but he also knew Lumas was depressed. He worried about his mental health but didn't know how to discuss it without sending him spiraling down.

Unlike Lumas, he came from a family of physicians, both parents were professors of medicine at prestigious universities. Dino Guitano was primed for an internship by his parents. When physical or emotional stressors crept up, he fell back on the supporting words from his parents. If he was overstressed, they sent him to their second home in Scottsdale. He had a three-year relationship with Nellie. In time they came to love each other and planned to get married after the internship.

Nellie had recently submitted her thesis in microbiology and was accepted. She was brilliant, amicable, and attractive. The grants supported her work, much to the disdain of her colleagues, who struggled with funding. Consequently, she kept her lab locked. It was not uncommon for researchers to discover their work published by a grad student or another professor as a result of sharing fax machines. She and Dino shared many interests in common: research, outdoor activities, and traveling. Dino graduated summa cum laude from Stanford as an undergraduate, and then stayed on for four years obtaining a PhD in biochemistry. Afterwards, he obtained an MD degree, not so much due to an interest in medicine, but rather in hopes of having a better chaofnce vying for grants.

Dino had secured a six-figure research grant before beginning the internship. He was likeable, not boorish, and while he enjoyed the pleasantries of a privileged upbringing, he understood he was fortunate. He knew there were brilliant minds all around the world who were struggling to keep food on the table for their families. There were plenty who would never have the opportunities he was born into. These and his other unconventional opinions about socioeconomics and political inequality kept him out of the good old boys club. This made little difference to him, as he despised narcissists.

There were no paramedic ambulances at the VA. Vets would walk in through the back entrance and ask to be seen. Occasionally, a car would pull up and push a vet out and drive away. On Fridays, dingy gray Army busses arrived, filled with homeless vets who were transferred from local shelters. All were malnourished and dehydrated.

Most illnesses were chronic infections, alcoholic liver disease, or psychiatric disorders. Ninety percent were preventable. The physicians knew there weren't adequate resources for addictions or psychiatric disorders, especially after hours, so patients were fed, medically stabilized, and discharged back to the streets. The staff were frustrated and angry at not having resources to refer veterans to in urgent situations.

If the weather was foul, the guards would set up a makeshift skid row in the lobby. Blankets were handed out, which sometimes had to be shared, but the vets never complained. The staff in the ER weren't trained for acute psychiatric interventions, therefore if a vet appeared to be a danger to himself, the staff kept him there until he no longer posed a threat. In these situations, creativity mattered.

When the hospital and emergency room beds filled, those still in need of admission were sent to the skid row lobby by gurney. The nurses would check in on the most seriously ill throughout the night. Food was pilfered from the cafeteria by the guards and passed around. Administrators left early and arrived late, by then the lobby entrance had to be emptied to avoid closer scrutiny and worst-case scenarios. This cycle repeated daily. Administrative attention to the vets lagged far behind the quality of care, but the vets never complained. They acted as if they deserved it.

Lumas was driving on the way to the emergency room when he received a text from Dino to evaluate a patient in the cell. He thought that odd. At that time of the morning, the physicians in the emergency would take the calls till the morning interns arrived. Dino didn't get much rest during the night, but there were still more vets to examine. He examined a man who had developed side effects from antidepressants, the patient was waiting in the emergency room for hours. He was on lithium for bipolar disorder and fell into the black hole for follow-up. Dino controlled his symptoms and asked the nurses to keep him for observation. There were more patients with the usual mix of congestive heart failure, emphysema, and cirrhosis. As a courtesy, he wanted to finish before the morning interns took over.

For years to come, Dino would remember the aesthetics in VA Medical Centers—filthy and depressing. Administrative leader- ship who should fight for veterans' affairs waned from Washington down. For a veteran returning from active service, it was a massive, monstrous, and monolithic mess. Those vets not acutely ill enough to require immediate attention fought the "service-related wall" and weeks to months of processing their paperwork.

Dino was exhausted. Finding the doctors' lounge empty, he fell on the couch. What seemed like a minute, turned out to be one hour of undisturbed sleep. His head in a fog, he stood and headed back to the emergency room for coffee. Anyone would swear he looked hungover from a night of partying. He swayed left to right, occasionally rubbing his forehead. His hair, at this point, had a life of its own and mimicked the barbs of a sea urchin, stiff and pointing in all directions.

One of the old-timers, Mary, sat at the nurses' station. Mary was a no-nonsense authoritative leader, a tough veteran of the Middle Eastern wars and MASH units. She had already seen more trauma than most emergency room physicians would see in a lifetime. She was a good instructor to nurses and physicians alike.

She acknowledged him with a barren smile. "We gave you some rest. Thank the nurses before you leave."

And with that curt response, Dino knew he was excused. "Okay, thanks, I appreciate it. I'm going to check on the lithium guy—"

"He's gone," she interrupted.

"Was he admitted to the psych ward?"

"Dr. Guitano, you aren't serious, are you? No, I went to check on him and he was gone." Again, she looked away and excused him. He left. If he pushed his luck, she could incapacitate him in a second and toss his limp body over her shoulder.

He left through the rear entrance, took a deep breath, and began walking toward Bobby's restaurant, an eatery within walking distance of the hospital. Bobby served a huge ranch breakfast that was greasy and delicious. The last thing he cared about now was the condition of his coronary arteries. He was beginning to feel human again, although sleeping on a couch caused his body to be painfully stiff.

He noticed a group of residents standing together, speaking with two security guards in the far corner of the parking area. This time of morning, residents were usually making rounds on patients. Curiosity got the best of him, so he turned and walked toward them. Bob Gold was standing with a security guard, staring at an old dark and dirty Dodge Dart, a relic. Dino guessed the car doubled for someone's home; it was full of clothes and papers were strewn everywhere, filling the front and rear seats. The windows were dirty and tinged with that yellowish film, noticeable with heavy smokers who rarely opened their windows.

"What's up, Bob?" Dino interrupted.

When Bob turned, Dino could see the silhouette of a head arched back and cocked toward the window. He squinted closer and saw the lithium man. His eyes were half open, his face ashen, and gray-black blood oozed from his mouth and ear, caking his beard into a matted bloody pillow. He looked down and saw a hand stiffened by rigor mortis and gripping a gun. Dino became dizzy and nauseous, and his knees buckled. Bob grabbed him by the waist before he hit the cement.

"Whoa, Dino. Hold on, buddy. Sit down."

Dino sat on the pavement with his vision blurry and his head spinning. He felt cold and began to perspire. He opened his eyes and looked up.

"Ah, shit, Bob I know this guy. He was in the ER last night."

A husky security guard leaned in and spoke, his tone was empa-thetic but there was something different about this guy. Dino looked at him hard for a second. The VA security guards were known to be frustrated wannabees without sidearms, a surly group. Consequently, most staff avoided them. This guy, however, sounded genuine.

"Dr. Guitano, why did he leave?"

How does this guy know my name? Dino thought, but he decided not to bring it up.

"He slipped out through the back door. No one knew he was gone."

"Why was he there, Dino?" Bob asked.

"Lithium toxicity. I was keeping him there until psych opened, and—"

"Okay, Doc," the guard interrupted. "Just sit there for a while. Don't try to move yet."

Dino couldn't move if he tried, his legs felt heavy and lifeless. Bob turned to the guards. "You guys need anything else? Otherwise I'd like to get Dr. Guitano inside."

The guard understood. Normally, Dino would have to give a detailed account of the emergency room visit. That would be sent to the chief operating officer and the chief of medicine. Thereafter, a formal investigation would begin.

The husky guard spoke to Bob. "I'll take care of him, pointing at lithium man. Please call if you remember anything important. Do you need help to stand? Can I give you a ride somewhere?"

"I think I will be okay, thank you."

After a pause, Bob and a couple of the others helped him up. They began to walk back to the hospital.

Bob stopped and turned. "Did anyone hear that?" he asked.

One of the other interns stopped and turned. "I heard something, it sounded like whimpering."

The guard turned and investigated the car. "God, please

don't tell me there is something or someone under that mess," the guard pleaded. The guard moved to the other side of the car. "I hear something from the back under there."

He pointed behind the passenger seat. "I'm going to have to break the window." It exploded with one hit. A putrid smell gushed out and quickly dissipated.

The guard gently moved the mound of debris away with his club until a small black-and-white snout appeared. The pup began whimpering louder and backed deeper into the mound. The guard was visibly shaken.

"Oh my god, it's a puppy! A baby shepherd, it's terrified." He lifted the pup in his arms. "God knows how long he's been in there." For a while, the pup continued to whine, then stopped and began licking the guard's face. The muscular guard's eyes watered, and he spoke gently, as if holding a newborn child. "Hold on, little guy, you can stop the kisses now. Anyone wants a new member of their household?" he asked the onlookers.

Guitano spoke up immediately. "I'll take him."

"Dino, you don't have to do this," Bob intervened. "We're not trained to be psychiatrists. Why do you think this guy blew his brains out right here in the parking lot?"

"I know, I know, but he needs a home now, and I can use the company sometimes. I'll teach him how to bite Jeremy."

"The VA just needs to do a better job, Guitano," Bob said in exasperation.

Dino took the dog and thanked the guard. The pup cried and squirmed all the way home.

CHAPTER FIFTEEN

Lumas finally read the text. "Go to the cell and see patient in room two. Give me a call later."

He was still reeling from the night before. Seeing Otis die in pain made him sick to his stomach. Maybe he'd call Frieda. They could have dinner together, that would be healthier than having dinner by himself. He missed her.

The Afro-American ward clerk eyed Lumas passing his desk. He knew something wasn't normal; Patrick never asked for a physician visit other than Jeremy. The psychiatric staff spent as little time with him as necessary, and Patrick stayed docile as long as he received drugs. He refused psychiatric counseling or placement in a halfway house.

Lumas walked into the room and caught a face full of cigarette smoke. Patrick attempted to stare Lumas down. It didn't work. Lumas had dealt with guys like Patrick growing up.

"Have it your own way," Lumas said with a shrug. He turned to leave.

Patrick smashed the cigarette on the bed railing and sat up. "I am a vet. You should be a little bit more respectful."

"What can I do for you? You asked to speak with a physician," Lumas said, ignoring the antagonizing comment.

Patrick spoke with an exaggerated twang. "Call me Patrick, Doc. I have a cough, you can hear it in my chest. Maybe I need some of those antibiotics."

Lumas was skeptical and didn't want to get anywhere near

Patrick. "What kind of symptoms do you have?"

Patrick coughed. "All kinds of yellow shit coming up my chest." He coughed and opened his mouth. A thick glob of greenish mucus hung from the side of his tongue.

Lumas decided he wouldn't get any closer. He was irritated and thought Patrick was white trash parading as a vet. "Close your mouth. I don't need to see it. Anything else bothering you? Any other symptoms, like fevers, chills, joint aches and pains, a rash, diarrhea, anything else?"

Patrick shot back with a quick sarcastic answer. "Ain't that enough, Dr. Lumas?"

"How do you know my name?"

"Jeremy," Patrick replied simply, a smirk on his face.

Lumas was even more skeptical now. His radar went up, he knew Jeremy was up to something. "Why did Jeremy tell you my name?"

Patrick turned and dropped his feet off the side of the bed. "Just listen to my lungs and get out. Give me some of that cough medication with codeine."

Lumas wanted out and away from Patrick as fast as possible. He pulled his stethoscope out of his pocket and walked toward the bed. As he approached closer, Patrick arched his back, raised his legs high, and kicked Lumas hard in the stomach. This knocked the wind out of him, and he fell to the hard linoleum floor.

Patrick was pleased. He looked down at Lumas holding his stomach and grinned. "That's from your boss, he wants you out of the VA or else," Patrick menaced.

Patrick lay back in the bed, grabbed his stomach, and began to scream. "Stop, get off me! Don't hit me again."

The ward clerk ran into the room. He knew he should have

gone into the room with Lumas. Now he was livid with Patrick. He took a step toward the bed with both hands tightly clenched. Patrick sat up and crawled backward, nearly falling off the far side of the bed.

"You can't touch me, you black son of a bitch. Get away from me," Patrick stuttered.

Lumas looked up.

"No, don't," Patrick feigned fear at Lumas.

He held his stomach and slowly struggled to his feet.

The muscular clerk grabbed his shoulder and lifted him effortlessly, leaning him against the wall. "You okay, Doc?" the ward clerk asked.

"Yeah, I'm okay, thanks," Lumas replied. He turned to address Patrick, a cold glint in his eyes. "Consider yourself fortunate," he said, his voice calm. "Not long ago I would've broken your neck with a bat. You got a sissy shot at me, but don't ever let me see your face again. Never again." Lumas walked toward him and the clerk decided to let the situation play out.

"You have no idea what I'm capable of doing to you, no idea at all. I don't care what Jeremy told you, how much he protects you, gives you drugs, your cigarettes, or whatever else. I will hurt you beyond hurt, and I really don't give a shit what happens to me afterward. You can report *that* to your boss."

Patrick moved back farther. Lumas faked a lunge. Patrick raised his arms awkwardly trying to cover his face.

Patrick screamed out at the ward clerk. "I wanna talk with Jeremy, boy, go call him now. Son of a bitch thinks he can threaten me," he said, his chest puffed up in anger.

The clerk ignored him and looked away. Lumas didn't. He was lean but had overdeveloped calf and thigh muscles from years of riding road bikes. He bent down, gripped the side of the metal bed, and lifted it sideways tossing Patrick over and under. The bedside table crashed onto the floor—cigarette butts, the water pitcher, urinal, and stacks of *Playboy* magazines crashed onto the overturned bed. One arm and one leg flailed out from under. Patrick began kicking the rail, the only part of the bed that saved him from being crushed.

The clerk looked down and spoke. "I wouldn't do that, dumbshit. That bed weighs about five hundred pounds. The rail is the only thing keeping you alive."

Patrick's leg went limp. Lumas turned and looked at the clerk. "Sorry about the mess."

"No problem," the clerk interjected.

When Lumas left, the clerk picked up the phone and pressed some numbers. "Lumas just left, you were right, sir. Okay, no problem."

At exactly eight p.m., the unlocked door to the cell opened. The man entered and gave the male nurse a nod. He wore a V-neck T-shirt that fit a massive chest of muscles, his meaty upper arms tearing at the edges of the sleeves. His gait awkwardly rotated side to side from overdeveloped thigh and calf muscles, and he sported a shiny bald head.

All the residents were sedated and tucked in bed. The doors were closed.

He walked into room two. Patrick hadn't been given his usual dose of Ativan and Demerol yet and was beginning to have minor withdrawal. He was irritated with the Afro-American nurse, suspecting he was taking his time because of the altercation with Lumas earlier. He heard the big man's footsteps, sat up in bed, and raised his voice.

"It's about fucking time… Who the fuck is you?"

The man smiled. "You must be Patrick," the man responded

in a deep baritone voice. "Who am I? Well, let's just call me pain."

He turned, closed the door, and walked toward the bed. Patrick's face turned red and flushed, and his voice stuttered. "Hey, man, what the fuck? What do you want? I ain't done nothing. Did that nurse tell you something? He's lying!"

The man smiled, then lunged, grabbed Patrick's neck, and squeezed. Patrick's face turned anoxic purple, like an overripened tomato. The blood trapped uphill caused his eyes to bulge out of the sockets, his jugular vein was engorged, and his face began to balloon. Patrick tried to scream but only mucus and garbled hissing sounds came out. His upper and lower jaw were locked together by the man's grip. He tried to push away and kick but with each thump, the man squeezed tighter and grinned wider.

His arms and legs flailed in all directions like a dying cockroach. The man began to laugh. Patrick peed the bed. He began to lose consciousness; his arms and legs went limp. The man loosened his grip. Patrick took a deep breath and fell to the bed. His head was clearing; the flashing streaks of light in his vision began dissipating as he limply crawled backwards.

"Stop, man. Hey, man, please. I ain't done nothing! Stop, you almost killed me. Shit, I pissed myself, man," Patrick coughed.

The man leaned in. "Take another deep breath; you'll feel better real soon. I heard you been fucking my sister."

Patrick looked at him, stunned but relieved, realizing there was some sort of confusion. Maybe he wasn't about to die right then after all. "Man, I don't know your sister. I been here, right here, for a month! Shit, you almost killed me, man."

The man straightened up. "Oh no. Shit, you're not McDonald?"

Patrick McDonald?"

Patrick coughed and sat up. "No man. My name is Patrick Greely, not McDonald. You almost killed me, man."

"Ah, shit, Patrick Greely. My mistake, sorry, man," the man said, taking a step back. A smirk remained on his face.

"Sorry, man? *Sorry, man?* What the fuck, you cuddah killed me, man. What the fuck!"

The man grinned and Patrick's heart skipped a beat.

"Just fucking with you, Patrick *Greely.* I know exactly who you are." The man grabbed him under his left arm and right thigh. Patrick screamed. He lifted him effortlessly over his head, stopped, and allowed Patrick to see what was coming next.

"Patrick Greely, can you fly, motherfucker? Let's just see."

Patrick screamed as his body was tossed upward toward the ceiling, then arched sideways, crashing five feet above the floor into the opposite wall, then down onto the hard linoleum. For a few seconds, he couldn't move and only whimpered.

The man walked over, lifted him by the butt of his pyjamas and his nape and threw him backward, overhead toward the opposite wall. Patrick screamed and hit the wall face first. His outstretched arms and legs struck the surface with enough force that it chiseled a relief of his skinny frame into the wall. The plaster cracked. He hung suspended for a second, then slipped down the wall, smacking the floor hard enough that his head bounced. The big man began to laugh loudly.

Patrick saw stars, flashing lights exploded, and excruciating lancing pain raced down his spine. He attempted to roll and lean against the wall but fell backwards, unable to support his body's weight with his arm. He looked down and saw a shard of bone sticking out at the wrist. He screamed loudly. "You broke my arm. Shit, man, you broke my arm!" he hysterically shrieked.

The man walked forward, pushing his booted foot into Patrick's chest wall. The air whooshed out of his lungs, and he turned blue.

"Enough fun tonight, Patrick Greely. Don't try to move or I'll break your chest. Listen to me or I'll be back and I'll stay longer. Next time, I'll fucking paralyze you. Get out tonight and I mean tonight. I'm only going to say this once, Patrick Greely. Never come back, never ever come back here. We are going to be watching you. Don't speak to nobody 'bout me or the doc you sucker punched yesterday, especially not to your bitch boss."

Patrick was losing consciousness.

"Can you hear me, Patrick Greely? Oh, I'm sorry. Your jaw looks broken, it's all kinda splattered thereabouts, some here, some there, and, oh, there's some on the floor. Your face is just kinda hanging on your neck. This is going to hurt a little. Say it, say it, motherfucker. Say you're gone."

A clump of bloody teeth fell out of Patrick's mouth. "I'm gone, man. I'm gone," he whimpered, his gums whistling over the words.

Satisfied, the man left.

CHAPTER SIXTEEN

Hello, Dearest Grandparents,

Something is very wrong. Today I was attacked by a patient. He was sent by Jeremy, the doctor who's trying to get me fired. I still don't know why he hates me so much. Life is tortuous at this moment. I know I'm out of my racial and socioeconomic comfort zone, but I don't deserve to be targeted. I drove and circled the city last night, sporadically parking.

I had nowhere to go and nothing to do and was disgusted with my life. I long for peace and forgiveness, instead, hatred fills my heart. I am so, so lonely. I drove through the old neighborhood, the hood. I was hoping to find distractions, anything, anyone, a fleeting respite from this pain. I've been having horrific dreams, all violent. When I wake in the mornings the bed is always wet with perspiration, the damn ghosts have returned, and I wake screaming, "Kill her! Kill her!"

As dysfunctional as she was, she was still my mother and I loved her. Even the beatings I forgave her, and I would have taken more and still forgave her if only she had lived past my twelfth birthday.

I recall seeing a child, who must have been no more than five years old, running after his mother in a parking lot. I could tell she was angry with him for God knows what. Each time he caught up to her, she turned and slapped him. Each time, the kid fell backwards, hysterically crying, but he'd get up and run to catch his mother again and again. The distance between the two expanded and still, the child ran faster. Not once did I see her look back. As far as she knew, the kid could have been hit by a car or fallen and been knocked unconscious. I have learned the love of a child for a parent surpasses inhumane cruelty.

After Mom died, stepfather number three booted me out of the house. I was thirteen and had nowhere to go, nor any food or clothes, but I was happy to get away, he was another mean and violent man. I rationalized that people like him get theirs eventually, whether here and now or in the hereafter. I believe in karma.

I bounced around and worked at numerous jobs and stayed, or rather hid, at Jerome's home until I could rent a small room in the back of an old lady's home above her garage. I shared the space with rats and spiders. I was sixteen then and on my own and had no one to depend on. I didn't mind much, at least I didn't have to contend with the idiot, and it was peaceful being alone, not lonely like now.

During the Vietnam War, I went to junior college, mostly to avoid the draft. Jerome kept in touch periodically through his sister, but that stopped when he became addicted. That poison was everywhere when I was growing up.

Jerome's ghosts were also powerful; he took a lot of horrific beatings from his alcoholic father. Those ghosts destroyed a gifted athlete physically, emotionally, and psychologically. I miss Jerome and enjoy the respite of recalling good memories of when sports masked the dysfunctional reality of our home lives. My life was on the same track as Jerome, but ironically the Vietnam War forced me into college, where I struggled for a GPA high enough to keep me from being drafted.

Eventually, and mostly out of curiosity, I took a basic biology course and fell in love with the sciences. The more I dove into mathematics, physics, and eventually, medical school, the easier it became to bury my damn pain—although always temporarily and with considerable payback.

There were lots of failed relationships, anxiety, and depression along the way, and the painful loneliness surrounded me. Each failure was not an opportunity to learn and improve but a testament to my feelings of worthlessness. Each success was a mistake, a fluke.

I am more depressed now than at any prior time in my life. The nights without sleep, long days, and constant criticisms by Jeremy just make me want to give up. But I won't. I am a physician because so many fought and sacrificed to open the doors, it would be immoral for me to give up. At the end of each day, I sit in the same obscure spot in the VA lobby. I can identify with these guys—we're all lost.

Good night,
    Elliot.

CHAPTER SEVENTEEN

The residential neighborhood outside the big city was perfect. There, young couples with one child and one dog lived in modest, well-groomed, two-bedroom homes. The streets were wide and lined by tulips and cedar oak trees, which had been planted in the early sixties, adding charm and aesthetic beauty. During the day, couples walked their dogs, kids played basketball in the street, and older folks sat on their verandas and read or conversed with neighbors.

Glenn Evans enjoyed driving through the neighborhood, he imagined buying property there someday. But now, he needed to stay focused. He was employed to eliminate another pedophile. Sociopaths have no remorse, and they are clever. The information was sent to him with the package of money left in his car, again. The same conditions applied, do the deed, research as necessary, and stay under the radar—meaning don't make it a spectacle and don't fuck up. The pay was good, very good, and Evans was glad they didn't want him to off someone with a questionable criminal background. All the prior hits were on seasoned degenerate child molesters, who somehow were able to rape and run. This guy abused his prowess for cunningness and sick, depraved behaviors, digging himself an early grave.

Evans surmised he had multiple employers. He had killed two pedophiles, one serial rapist, and two homophobes who stalked and beat gays. One gay died, and two most certainly wouldn't regain full motor or cognitive function. However, the jobs were too heterogeneous for a single person and disposal was not revenge as much as abject justice. All the hits were repeaters. Evans had, by this time, trusted the background checks he received.

There were no streetlights for blocks; that was a plus and very few residents walked in the dark. But killing the guy in this neighborhood and possibly on the street would terrorize the community. These people didn't deserve that, he had to think of something more creative and outside the area.

Evans followed his target for an entire month, switching rental cars to avoid him becoming suspicious. Finally, he caught on to the man's one convenient habit. Every other Thursday at eight p.m., he'd go to a local bar called Pineapple Station and converse with the regulars while downing three gin martinis.

Evans grasped, early on, that this guy was not only a crook but also a disgusting racist. Most sociopaths were affable and engaging, but cold and calculating. This guy was dirty, obnoxious, and a drunkard. The other regulars gravitated away as his blood alcohol level rose. To his credit, he was an equal opportunity bigot. The bartender frequently asked him to lower his voice, as he berated Afro-Americans,

Latinos, Asian-Pacific Americans, and Jews, of course. That lasted for a few minutes but corresponded with his last martini.

Then he left by way of the rear door to a poorly lit parking lot, all good for Evans. He would exterminate him away from the neighbor- hood and while he was drunk. This guy would never be missed, in fact, the bar would probably offer drinks on the house for getting rid of him. Motives would be too numerous to count and following every lead would turn out to be a detective's nightmare.

His Smith & Wesson .20 caliber handgun was his personal

preference for close killings. It made little noise and was highly effective. The bullet lodged in the substance of the brain rather than exploding the skull like dynamite in all directions. That night, he dressed in dark sweats with a hoodie, which partially covered his face, enough for anyone to have difficulty accurately identifying him. He had dinner at home and took a long nap, which would help him stay awake and focused. Timing was somewhat difficult to plan. He knew he had to kill the guy at close range but not linger around the parking area waiting for him to stumble out. Sitting in his car for an extended period might result in a cautious female requesting an escort from the bar.

He decided to kill him in his car. Over the years, he'd collected a cache of devices to open doors and turn off security cameras. Recently, he had procured a palm-size remote control device that inactivated car alarms and unlocked doors. Even recent models were vulnerable. The device was not easy to come by, was expensive to purchase, and entailed considerable exposure in order to find the right dealer.

With each hit he became more astute, observing his own physical and emotional responses prior to committing the deed. Evans, still an avid student of philosophy, read from Cicero and extrapolated the meaning: *The right of killing was pondered, there would be no discussion nor diplomacy. Further, other children would live in peace.*

He was born with emotional strength, both constructively critical and reassuring at other times. Consequently, he settled into a comfortable balance of values, which otherwise violated the usual standards of societal norms. He slept well, ate healthily, exercised, laughed with the old guys at the park, and occasionally dated. When he left home, his brain was quiet, his heart content.

He lucked out. There was cloud cover and the parking lot

was even darker than usual. He decided to use the remote control and crawled into the compartment section of the man's BMW X5 SUV. Evans wondered how this guy could afford to drive a sixty-thousand-dollar luxury car. It was cramped but not intolerable. He settled in and estimated when the man would exit the bar.

He was punctually drunk and slowly found his way to the car, occasionally stumbling. Evans quietly pulled out the Smith & Wesson and took a deep breath. Something was off. He stopped short of getting in the vehicle and looked around, then unzipped his pants and peed. He got in and closed the door. Evans knew now was the time before the fool started the engine. He began to rise to take aim at the back of his skull when two women passed between them and the next car. Evans crouched again, but the man had already started the car. The women were walking too slowly and might still hear the shots. And if the fool started driving, Evans could get stuck in the back seat after shooting him with the car moving and his body slumped over the wheel. Staying there was not an option, the fool was drunk and might kill him if he ploughed into a parked car.

The man pulled out into the street. It was still dark when he made the turn. Evans sat up and shot three times, all three bullets hit the intended area. The man's head banged against the wheel, his body slumped to the right side, and then the car accelerated. Evans was thrown back against the rear hatch window and banged his head, hard. The man's dead weight must have forced his foot against the accelerator. As Evans pulled himself up and over the back seat, the car accelerated faster.

The car hit the curb, it reeled high, then down hard, tumbling him sideways and back and forth. He straightened just as the car piled up some house steps and crashed into a front door, exploding a large glass-paned window. Someone screamed inside the house, and Evans began kicking the back door—it was stuck. He crawled over the rear door and kicked hard at the hatch top. It finally began to crack open, enough for him to crawl out. An elderly old woman with curlers on her head stuck her face out of what was left of the front window.

"Oh my god, oh my god, is anybody hurt?"

Evans stood up and pushed hard, closing the hatch. He was gloved and didn't worry about fingerprints. He squirmed out and away from the vehicle, repositioning his hoodie.

"Lady, I almost got run over. Call the police."

"Okay, mister, you hurt at all?"

"No, just shaken up. Go call the police. The guy in the car isn't moving."

No one else had immediately run over from the surrounding homes. In the distance, he saw people exiting the bar and starting to walk in his direction, but they were a good half block away. He walked in the opposite direction and disappeared into the darkness.

CHAPTER EIGHTEEN

"I don't know what happened. Patrick told me he did exactly as I told him. I went there today to have him sign a formal complaint against Lumas and he was gone. The staff there said he'd escaped and made a report to security, but nothing happened. I mean they didn't find him. When I pressured the night nurse, he said the same thing and told me to get out or he'd fuck me up."

Jeremy regretted saying that immediately.

Karlson turned his back and spoke condescendingly as if he were speaking to a child. "You let a nurse threaten you and you did nothing? What kind of a spineless wimp are you, Jeremy? Why didn't you have him fired?"

"I can't find Patr—"

"Don't tell me his name, idiot." Karlson cut him off. Karlson turned and walked toward Jeremy, pointing his finger in his face. "That's bullshit. The clerk knows everything. He won't tell you anything about why your gofer disappeared."

Jeremy had endured Karlson's indignant rants many times. He hated and simultaneously adored and emulated him. He believed the constant berating was akin to a loving parent disciplining a child, a parent who only wants the offspring to achieve greatness. He had endured the castigations, believing Karlson would nominate him to be the next chair of medicine.

"I made it clear to…"

Karlson stopped him, palming both ears. "Don't tell me anymore, dammit. I'll get someone else to finish this."

Jeremy sat up straighter, his voice stuttered. "I-I-I can end-end this, this week, I-I-I promise."

"How can I trust you?"

This was Jeremy's chance to redeem himself. "Haven't I always come through for you? This is the sixth year you've put me in charge, and I've fired seven interns. Lumas is protected by Guitano. If you give me the go-ahead, it would be easier to fire both."

Karlson knew he couldn't. Guitano was paying his own salary and he had that large National Institutes of Health (NIH) grant. Calling undue attention to Guitano was dangerous. "No. Stay away from him." Jeremy was angry and envious. He pressed Karlson about it.

"Why, who is he to you? Why are you protecting him?"

Karlson's face turned red and he began screaming. "Don't question me! Who do you think you're talking with? I am not one of your interns. I don't have to explain my reasons to you or anyone. I am the chair. What I say to do is not questionable or negotiable, only doable. If I say jump, you jump. If I say fire an intern, you say, 'Yes, Dr. Karlson.' The word *why* doesn't exist in my presence."

Jeremy pushed back tears and Karlson caught a whimper in his voice. "Okay, okay, I'll get it done this week I swear or…"

"Or what, Jeremy? Will you be the next to disappear? All I need to do is snap my fingers and your position is history. Try getting a position at another academic institution. Your career will be gone forever." Karlson looked at Jeremy's boggy eyes and pastel face. He sat next to him and put his hand on Jeremy's shoulder. "This is important, critically, critically important. I know you can do it," Karlson said, his tone suddenly changing. "I depend on my golden boy…"

Karlson and Jeremy were startled as the door swung opened and smashed into the wall of bookcases. Jennens stood in the doorway and didn't immediately speak. He turned, told the assistant to go to lunch, and waited until the door closed.

"You're both idiots, arrogant idiots," Jennens began. Karlson spoke up. "Hey, don't come in my office and—"

"Shut up. Get out of my way," Jennens shouted, interrupting him.

He shoved Karlson aside, sat at his desk, and inserted a CD into the computer hard drive. The voices were distant but discernible.

Karlson slouched into the chair next to Jeremy. "Where did that come from? Who recorded it?"

Jennens didn't have patience for Karlson on a good day. "She has been recording you for months, maybe years. Did it ever dawn on you two to check her desk sometimes, or ask her a question that throws her off so you can see what she is thinking, whether she is rooting for you or trying to get you booted?" he shouted. "Is she fucking you over?" he went on. "Did you ever think a nobody could bring you down, Karlson?" No one spoke for a full minute until Jeremy broke the silence.

"None of this makes any sense."

"Shut up! Stop feeling sorry for—" Karlson barked at him. Jennens interrupted Karlson and got up and walked toward Jeremy. "What are you talking about? Tell me."

Jeremy looked at Karlson for permission. Jennens saw the look and leaned into his face. "Don't ever do that again. Now, what's going on?"

Jeremy told Jennens everything, from picking one intern yearly for disposal to Patrick's disappearance.

Jennens screamed, "I knew about the intern scam, idiot, but you morons didn't cover your tracks. Arrogance and ego are a lethal combination."

Jennens picked up the phone and pressed the numbers. "It's Jennens. Bring me the security recording outside the psych ward from last night. I'm in Karlson's office. And hurry."

He sat in Karlson's chair and propped his feet on the desktop. "So, you boys been scamming the university for years, and I thought you were novices all this time. Noble of you, very ethical and professional I might add. As I've said before, Karlson, you're just like my old man. He was very noble and ethical, beating the crap out of me every damn night between shots of gin. Beat me more if I came home with average grades. If I got anything higher than average, he beat me harder. The son of a bitch didn't want me to succeed at anything. He could not have a son who accomplished more than him. Can you believe that son of a bitch was jealous of a kid? He died of cancer. After my mother died, I refused to allow you doctors to give him anything for pain. I enjoyed every second when he screamed. I kept him home on hospice. I made sure he had a painful death."

Neither Jeremy nor Karlson were struck by his comment. To them, it sounded like the norm for end-of-life care. Interns still were taught addiction was an issue that needed oversight even at the end of life. "What are you talking about, scamming the university?" Jeremy challenged. "I, *we* fire interns because they don't fit in or they function lower than the standards we set."

Jennens laughed loudly.

"What did I say that's so funny?"

Jennens pointed to Karlson. "Your boss is pocketing the cash. He didn't tell you. How naïve of you. That would have been your insurance policy, idiot." He stopped and looked at Karlson straight on. "And I'll bet he's not sharing a penny with you, no bonuses, sabbaticals, nothing. Typical Lone Ranger hero stuff, but Tonto gets fucked. Ask your boss how he gets the bucks to go on those extended vacations every year. Hey, Karlson, are you telling them you have a rich auntie who left you millions?" Jennens laughed again.

Jeremy looked at Karlson. He began to speak. A knock at the

door sounded, and Evans entered, carrying a disk.

Jennens looked at Evans awkwardly and spoke. "Did you listen to these?"

Evans regarded Jennens. "No," Evans didn't care what was on the disk.

Jennens looked at him for a split second. Evans maintained eye contact. He wasn't intimidated. Jennens opened the disk and scanned through hours of nothing. No one entered the cell between ten a.m. until eight p.m. At exactly eight p.m., the bald man entered and left at eight-thirty.

Jennens looked around the room. "Anyone recognize this guy?" No one answered. He looked at the guard again. "I want you to find out as much as you can. Something is wrong here. Did you find out if she made copies of the disk?"

"Yes, five. But that doesn't mean she didn't burn more copies."

Jennens leaned back in the chair. "Yeah, I know. And therein lies our problem. Get back to me when you know something more."

"Like what?" Evans challenged. "I'm not a detective, and I don't like the way this is heading, do you understand, Jennens?"

Jennens, Karlson, and Jeremy became nervous. Evans, the security guard, was not another one of Jennens's cronies. He wasn't intimidated.

Jennens's voice cracked. "Okay, yes, I understand."

The guard walked out, Jennens took a deep breath, stood, and left. Karlson told Jeremy to stay.

CHAPTER NINETEEN

Evans woke the next morning with a painful stiff left shoulder. He guessed he tumbled hard in the back seat when the SUV went airborne, crashing him into the door. He thought it could have been worse. He might have lost consciousness and gotten trapped in the car. All in all, besides leaving a mess, the jerk was dead and Evans got away without any major complications.

There was the mandate from his unknown employer to stay under the radar. He wondered how far under the radar was considered acceptable. He scanned the local newspaper and watched the morning TV news—which reported drive-by shootings, hit and runs, accidents, any murders that had occurred overnight—but nothing was mentioned about his hit, just like with the other exterminations. It was as if he'd squashed a roach, the deed was very ordinary.

Jennens called. "Stop by my office this morning."

Jennens didn't demand anything from Evans. He was careful not to piss him off for two important reasons: first, Evans knew too much, and second, the guy scared him. In retrospect, it was a mistake to ask him to occasionally sleuth around. He was unpredictable, aloof, and Jennens couldn't find anything in his employment history to blackmail him. In fact, the guy just seemed to have materialized out of nowhere. That made Jennens vulnerable and uncomfortable, someday he would have to tidy up the situation.

Evans stood and walked around his desk as Evans walked in.

"Have you seen Tina Moore?" Jennens asked.

"No, why?"

"She didn't show up for work today." Jennens was edgy and spoke fast.

"And..."

"And, she hasn't missed a day's work in twenty years. I don't like it, I'm concerned about her."

Evans knew that was a lie. "So why tell me? She's your assistant." "Can you go by her place and check on her?"

Evans was annoyed. "I keep telling you, I'm not a private detective. I did you one favor, now you're making me regret it."

Jennens stepped back to his desk and sank into his chair. He was anxious and squirmed. "Okay, this last time, just drop by her place. I won't ask you to help me again. It's my job to look after the staff."

Evans looked at him and smirked another lie. He turned and walked toward the door.

Jennens stood and grabbed his arm and pulled hard. Evans turned, clutched Jennens's hand, and squeezed. Jennens's face turned red. "You're breaking my hand!"

"Don't do that again, unless you want to lose a handful of your teeth. Don't ever put those paws on me, Jennens."

"Okay, let me go, now!"

Evans released him. Jennens rubbed his hand.

"This is the last time. Don't contact me again," Evans said.

Evans waited outside Tina's condominium until he was certain the morning crowd had left for work, or at least he hoped they had. He had no idea what Jennens was up to, but he didn't trust him.

Jennens was desperate and dangerous. He could make her disappear.

And he had enough cronies working for him who would be forced to assist, or they all would go down together.

Evans thought the entire situation was surreal, something out of a TV soap opera. Now, Tina knew everything about Jennens, Karlson, and Jeremy. However, Evans was thinking about ways to extricate himself as soon as possible.

Tina probably had enough recorded to put Jennens in jail, Karlson and Jeremy also. She had likely realized that Evans had gone through her desk and found the recordings. It was either that or she wanted Evans to find them. Tina did not seem like a sloppy spy, so he chose to think the latter. Why him though, and why now? Nothing made much sense. She could have sent all the information on the three of them to Washington long ago. So, he guessed she must not be done collecting incriminating evidence.

Tina's condo was the last unit on the ground floor, located around the back. Thanks to the shrubbery, which covered the path left of the walkway, nobody could see him from the adjacent building.

The door was only partially closed. *Thanks much, Tina*, he thought. That saved a lot of work picking her lock.

"Hello," he called out. "I'm Evans, the security guard from the VA. Anyone home?"

No answer.

He pushed the door all the way open. The living room was meticulously organized. No obvious signs of an altercation. He walked in farther. The kitchen was undisturbed, glasses and dishes stacked neatly on the island.

He walked up the stairs, careful not to touch anything that could be powdered for fingerprints. The bedroom was undisturbed and neat. He couldn't find her purse or keys. He left quickly, leaving the door partially opened. He did not want to be there in the event Jennens called the police. He was capable of anything.

Evans drove back to the hospital and mulled over a plan for the rest of the day. He headed to the lobby.

The old vet was sitting alone. Evans knew he was waiting for Tina. The man looked relaxed, barely repositioning at all for a full hour. He didn't look at the clock or turn to see if she was exiting the elevator. At half past five, he stood and left. Evans decided not to follow him, the old guy was there for a purpose and would probably spot him, and he knew this guy had a lot of gray matter. But most important, Tina didn't show and the old man did.

Evans saw Lumas sitting in the corner. He'd noticed him taking up that spot three or four times weekly. They'd never met, but Evans had memorized the faces and names of nearly all the medical and administrative staff, a mental exercise he was exceptionally good with. He enjoyed calling them by name. It startled most and sent a creepy, eerie chill down their spines.

Maybe Lumas had seen something, or there was an outside chance he'd spoken with Tina or the old guy.

"Hello, Dr. Lumas. May I take a seat?"

Lumas was in deep contemplation, caught himself, and looked up. "Evans, right?" Lumas asked.

Evans was surprised. "How do you know my name? We've never met."

"I saw you pick up one of the homeless vets some months ago and take him to get a meal. That was nice of you."

"I get the first part, but I don't publicize where I take them afterwards."

Lumas took a deep breath. "This looks like a big place, but it's actually not, in a pseudo-philosophical way."

"Oh, you mean people talk a lot." Evans and Lumas laughed.

"Sort of, but more. For instance, I dropped a line about you to HR, none of my business but someone should recognize what you do, and I suspect this has happened many times before. The assistant there said she gets a lot of drop-by compliments about you. It should not go unrecognized. I got a mouthful of it from a ward of vets when you ordered delivery one night. This place has a soul, with exception."

"What do you mean?"

"Look around, some of these guys have been sitting here for hours. The registration window is closed. I don't know how these guys even know how to get the attention of a clerk. And I've seen the people behind that window on the phone all day long trying to get service-related approvals for care. I think they try to do their best, but the place is a mess. There are not enough people to handle the workload, and the guys at the top don't seem to care at all. For the guys who make it past service-related approvals, the fortunate few then must wait for an appointment to get in the clinics, which can take months. We have enough medical staff but again not enough ancillary people to schedule lab tests or studies. The outpatient physical and occupational staff have been cut back to a skeleton crew.

"Some of these guys wait months for a simple test. We must miss so many bad things that could have been handled much earlier." Lumas went on. Evans couldn't stop him even if he tried. "Then there are the inpatients. You've already seen some of that mess. Most of the time, the food is delivered an hour late and cold. It's not the staff's fault, some jerk at the top fired a bunch of people in the kitchen. Some of the staff are vets, and others just respect them, but all the employees want the best for them. As I said, this place has a soul. The problem is administration and the medical hierarchy, who don't give a crap."

Evans caught himself getting angry but quelled his emotions. For now, he needed to let Lumas vent and maybe say something that would help him find Tina. Lumas was observant, maybe he recently saw Tina talking to the old guy, hopefully within the last few days.

"The idiot chief of staff and his kiss-ass have made our lives more difficult, which translates into less efficient care."

Evans had no idea what that meant but it didn't sound very empathetic.

"Now, we transport the vets to the lab and X-ray departments, do our own blood draws, and run the lab equipment. It takes hours to do simple things that should take minutes, if you know what you're doing. Administration couldn't manage that one without the help of Karlson."

"Who's he?"

"He's the chief of staff. They are all in bed together."

Evans knew it was time to redirect Lumas. "I'm looking for an employee who went missing, an administrative assistant in your boss's office. Maybe you can help me. There's an old guy who sits over there every day. Tina sits with him and talks for an hour or so."

Lumas looked at Evans and tried to sense if he was honestly concerned. He seemed genuine. "Yeah, I know who you're talking about—older guy, looks and dresses like a farmer, scruffy yellow beard. I had a conversation with him once. He's a nice guy."

"I need to speak with him, maybe he knows where she is. Does he ever come back later in the evening?"

"I usually take up this spot till seven, never seen him return. Do you want me to call you in the unlikely event he does this time?"

"Yeah, that would be helpful. You want a ride home?"

"Thanks, I have a flat tire, so—" Lumas stopped mid-sentence, fixing his eyes on Evans. "How did you know I've been waiting for a ride?"

Evans stood and leaned toward Lumas. "You're not the only observer here," he said before he turned and walked away. Without turning back, Evans shouted, "Hey, Doc, you are the only person who can allow them to fire you. It's all between your ears. Read a book called *How to Think Like a Roman Emperor*. Put down the textbooks for a while. No offense. I know you are a good doc, but… give it a little thought. See ya."

Lumas was surprised for a second. "What? Hey, stop! Where did that come from?" he called out after him.

Evans kept climbing the stairs.

CHAPTER TWENTY

Lumas had to bypass his ego with effort and took the guard's recommendation. *How to Think Like a Roman Emperor.* What did that have to do with the vets or the inefficient VA system or him? The truth was that the book was a testament to the virtues of ancient Romans and had very little to do with the history of Roman civilization or conquests, something one would realize if he or she carefully read between the lines.

Stoicism, the prevailing philosophy, was how to think like Romans who lived in harmony with nature. It consisted of the endurance of pain without complaint. There were a great many Stoics who had differences of opinions about how to practice the ancient Greco-Roman philosophy. However, Lumas was most impressed with the concept that the highest good is based on knowledge and living in harmony with reason and indifference to fortune and pain.

He knew what it would take: practice, practice, practice. It was not easy to reorganize his way of thinking.

He was angry at the world and essentially felt sorry for himself, dolefully thinking his childhood was the worst anyone ever endured, and that his loneliness and depression belonged to him and him alone. He was certain he was born by accident, a fluke of nature destined for a life of misery.

Simplistically, his self-inflicted and erroneous beliefs that he was different, the ego, led to self-destruction and the cycle of despair and loneliness. It was, in fact, more cowardly than noble.

He succumbed to the dark side of human nature, resignation.

He could not change Jeremy, Karlson, or his destiny. Therefore, better adapting and not stressing over the impossibility of the situation here and now, especially that which he had no control of. He could, and should, only control his response to ignorance and injustices. Other than changing the way he thought on a second-by-second, minute-by-minute, and day-by-day basis, by rebooting his subconscious, could he possibly alter his self-destructive behaviors.

CHAPTER TWENTY-ONE

A nurse unassumingly walked through the lobby past the veterans into the elevator. She exited onto the oncology floor and slowly walked past the nurses' station. It was shift change, and the day and evening nurses were all in the conference room. She continued without being noticed and entered room nine. The room was dark, and the patient, Betty, was asleep and snoring loudly, occasionally jerking in pain, moaning, and groaning. The nurse took a deep breath, closed the door, and walked toward the bed.

Betty was weak and sedated from pain medications programmed through a pump to deliver one mg of morphine per minute. The nurse was aware that Betty was receiving low doses of pain medication for her severity of pain but could not convince the physician on-call to give adequate amounts so Betty would not have peaks and troughs of severe breakthrough pain.

She unlocked the pump and tripled the hourly amounts and immediately gave Betty twenty milligrams of morphine. Within a minute Betty settled down, her limbs became limp and her respirations shallow. She waited and held her hand until Betty died, left the key in the pump, and disappeared out and down the stairwell undetected.

The nurses knew Betty had the choice to die with dignity, under her own volition, and not in pain.

CHAPTER TWENTY-TWO

"What do you mean you just found her dead? Why the hell did you call me? Why not call her physician?"

Jennens was irate, the charge nurse on oncology sounded panicked and refused to notify the on-call doctor. The nurse told Jennens he needed to come there right away. He took his time.

The charge nurse met him at the entrance to the ward.

Jennens started to speak in his most authoritative, condescending tone. "What's so important?"

She turned and walked toward room nine. "Just follow me."
"I don't have time for…"

Clearly, he did not intimidate her. "You do now."

He followed, but the putrid odor stopped him. Even Jennens knew the smell of a decomposing body. He stopped, coughed, and stepped backward out the door.

The nurse stuck her head out the door. "There is a face mask on the table behind you."

He looked at her, angry for not having been warned about what to expect. He grabbed a mask, slammed the drawer, and reentered. The mask only partially blocked the smell. The nurse, seeing him turning pale, disregarded and rolled her eyes. She pointed at the bed and said, "She's dead."

"I can see and smell she's dead," Jennens shouted.

Jennens moved closer to the bed and noticed the key in the pump. "Your key—"

"No, dammit, I have my key right here in my pocket," she

interrupted him.

She pulled it out and held it up in front of Jennens's face. "Every charge nurse on all the wards has a key to the pumps, only the charge nurses. Someone else came in during shift change or after midnight and did this, probably after the last patient evaluations."

He coughed as they both walked out of the room.

"Why would someone leave the key in the pump?" he quietly asked. The plump nurse rolled her eyes again and answered. "I don't know, that's your job to find out. But whoever the nurse was, he or she increased the dosage of morphine. I'd say leaving the key in the pump made quite a statement. Wouldn't you agree?"

"Who was she? And keep your voice down, dammit," Jennens demanded.

"Betty was a pilot during Desert Shield and a tough old girl. She was dying of colon cancer, basically any day. She was homeless. We knew her well."

Jennens seemed almost elated at the mention of Betty being home- less. "So, she has no relatives or friends?" he asked.

"To the best of my knowledge, she has no family but a shitload of friends here."

Jennens chuckled and smirked, his sardonic response caused the nurse's face to flush red. She balanced her stance and took a step toward him. Grabbing his left arm above the elbow, she squeezed. Jennens pulled back but found himself caught in her painful grip. The cherub-faced nurse was too strong, she didn't budge.

"What is so damn funny?" she asked.

Jennens pulled back again, but the vice grip only tightened. "You're hurting me, lemme go… now!" Jennens hollered.

She turned her head right and left, scanning the hallway. A small group of nurses and orderlies had collected at the nurses' station and were watching the situation as it unfolded. Not a word was uttered, and they didn't attempt to help or hinder. Except for a few abject and irritated expressions, they stared like the living dead, emotionless.

The nurse squeezed tighter, turned toward the gathered group, and escorted Jennens to the service elevator, into which she forcefully pushed him. She stared at his eyes as the doors closed.

Jennens stepped out of the elevator, rubbing his arm, he picked up his pace to Karlson's office.

"I need to speak to you, now. Call your boy," he declared once he arrived. Jennens had by now taken to walking into Karlson's office unannounced, mostly to disturb and irritate him. Now he was fuming.

Jeremy came right away. He sat in one of the chairs.

Jennens locked the inside and outside doors and then promptly began screaming. "What the fuck is going on here? I want to know the truth, now."

Jeremy stood and faced him. Jennens pushed him back in the chair.

"Sit there and talk, both of you. Which one of your lackeys is capable of murder?"

Karlson sat forward with a stunned look. "What are you talking about?"

"Someone killed an oncology patient this morning, got in and out before anyone noticed. Someone who knew the nurses' schedule."

"Which patient?" Jeremy asked.

"Does it matter, idiot?" Jennens screamed in response. "Are

you retarded? The feds will come down on this place and interview every one of us. And that will spark an internal investigation about ledgers, payroll, accounts receivables—you two get where I am going. They'll interview the doctors and with your rotten credibility that will initiate an investigation of this entire goddamn program."

"We haven't killed anyone!" Karlson shouted in defense. "Really? What about Hanna Choy? What happened to her?"

"Wasn't she last year's target? Didn't she jump off the tallest building on campus last year? Nothing goes on here I don't know about. I don't care what you two idiots do unless it conflicts with my plans."

"We had nothing to do with her suicide, nothing," Karlson insisted.

Jennens sat and crossed his legs. "I know you two set her up to appear she was incompetent until you had ammunition to fire her, then she committed suicide."

"We didn't know she was unstable," Karlson responded. "Besides a depressed physician is a dangerous physician. Eventually, she would have done it anyway."

"God," Jennens spoke, exasperated. "I will never understand how stupid doctors can think and behave. You know what the suicide rate is for medical students and doctors in training? Astronomical, twice the rate for the same age group. And not one medical school has done a damn thing about it. You academicians are the cause of the problems; your narcissistic egos are literally killing people. Suicide is murder if you forced her to jump; it's the same as pushing her out a window. Look, you two, nothing is sacred if the feds get in here. They will locate and question all the disgruntled physicians you two fired and look for a pattern. Eventually, someone will put together you canned physicians to line your pockets. Do you want to justify firing those physicians under oath?"

He looked at Karlson and screamed again. "You understand we all go down together! Now, I want to know who you two Einsteins have been torturing this year."

Karlson looked at Jennens. "His name is Lumas."

Jennens walked through the hallways, taking his time to mull over what he'd learned about Lumas. No matter what Laurel and Hardy typecast, he didn't sound like a murderer, but it was useful information anyway. During an investigation, someone would eventually express their opinion about the cutbacks, employee complaints he had successfully suppressed, and general disdain for administration, primarily him.

If left as the situation was now, he would also have to explain why it took so long to report a murder, but maybe not, if he handled things right as quickly as possible. He knew Karlson and Jeremy were stupid and egotistical enough to believe their own curriculum vitae. Left with their unsubstantiated opinions of Lumas, it would lead to a lot of unanswered questions. And, of course, Tina's disappearance was still a mystery. He picked up the pace to his office. There were too many loose ends.

CHAPTER TWENTY-THREE

"What did you find out at Tina's home? Why haven't you called me?"

Silence on the other side. Jennens took a long deep breath. He had stepped over a line and had to backtrack. He stuttered and held the receiver tightly. "Uhh… I'm sorry. I meant, have you something to tell me about her? I have a lot going on and I may need your help again, please."

Evans still did not answer.

"Are you there? I can pay you well, very well."

Evans breathed into the receiver purposefully and let Jennens sweat for a few more seconds. He spoke as coldly as he could, for effect. He wanted Jennens to feel vulnerable. "I'm coming over, now," Evans finally said.

Jennens hung up the phone. "Shit."

Evans arrived thirty minutes later, opened the door without knocking, and stood facing Jennens.

"Do you want to sit?"

"No, what do you want? I told you the last time, no more sleuthing around for you. Did you understand I meant it?"

Evans had decided to stay in the loop since going to Tina's home. As far as he knew, Jennens was trying to implicate him in Tina's disappearance. It would be just like him to think Evans left fingerprints everywhere. He despised him and had by this time developed strong feelings for the vets. He thought it was just like Lumas said, they deserved better. They were soldiers.

Jennens was stuttering again. He sipped water while trying to control his shaking hands. "You sure you don't want to sit?"

"No."

"Okay, can you tell me what you found at Tina's home?"

"Nothing," Evans replied, stone-faced.

Jennens thought for a moment, then leaned forward. "How much do you want?"

Evans thought that this was just where he wanted him, scared and desperate. "I'll give you a bank account number and a dollar amount this week. You are to memorize it, nothing by email or texts from now on."

"Okay."

"And I want unrestricted access to the system. That means access to everyone's emails and the secured emails also."

Jennens looked startled then composed himself. "Why? I can tell you everything you need to know."

Evans just looked at him, didn't answer. "Okay, can I ask why you need access?"

"You want my help or…"

"Okay. I'll have your password set up tomorrow morning," Jennens conceded.

"Make sure I can change it." He leaned forward into Jennens's face. "Jennens, don't let me catch you trying to hack me. That would be bad for your health."

"I won't, now tell me what you found."

"No."

"But you said you would…" Jennens protested.

"Stop talking and listen. I want the money and access first. And, Jennens, I want to know everything. If I think you are lying to me, well then…" He straightened, stared at Jennens, turned, and walked out.

The next morning, he went to Jennens's office, gave him the account number, and took the username and password. Evans told him what he had found at Tina's home and that she had not met the old man at their usual time for the last three days. He waited an hour, then left. None of it made any sense, except that Tina left quickly and must have known someone listened to the recording and went to her home to find duplicates. Who it was, was a no-brainer—Jeremy sent by Karlson.

Evans spent the rest of the day reading through Tina's emails. He had no idea what he was searching for or why, it was not his business. Evans decided to give his brain a rest, something would come to him. Tracking down what Jennens was really worried about kept his mind active. Jennens wasn't tracking Tina for benevolent reasons; there wasn't a compassionate bone in his body. From the beginning, he had asked Evans to beat vets, employees, and even vendors. Evans refused, but Jennens was persistent.

After a while, he realized Jennens was all about loyalty. Once bought, there was no going back. And Evans did accept the under- the-table bribe when he first met Jennens. It was all a test from the beginning. To keep Jennens off his back, he agreed to make a show of being his personal assistant. With Evans's stature and pseudo-aloof demeanor, the staff considered Evans an enforcer. However, Jennens knew Evans was not one of his minions and that was a problem. He could not trust him—Evans had threatened to snap his neck one too many times.

CHAPTER TWENTY-FOUR

Lumas entered the doctors' lounge and sat facing one of the computer screens. He did not scan his ID card to open the program but instead sat motionless, staring at the blank screen. Amin walked over and began bumping his hand with his huge doggie snout, wincing as he sensed Lumas's tension.

Dino turned to talk to him. "What's up? Why so grim?"

Lumas turned and spoke softly and dejectedly. "I'm finished seeing my patients. I am going to check out to the on-call doc and get out of here."

Dino stopped him from leaving. "Whoa, buddy, the best thing for you to do now is stay right here. Do not go running off by yourself. Jeremy is trying to do just this, make you crazy and depressed enough to withdraw and disappear. A couple of days of missing in action, and they have you. Go downstairs to the on-call rooms and crash for a couple of hours. After I walk Amin, I'll drop him off in your room. He's good company, and it's about time for his afternoon siesta."

Lumas agreed and left. He sank into the hard, unforgiving metal-frame bed, feeling dejected. But he knew Dino was right, if left alone, he would think of some way to punish himself. He microwaved the last cup of chamomile tea from his thermos, and then passed out in a heavy sleep.

Dino thought Lumas was right. Very soon they would find some way to fire him. He needed to find the reason and take it to the dean. He leaned back and began to stroke Amin. The rescued shepherd pup had grown to be a muscular seventy pounds of heart and playfulness. He loved children, diving into waves at the beach, and playing Frisbee in the park. Overall, he was a true friend and had good company.

Dino named him Amin, French for a friend, a descriptive, solicitous, and regal appellation for a big teddy bear. He excelled in therapy school, so Dino took him to the hospital daily where he immediately became a star. Patients, nurses, and physicians loved seeing him roam the wards, going from one depressive stark room to the next. He always got a good scratch on the head while sitting next to a patient's bed and was an exceptionally gifted shrink.

Dino forced his brain to focus on the upcoming evening. He and Nellie were invited for dinner with her parents and he promised to be there on time. He enjoyed their company; they were a pleasant couple. But Dino never enjoyed sharing a good meal with other physicians, especially university physicians. Academicians were boring and wasted his time incessantly talking about their research projects. Other than at barbecues, he avoided mixing dinner and a good Bordeaux with boring people. Instead, he coveted his time with his future wife.

Jeremy walked in.

Dino felt a flash of electricity shoot down his spine. He immediately began thinking of ways to hurt him. Maybe he could catch him in a lie or maybe he should threaten to pull the grant if the university didn't terminate his ass. He would be glad to do anything to discredit and dismember both Jeremy and Karlson.

"So, where is Lumas this morning?"

Dino turned his back to Jeremy, focusing on the computer screen before him. "He's around, probably still making his rounds."

Jeremy's curt and pejorative voice grew louder. "I asked a question of you, Dino. Where is Lumas?"

Amin's ears straightened vertically and cupped toward Jeremy. Dino turned his chair toward Jeremy. "He's probably trying to clean up your fucking mess from yesterday."

"A mess," Jeremy retorted with a chuckle. "I take no shit from these vets. They get sarcastic with me or question me, they pay."

Dino went from being annoyed to angry. Amin looked at him, sat up, and whined. "Why did you have to embarrass the guy? There was absolutely no reason to do that."

Dino was the only intern who got away with questioning Jeremy. "Fuck off, Dino. If you weren't protected by Karlson, I would have ripped you apart a long time ago."

Dino's immediate reaction was to confront Jeremy, instead he kept composed.

Jeremy continued, "You can keep that straight face, but I know about your deal with the university. All the while you thought I didn't give you shit because you have a PhD."

Dino let him go on. He knew Jeremy was a sick man and needed to be institutionalized. Arguing with him would lead to nowhere except frustration.

"I have been protecting you from your fuck-ups all year long. That was my job, Dino. You would not have made it through this program without me. I suppose someone on campus wants your grant money badly. Congratulations, you just bought yourself an internship. You owe me."

Jeremy waited to see a stunned look on Dino's face, but it didn't happen. Amin sensed the hostility in the room, sat up, and barked once.

"I'd buy another internship rather than be a psychopathic

whore for Karlson. Yup, I paid a small portion of my grant to get into this program. I'd do it again, especially because I opened a position and didn't eliminate a candidate better than me."

Dino's response took the steam out of Jeremy. Seeing the look on Jeremy's face, Dino decided to go for the jugulars.

He gave Amin a command and pointed at Jeremy. "Amin, teeth."

The animal stood deliberately, bent low in a concentric mass of muscle, growled, and slowly hunched forward. A thick crop of hair terraced from neck to tail, jowls retracted with upper and lower cheeks displaying sharp, white-fanged canines. He lunged forward whenever Jeremy exhaled.

The nurses sitting outside recognized Amin's growl, what was once playful was now viciously primeval. No one moved, knowing Dino had probably just had enough of Jeremy's harassment this time. Jeremy reached out for the arm of the next chair but froze when Amin lunged closer. The dog would strike and gnaw his arm if he moved too fast. Dino watched, calculating enough time to terrorize Jeremy but not letting Amin loose.

Amin crouched lower. Dino was stunned to see this level of ferocity from his animal.

Jeremy's face was gaunt and sallow. He was afraid to move or talk, his voice cracking. "Get your fucking dog off me. Call him off now." Dino would later revisit the instant when Jeremy said, "Fucking dog," and swear that Amin understood the expletive. The shepherd lunged forward, his canine teeth mere inches from Jeremy's testicles.

"Stop him, stop now!" Jeremy protested.

Dino knew the timing was critical, he didn't want to call off his dog too soon.

Jeremy was shaking uncontrollably. "Say please."

Dino knew that was a mistake, however, he could not help but embarrass Jeremy, even if it was just between them.

He called off the dog. "Amin, heel! Come," he ordered. The shepherd did not relent.

Dino repeated the command.

The dog targeted Jeremy. Amin didn't move but kept a predatory stare at his eyes. His ears slowly began to rise, twisting and turning like two gigantic radars homing in on any aggressive moves.

Dino tried once again. "Amin!"

What was seconds seemed like an eternity to Jeremy. The dog raised his head and backed away. Amin glanced back at Dino. The dog's eyes revealed that killing this man was normal, like stalking a meal. The dog continued to back up, not surrendering his posture until he reached Dino, then sat next to his master, keeping a piercing watch for any quick moves or angry intonations from Jeremy.

"Get out very, very slowly and don't look into my fucking dog's eyes."

Jeremy walked halfway through the doorway, grabbed the handle, turned, and slammed it with a thud that rocked the hallway, startling the nurses at the desk. Amin charged, slamming into the closed door with his massive torso. He sniffed below the door and barked, whining at Dino to open the door.

As Jeremy passed the nurses' station, one of the students let loose three loud barks. He turned, extending his arms, then fell backward on the linoleum floor. Those sitting had to stand to lessen their painful guttural laughter; others leaned over and held their stomachs, laughing uncontrollably.

The charge nurse strolled out of her office having seen the spectacle through her door. She leaned over the counter and eyed

Jeremy, grimacing in pain. She casually turned to her nurses. "Well, well, students, let us break for lunch. Make sure your documentation is completed and meet in the lounge in fifteen," she said, her voice chipper.

CHAPTER TWENTY-FIVE

Dino was not sure if Lumas went down to the on-call room. He was depressed. He was better, but still unpredictable. He leashed Amin and went down the back stairs to the dungeon, branded for the similarities. Amin winced, barked loudly, and began sniffing corners, as Dino turned right at the last stair. The shepherd crouched low and homed in on three empty pill packets in the corner. "What's up, Amin?"

He crouched and picked up each packet, all were empty. "What the hell is this doing here? Lorazepam, two milligrams,"

Dino said aloud. "No way, Lumas, you didn't…"

Amin turned and fixed his vision down the long, dark tunnel behind them. His oversize oval ears rotated right and left until he fixed on the movement, then he reared on his hind legs, growled, and barked viciously. The animal startled Dino, but his reaction was too slow. Amin barked persistently and began charging down the hall.

Dino screamed when the leash tightened around his wrist and he fell face down, getting dragged behind by the big shepherd.

"Amin, stop, stop!"

The shepherd ignored his commands, transfixed on the sound ahead, as Dino barrel rolled over and over, smashing into the walls. "A… MIN. Heel! Stop!" The animal was in another place and out of control.

The hallway was sloping downhill and leveling at each turn,

as Amin sped faster and faster. Dino screamed again as the leather leash tightened and burned his wrist. The dog turned sharply left, following the serpiginous path down the hallway. For a second, Dino saw the silhouette of a human body running some thirty yards ahead.

"Stop, goddamn you, the dog is pulling off my arm," he yelled out. "Stop, asshole!"

The ghost ran left, and Dino rolled and screamed in pain. Amin turned his massive head for a second, as if to remind Dino to hold on tight. This gave him a second to react, and he pulled the leash with all his strength. Amin's neck tilted enough to grab his collar. The dog tripped and fell sideways, sliding to a stop. Dino wrapped his arm around the dog's neck and held on. The dog continued to stare down the dark hallway, his mouth began frothing with thick white sputum. He winced and barked again. Dino held on.

"Amin, stop. Calm down, buddy."

He heard a door slam in the distance, but it was too dark to see anyone. "What the hell, who's down there?" he yelled. "Goddammit, this is like *Freddy's Return*!"

He stood and looked back down the dark hallway, realizing Lumas hadn't come out of the room when Amin went berserk. Something was wrong. He ran back and burst through the door. Lumas was lying crossways on the cot, face up. Dino pushed him hard.

"Hey, wake up." He pushed down on his chest. "Wake up," he repeated. Lumas's breathing was labored.

Dino found an empty thermos on the floor beside a puddle of water. Amin put his big snout to the floor and sniffed. He sat and looked Dino in the eyes and began to bark nonstop. The dog jumped on the bed and continued to bark, snatching the blanket under Lumas's limp body and pulling with enough force to rock the entire metal bed. He barked and pulled hard enough that it caused Lumas to tumble to the floor, bouncing his head against the hard linoleum. Dino was initially concerned when he heard the thud of Lumas's skull bouncing.

Amin jumped off the bed, grabbing Lumas's arm and began to drag him. He moaned and moved his arm in response.

"No, this isn't happening," Dino said, realizing what was transpiring.

He picked up the phone and called. "Is Robbis there? Put him on the phone and hurry."

He waited, tapping nervously on the receiver until Robbis picked up.

"Grab a vial of Romazicon. Yeah, yeah, the antidote for Ativan. And bring a syringe. Get down here to the sleeping rooms now, hurry up. No, you'll see. Just hurry. And don't say anything to anyone."

Amin growled, barked viciously, and simultaneously pulled Lumas in circles. Dino watched in amazement. The dog smelled the chemical in Lumas's body and was tossing and turning him, barking and smacking his long paws against Lumas's face. Lumas moaned again, the dog did not relent.

Robbis ran in and jumped in the corner as Amin turned his attention toward him and barked.

"Dino, grab Amin," he screamed. "No, give me the vial. Amin, heel."

The massive shepherd ignored him. Consequently, Dino chased the two in circles attempting to give the dose as high in Lumas's upper arm as possible. Dino lunged at Lumas's torso, holding him in place. He and Robbis waited until Lumas began to move his arms.

Amin grabbed his collar and pulled rhythmically again. Robbis initially thought Amin was attacking Lumas. His hospital garb was torn from head to toe and his face was scratched. The dog continued to bark until Lumas muttered incoherently, at which point he sat next to his face. He wagged his tail, smacking Lumas's face with whip-like swipes.

Robbis spoke softly. "Can you call Amin off now?" Amin eyed both.

"Uhh, I'd rather not touch Lumas till Amin is finished." Robbis did not understand, after all he was Dino's dog. "Just wait and don't move," Dino instructed.

Amin licked Lumas's face, leavings slobs of thick, frothy mucous from his eyes to his mouth.

Dino saw an instinct in Amin that amazed him.

"Ow, where the hell am I?" Lumas uttered as he rolled over. Amin gave him an additional round of thick licks. Lumas gawked at Amin, grabbed his ear, and rubbed it. Amin barked.

He looked at the two men in the corner not moving. "Hey, what the hell happened? Why are my clothes torn apart? I have Amin's slobber all over my face, and why the hell does my head hurt? I have a lump here," he pointed to the back of his head.

Dino moved forward. "Amin just saved your life," he informed him.

Lumas was confused and pissed. The sedation reversal for benzodiazepines took ten minutes until he began to regain full consciousness. For now, he was still very groggy. Robbis shoved him once. Amin growled, and the dog's disposition was evident. Dino chuckled.

"Whoever did this," Dino began, "and it's probably Jeremy, didn't want to kill you, just numb you, make you stupid, and appear to be under the influence. Amin smelled him in the hallway and took off. I should have dropped the leash, but I didn't think fast enough. This is out of control; we should do something. The idiot's a psychopath."

Robbis stood and paced nervously. He was terrified and thought he needed to extricate himself quickly. His voice quavered when he spoke. "Do you know for sure it was Jeremy? We can't do anything without proof. And if we thought we did, no one would believe us, we are nobodies. Karlson would fire all three of us just for accusing Jeremy. Those two are in bed together, maybe literally."

When Dino spoke, it was clear he was impatient with Robbis. "I know it was Jeremy, but I can't prove it. None of us has access to controlled medications, only nurses and the bosses. And no one else has any reason to do this except them. But I cannot figure out why." Lumas sat up and held the sides of the bed, trying to steady himself. He lifted his head. "You can't, I can't, no one can," he dejectedly said. He held his head and moaned. "I feel like shit, my head is exploding."

Robbis began to leave and stopped short when Amin sat upright and growled.

"Shit, Dino, control your dog."

Dino scoffed at him. "He smells something in you."

Robbis raised his voice. "That's not fair. I brought the Romazicon, didn't I? What are you trying to say?"

"Thanks for your help, you better take off," Dino replied in a dismissive tone.

Lumas tried to stand but swayed back and forth and grabbed Dino's shoulder. Amin whined again.

"I think that dog loves you more than me, and I feed, bathe, and groom him."

Lumas gave Amin a scratch on the head.

"Judas," Dino said. The animal whined again. Dino thought he understood every word.

"Don't start feeling sorry for yourself, the year is almost over and you survived. You've changed, and we've all noticed it, especially Jeremy, and herein lies his fear and dilemma—what next to do to get you. A lot of people want to help. They see the crap Jeremy is putting you through, but they do not know how to help. I hate to lay this on you, but if you leave, either terminated or willfully, we all lose. Jeremy might need a second victim or maybe someday someone will find he's been doing this for a long time before and after we're gone. We must find out why. And another thing, don't take this so personally—you're a nonentity, just a means to their end, whatever the hell that is."

Lumas, still groggy, spoke softly while simultaneously scratching Amin's head and his own. "I am, I do, but that's easy to say when you're not in their crosshairs all day, every day, or being euthanized like an animal. Isn't this enough to go to the dean?"

"No, it isn't," Dino responded flatly. "As much as I don't trust Robbis, he's right. We are minimally paid house trash. No one will ever believe us."

"I didn't think Jeremy—"

"Get over it," Dino interrupted. "He's probably done a lot worse and there's nothing personal, Lumas. He doesn't give a crap who was picked this year. He's an equal opportunity sociopath. It could have been any one of us. The guy is blinded to bias, your name wasn't chosen for any particular reason. Jeremy is one of those people who just follows orders and no better than the trash who dropped the xenon pellets, it is just a job to him. However, I believe he enjoys inflicting the pain, think it gives him a sense of immense power or something. He's desperate now, running out of time before the internship ends. Look, we should get upstairs and make sure he sees you mobile. That will piss him off, and he's already had a bad day."

Lumas had no idea what he meant.

"I'll call Ganz; he may be able to help. He hates Karlson. Turn around, I'll give you the last shot of the Romazicon. It'll keep you going till you get home, then you'll crash hard, but you have to get back here in the morning, on time," Dino stressed.

"Shit, this is gonna hurt," Lumas said, looking at the syringe. Jeremy looked over his shoulder as Lumas and Dino stepped out of the elevator. No one saw the anger in his face, his jugular veins stuck out, engorged, full of blood like thick ropes. He was seething and clenched his fists until his knuckles turned white. He ground his teeth till his jaw throbbed. He pushed a vet aside, entering the elevator. When the doors closed, he screamed. "Son of a bitch, you're dead!"

Lumas became groggy before he left the hospital. He had a difficult time walking straight and steadied his frame by leaning against the chairs and wobbling his way through the lobby. Most of the vets had their heads bent, reading outdated magazines or sleeping.

He was pretty sure no-one paid much attention to him. Only Evans hidden in the dark stairwell watched him leave. Lumas was too hung over to notice the VA cruiser following him home.

Dear Grandparents,

Another horrible night. As soon as I closed my eyes, there was a blinding flash and I was running around in circles as mother was trying to kill me. She had a knife, and I was naked and very young, maybe five or six. She kept stabbing and cutting me, I was running around that small room in the house back in New Orleans. But there was nowhere to run. I was in a space the size of a closet.

I felt cold and hungry and tears poured down my face. I screamed, but she laughed even louder. I felt the pain of every strike in my dreams. I could see drops of blood on the floor, and she laughed as I screamed, slipping on the blood puddles. She kept trying to kill me.

Grandparents, I do not remember hurting her. I never remember hurting her. I ran and screamed louder. Then the apparition of the man pointed at me. He laughed louder than Momma. My ears hurt, I held my head tightly. She caught me and cut me in the chest. I felt the pain even though I knew it was all a dream, but I couldn't wake up or move. My arms hung, paralyzed, like the branches of a willow tree. The man told her to cut deeper. My knees buckled, and I died. The pain stopped as soon as she cut as hard as she could.

I think I woke my neighbors, again. My bed was wet with perspiration. I loved her so much. But I know she did not love me.

When life is good, humans feel ashamed. For the most part, humans spend valuable time terrified of what they could lose or never acquired. Very few are grateful for all they have and for each new day.

Good night,

Elliot.

CHAPTER TWENTY-SIX

Lumas had to force himself out of bed early that morning. He was terrified to be late. Yesterday, Jeremy put a sedative in his thermos.

If it had not been for Dino, he would have slept forty-eight hours and been fired for neglecting his responsibilities. It was all planned that way. His mind raced, medicine was not what he had wanted after all, it was not a profession of empathetic and dedicated caregivers, instead it was exactly the opposite. It was treacherous and ugly. He thought physicians were not much different than Wall Street butchers. Patients were commodities, and the less money spent on them, the faster an administrator or department chiefs, like Karlson, could move up the ranks. Both sides worked to cost control vets to death.

The researchers did not want to waste time on veterans they assumed were uneducated and high maintenance. They had no understanding of the patients and no interest in learning. In their eyes the vets were all "wretched" and forgotten people. Life was painful enough for the wretched, much less having to fight the ignorance and indifference from physicians who have negligible socioeconomic ethnic, racial. or cultural similarities.

Veterans Affairs physicians, although having staff positions at the main campus, were regarded as the academic underclass. Academic medicine has a subclass of untouchables, which the higher-ups need to demean and stroke their own egos, one of the ugliest traits of human nature. They were the untouchables. The chiefs covertly pronounced them substandard academicians and sentenced them to the VA. The ones who got it always left, the others were either delusional, or delusional and retarded if they thought this purgatory was temporary.

Lumas thought maybe he had made a mistake and should have pursued research. He could have hidden out in a lab somewhere quiet, like Greenland, far away from the bullshit of US medicine and America. He regretted becoming a physician. He thought he had been through enough pain for eternity. But feeling sorry for himself did not help. If it were not for the veterans, he would have quit a long time ago, they gave him purpose and strength.

CHAPTER TWENTY-SEVEN

It was raining and cold, unusual weather for the city, and the sidewalk under the overpass was crowded with the homeless. Tents were stacked side by side with barely enough space to walk. Polyester dilapidated tents were the remnants of better days when the Scouts camped and relished the tight spaces, laughing all night. They were shelters for rich kids, since turned into faded rags supported by bent metal poles. Crumbling brown bags, rusted shopping carts, and empty wine and beer bottles were thrown in the few empty spots between tents. Dirty withered feet stuck out here and there from tents or makeshift beds piled together with dirty newspapers. Homeless families stood or sat staring into the passing cars or conversed with invisible demons, expressions of total disdain for oglers embarrassed the most inconsiderate passersby. Mothers shunned the same embarrassing questions from curious children. Passersby turned and looked away, indifferent. All had stories, but no one cared, even they had long ago forgotten.

Across the street, a child cried and held on to his mother's skirt while she argued with one of many dealers.

White cops on cantering horses rode apathetically and authoritatively, flaunting cowboy hats and boots, their demeanor and stature akin to royalty. The mounts galloped like champions, and the kings spoke pejoratively and condescendingly. They eyed the wretched, their body language brandished the peasants into submission in their own warped minds.

No one would take Patrick into their homes; he had burned all his bridges. With no real friends and no money, he was desperate after drinking and shooting every cent he had left from his Social Security checks. One of the volunteers from the shelter gave him a blanket and a tent and closed the door hard. He was not welcome there either. Now he was terrified to go back to the VA. The monster would surely kill him the next time.

Up the pavement and intentionally avoiding eye contact with anyone, a person walked slowly, occasionally stooping low to look inside a tent. As usual for the homeless, most slept during the day and were up at night for protection.

It was not difficult to locate him. One side of the street was occupied mostly by Caucasian vets, which gave him some protection. Patrick initially flinched when the gloved hand with a loaded syringe stretched through a gaping hole in the fabric. For a second, the shakes abated.

"Hey, thanks, brother, thanks," he said.

"Yeah, vets stick together. You can count on me whenever you need something, man. Yeah, count on me."

Patrick untied a shoelace and wrapped it tight above his left elbow. He became frustrated and angry when he could not find a cooperative vein and began to shout out. "Skin pop!" He looked up and out of the hole but only saw the outline of hospital scrubs.

"Yeah, man. That's a good idea. Man. Thanks, man; thanks, brother."

After jabbing his left thigh, Patrick lay back and waited for the warmth to settle in. He loved the high of heroin, it was better than cocaine, meth, or alcohol. Heroin made him feel immortal and impenetrable. He wanted this to be his best high, he deserved it.

"Hey, man, thanks. This is good H," he said.

Patrick felt the warmth as his facial vessels began to dilate. He felt the euphoria begin to kick in, lightening visions of paradise streamed through his mind—women, cars, fucking. He circled higher and higher and smiled.

"Yeah, man, this is good shi…"

He coughed and felt nauseous, then coughed repeatedly. Patrick began to feel like he was drowning as he coughed thick white mucous. The world spun, he grabbed his neck and squeezed. He spit and rolled, coughed once more as his eyes rolled back in their sockets. He was dead.

The person wearing the scrubs looked through the hole. "That was good shit, Patrick, good shit. Better than Demerol."

It took three days until the stench of Patrick's decomposing body was putrid enough that the mounted police were distracted enough by the wretched to pay attention.

Patrick was still wearing the VA patient name tag when his body was sent to the coroner. The cause of death was determined to be a heroin overdose. Jennens was contacted as per protocol.

Jennens cringed when he received the call from the local police about another fuck-up. Vet disappears from a locked psych ward and committed suicide on skid row. This would dictate an immediate review of the incident of events, security protocols, and implementation of changes, none of which were good for Jennens. He was sure this was Karlson and Jeremy's work.

CHAPTER TWENTY-EIGHT

Robbis locked the dungeon door and headed toward the stairwell. All was slow for him today. He was pleased since Jeremy had given him laudatory praise, so much so, Robbis was embarrassed.

After his presentation, Jeremy gave him the rest of the day off.

It was still cold and dark as he exited the main building through the back. He always parked in the farthest spot in the corner, other- wise with his poor vision he would lose his car in the huge parking lot. The darkness and cold reminded him of reading *The Legend of Sleepy Hollow*. The moon was blanketed by thick cumulus clouds, and the ground had those tiny rocks that crunched as he negotiated bumping around the parked cars.

He was between shifts and the lot was full, which made the walk even more eerie. It was not unheard of for an employee to get accosted by a drunk vet at similar times. The yellow dim of the parking lot light poles made matters worse, giving the illusion of movement around parked cars. He wanted to get to his car as soon as possible and picked up the pace, nervously stopping after a few steps and tiptoeing to spot check his trajectory.

"Thank you very much, Jeremy," he nervously mumbled to himself. "I should have stayed and left with the crowd. I'm an idiot. There's a yin and a yang to the universe and I'm going to get yanged if I don't get to my car."

He stopped when he thought he heard movement up ahead. "Hello, who's there? It's Dr. Robbis here, who's there?"

No answer.

"Schmuck, you're hearing things," he muttered.

He picked up the pace only to smash his right thigh into a bumper.

"Shit, that hurt. Goddammit, goddammit," he hissed in pain. A blot of blood began to expand over his left thigh pants leg. "Fuck. Look what I've done—fuck, fuck, fuck."

Excruciating lancing pain shot down his spine, his knees buckled, and he grabbed his neck and screamed. Another hit to the same area sent him toward the ground, he stretched out his arms instinctively to avoid smashing his face. His right wrist snapped in hyperextension.

Robbis screamed in pain. "Ahh, ahh, stop. Don't kill me!" A blow to the left wrist was next.

Robbis began to whine like a child. "Uhh, uhh, stop. It hurts. Uhh, stop, please!" He felt the warm oozing of blood dripping down his neck. Robbis dared not look back, fearing that the perpetrator might strike him in the face. He crawled toward a car and could hear the crunching of footsteps as the next blow hit him in the thigh.

Robbis screamed. "Someone help me, please, help," he called out.

He grabbed the left front tire and pulled hard, managing to crawl under the front bumper. The painful blows finally stopped. He continued to crawl.

"Uhh, don't hit me again. Why are you doing this? Stop, please, you're killing me, stop." Robbis heard the crunching of the rocks again, but he couldn't see anything. The slight lighting from the parking lot was gone—he was in total darkness.

The crunching started again but became fainter, and he realized the perpetrator was walking away. He began to cry and lay perfectly still. His body throbbed in pain, but his left wrist was deformed, a fractured bone jutting through his skin like a stiletto. His mind was too distracted before to notice the extent of the deformity. He screamed again but no one heard him.

He waited and waited until he heard the day nurses leaving and walking toward their cars and screamed out for help.

CHAPTER TWENTY-NINE

Mania and hypomania, Lumas knew his diagnosis, though he resisted admitting it, especially being a physician. He was ashamed. His inability to control the highs and extreme lows left him exhausted at times and the symptoms were coming more often. He forced himself to read about people with similarities. That gave him some hope that he would not suffer forever.

He was profoundly influenced by Amy Shively Hawk's book, *Six Years in the Hanoi Hilton: An Extraordinary Story of Courage and Survival in Vietnam*, with a foreword written by Senator John McCain, who had been a prisoner of war in Vietnam. Who could possibly survive as these men did, hungry, cold, and tortured? But they did survive, even the men who were murdered still survived in the hearts of all Americans. The captors took everything, except they could not take their camaraderie, courage, and dignity. They had the courage to persevere and survive and hope against hopelessness.

Lumas had not picked up a philosophy book in a week. They were his bibles. Poetry also took the place of the great Stoics, albeit infrequently, never not Aurelius. Lumas had a special love of poets and poetry, including Dickinson, Grayson, Kipling, and Yeats, of which he felt deep consolation and love.

"An aged man is but a paltry thing, A tattered coat upon a stick, unless soul clap its hands and sing, and louder sing For every tatter in its mortal dress."

—William Butler Yeats, "Sailing to Byzantium."

Drinking made the wide swings in his behavior worse, as did Jeremy, lack of sleep, and other self-destructive behaviors. Shame was the essence of contemplating suicide. It gave him some semblance of peace in an otherwise pathetically dead-end existence. He avoided relationships and had not seen Frieda in weeks. He was avoiding her, and he knew that was cruel, but the downside was breaking her heart and his.

Driving nightly looking for a reprieve from the loneliness was cathartic in an unhealthy disposition and was both dangerous and degrading. He would stop at dive bars and after too many martinis go home with any woman as drunk as himself. Too many times, he tried the illicit recreational drug of the night, drugs were easy to come by, but he quickly gave that up when Dino made a comment that he smelled like marijuana and looked like shit. Besides, it took him two days to recover from an all-nighter, and he became unnerved with his all-too-often missed diagnoses. The vets deserved better.

He was self-destructive, he knew it, and he felt and dreamed that everyone knew it also. But there was no way out except the obvious. It took more courage to live than commit suicide, at least for now.

CHAPTER THIRTY

Evans drove down the dry unpaved road to the shooting range.

The terrain was poorly maintained, dry brush whooped off the front of the bumper and shady oak trees with gigantic branches stretched overhead. The road was hashed out with sharp serpiginous switchbacks and steep drops on the left. Evans' mind was fixed on the road. It was a good distraction from Tina and Jennens. Besides, he had not used his gun since killing the pedophile.

He could hear the popping rounds in the distance when he made the final turn into the parking area. For the most part, the shooters sported .22, .45, or .50 caliber rifles, but interspersed he heard the boom of a .270 or 6.5 magnum deer rifle. Evans avoided the spots anywhere near such powerful weaponry. The blasts temporarily paralyzed him, the ground shook, and the concussion waves traveled through his body causing his heart to skip beats.

He had no interest in hunting or hunters, what kind of sport was it to kill a deer from a quarter of a mile away with deadly accuracy?

That was not sport to him; he considered it no less than murder. His murders were for a purpose; they were disposals.

Shooting ranges always felt like purgatory to Evans, between heaven and hell. Shooters could be broken down into groupings. Some were just casual weekenders, father and son or husband and wife enjoying target practice. They laughed a lot, to them shooting was just a pleasurable way to pass the time, no different than playing baseball or camping.

Next were the semi-serious hunters, two buddies, no pretenses, good-to-very-good hardware, and seemed to be all about the outdoors. If they shot a deer, fine. If not, it was good to walk through the forest. In general, these were nice people, middle-American family folk. Although he still didn't agree with killing for fun, he understood the lot.

Then there were those who terrified him, people on the edge with big formidable guns. They had weaponry he knew was above their skill levels, although they attempted to look otherwise. They were scary, always alone, never made eye contact, and smelled of psychopaths. Evans could spot these guys and kept his distance. Guys who could flip out anytime, and heavy artillery made them feel powerful. Every shooting range had a sprinkling of psychopaths. He walked to the farthest lane available and set his handguns out and shot off a few rounds with the .22 caliber handgun. Then he spotted her, a police officer. She was obvious and either dumb or all too sure of herself. She casually walked behind the shooters, eyeing their guns, her first obvious mistake. Then she interrupted their conversations, which seemed rude even from a distance, second mistake. She was working above her pay level.

Evans wanted to avoid her seeing his .22, it was the weapon he used to eliminate the targets. She might get lucky, and he could get some unwanted attention. He dropped the gun in the case, put on his cap and sunglasses, and walked toward her.

"Hey, beautiful, what's your name?" Evans was loud, obnoxious, and tried to sound as thick as possible. "What is your name, honey, and why is a pretty young lady as cute as you out here all by yourself? My name is Patrick, Johnathan P. Patrick, and I am as American as apple pie. I was watching you come in, hoping you would stop by me and here you are, lucky me. Hey, what did you say your name was? You can call me Pat, short for Patrick. Yeah, boy, you are a honey all right!"

By now he had attracted enough attention that some shooters dropped their guns and began to laugh loudly. She was stunned and tried to compose herself, fidgeting about, at a loss for any coherent response. She took a step back.

"Uhh, what, uhh, my name is Susan, Susan Turner."

Evans stepped forward into her comfort zone. "Well, hello, Susan Turner, that is an awfully beautiful name. My mother had a beautiful name like that. Her name was Martha, Martha Patrick. Well, what a coincidence that is, Susan Turner. Hey, you out here by yourself? Because I would sure like you to come join me right down here. I'm by myself also. Oh, did you say you are all by yourself, Susan? Hope you are. Yes, sir, I hope you are. It's okay if I call you Susan, right?"

She stepped back as he stepped forward. "No, what? Yes, I'm with someone."

"Oh, come on, Susan. I think you're funning me. I didn't see you with anybody. I think you're just shy."

By now the woman's face had turned beet red.

"Look here. I want you to see my gun." Evans put an emphasis on "see my gun" then winked and laughed loudly.

She snorted, turned, and walked away.

Evans raised his voice. "Susan, where you going, honey? I didn't mean nothing."

Evans packed up his weapons. Susan had put a damper on the day. She was obvious and stupid, but she was there looking for someone, someone like him. He knew there had to be an investigation and one of the obvious places to start searching for suspects were the firing ranges. He screwed up going there. She probably overheard someone with experience discussing plans to blanket the ranges and decided to try and get some brownie points. He thought she was an idiot and deserved an injection of terror up her arrogant ass.

The skeet range was situated at the farthest corner of the range, away from the crowds. It was closed that day due to high winds. Evans parked behind the bungalow that functioned as the check-in area. The hike ended at a ridge overlooking the winding entrance to the range. There she was, as he expected, her car partially hidden behind a big oak tree.

She didn't hear the shot smacking the hillside; the poof of dust caught her attention over her shoulder thirty yards to her back. She shrugged and turned to grab the bottle of water she had just placed on the roof of her car. It wasn't there. She walked to the opposite side, still no water bottle. She rounded to the back and saw the bottle with a hole through it in a puddle of muddy water. She hesitated but picked it up and saw the round hole through both sides of the plastic container.

"What the fuck?" she asked.

She stood and walked quickly toward the passenger door. Two puffs of dust exploded at her feet. She froze, wet warmth dripped down her inner thigh. The rearview mirror exploded, and two more poofs of smoke went up her right and left sides over her shoulders. A bag on the hood of the car flew upward, twisted, and rotated like a spinning top, sending bits of hamburger and fries spinning in all directions.

She screamed. "Stop, okay, stop. What do you want? Don't shoot me. I am an officer."

Evans decided to let her shake for a minute. She had tears rolling down her face now. Perfect, he had her attention.

She screamed again. "What the fuck do you want,

goddammit?"

"Still a little full of yourself, aren't you?" Evans said under his breath.

The next shot grazed her left arm. She fell to the ground and began to sob loudly. "Don't kill me, please."

"That's better," Evans continued.

The next three shots hit at quick intervals of ten, five, and then three feet away, forcing her to logroll toward the car door. Her face was covered in powdery dust smeared with muddy tears, as she kneeled facing the bluff and raised her arms high.

"That's better, my dear," Evans said.

She slowly stood and slid into the car. Evans watched as she drove down the long highway to the freeway. He knew she wouldn't report it to anyone. The terrifying foray was too embarrassing for an officer to admit.

CHAPTER THIRTY-ONE

Evans was frustrated and tired. He decided to pay a visit to the old guys at the park. He had avoided them, or at least the location, for some time, fearing the cops would make occasional surveillances. They were a queer group, but entertaining, and he needed the distraction. By now any semi-competent officer would know someone had been watching the pedophile for a while before killing him.

They were always laughing and ribbing one another, but at times he would catch one of the men ogling him intently, then not so coyly looking at one of the others and nodding or shrugging their shoulders. Evans didn't understand but thought it best not to confront any one of them. They made him laugh and besides, he thought them pretty ballsy after they ripped the detective a new one. Ben spoke without losing his stark gaze on the chess table. "Evans, you see that police car over there?"

"Yeah, I've seen them before, the last time I was here and once before that."

Ben looked at Larry, he spoke to Evans. "Why do you think they're still hanging around?"

"Probably because of me."

"Yup, that's what we think also," Ben interjected. "They're looking for the hero that shot the child rapist across the street. You think they'd have something better to do, but someone got the guy before them and all the notoriety beat them to the kill, and really pissed them off. They been photographing lots of men here every day, probably got you on their list also. So, Evans, we were wondering if they think the guy who killed the molester is stupid enough to come here again or just that clever enough to come here again. Anyway, what do you think?"

Evans didn't flinch but looked down at the chess game. "I think they have no idea one way or another. Their investigation probably has gone nowhere and now they are fishing. If the guy was on this mission to kill, then job done and now is the time to become invisible in broad daylight. Rook takes queen, checkmate."

Ben's eyes opened wide enough to see most of his globe. "Muthafucka, muthafucka," he cursed.

The table burst out laughing.

Ben smiled deeply, then his expression changed to serious. "Listen up, Evans. You better go now. We'll take care of the cops."

Evans was obviously taken aback. "What do you mean by that, Ben? You guys don't have to do—"

Ben interrupted him. "I said you should go now; we'll see you here in two weeks."

The men all looked down at their boards and began idle chats among themselves, to the exclusion of Evans.

"You read a lot?" Ben asked Evans.

"Yeah, I don't look at the television, especially not the news. I know what to expect daily."

Ben gave a broad smile. "Now that is an interesting answer. Read about Augustus and Marcus Aurelius and a philosopher called Seneca. Will make you a better chess player, I guarantee it," he advised.

"I beat you," Evans retorted sarcastically.

"That's true, but I don't expect to win every time, and I don't let my ego cloud my rational thinking, Evans."

As Evans walked away, he felt a twang of rejection and confusion. He never allowed anyone to excuse him, but this was a demand and unusual, it was nonnegotiable but had a feeling of paternal supervision. It was as if Ben was telling him: *We're watching out for you. Now, go on with your business.* But it was said as if he was in the military—no excuses, no forgiveness, no fuck-ups. He knew there was always something strange about the old guys, but he still chose to file it and appreciate them for who they were, whoever they really were. He trusted them, and he needed their trust and friendship.

He sat at the computer that evening reading the emails, searching for anything that looked like a cogent trail of conversation leading to the disappearance of Tina. Prior to going missing, she wrote to dozens of employees, primarily in the secretarial pool. Other than confirming meetings and other administrative chitchat, she didn't veer into idle conversations about family or hospital politics.

What was unusual was that she was verbose and redundant, which struck him as unusual. Her reputation was all business and to the point. He dissected her run-on sentences, looking for hidden messages or codes until he felt his brain exploding. Not infrequently he'd stop, rub his temples, and wonder why he should even be concerned. It wasn't his business, and he wasn't being paid, but he found himself ruminating on her whereabouts and sat at the computer every day for hours.

He slammed the laptop closed and cursed himself. How the hell did he get into this mess? Who sent him the messages with the instructions? Was it the old guys or were they just a bunch of wannabees feeding on their morbid made-up curiosities?

Evans had survived on wit and resourcefulness since youth.

He had empathy for the vets who barely survived in their miserable worlds— something he knew he could never endure. In a way he felt as if he was protecting them and the young doctors from the indignities and condescending treatments they were being subjected to daily by Jeremy and Karlson. He wasn't tolerant toward bosses, especially Jennens, whom he detested, and realized he needed to keep a closer eye on him. Evans was a prolific reader. He was aware of the Stoics well before Ben said to study the emperors, especially the Greek and Roman philosophers. He believed allowing a pedophile to live would invariably result in a catastrophic snowballing effect that would last for generations, due to all the victims' shame, anger, depression, and maybe some suicides. Evans wasn't a serial killer and didn't think of himself as the hand of God. He was practical and would deal with situations as they occurred in the now and not ponder the past or the future, one unchangeable, the other unknown.

Evans was a Stoic. He had studied and navigated through complexities since childhood and was courageous enough to oversee a toxic situation he had no personal nor fiduciary interest in. In the past, he was paid for his services, but his involvement now was personal, and it felt foreign and uncomfortable. He thought he had a purpose in making positive changes for the vets and the young doctors, if only he could find Tina and gain her trust.

CHAPTER THIRTY-TWO

Lumas sat on the edge of his bed, suicidal and deeply despondent. He knew no other way out than ending his life. All his will to fight was gone; there was no joy left in his heart; he was exhausted. At least it would be over, he would not suffer any longer. He stared at the floor, the carpet worn from constant foot traffic reminded him of how beat-up he felt, the way he envisioned his sorry existence.

He thought of how many people suffered similarly. All those nights he had pored through the biographies of brilliant individuals who lost and chose to leave, maybe that next place would be kind and loving, somewhere he never knew. But this life was hell, cruel, and unforgiving. He had nothing to lose. A second of discomfort, then nothingness. His friends would go on, there would be a short memorial, of course, memories of camaraderie, short speeches admonishing the belief that he was a good physician. Death consoled him.

He closed all the windows and put towels under the doors. Then he walked to the kitchen, opened the oven, turned on the gas, then the burners, then lay on the couch. Finally, his soul was silent, at peace.

Frieda began banging at the door just as he was beginning to feel the warmth of succor. "Lumas, open the door. I know you're in there, open the door, it's Frieda."

He was startled, how did she know? Questions raced through his mind. What was she doing here? Who told her I was home?

He felt anger, his impetuous plan for committing suicide gone, spoiled. How dare she? Frieda had no right to interfere.

She pounded harder. If she continued, someone would call the cops, that would be worse. Being caught trying to commit suicide would invariably result in being committed to a dungeon, just like the wretched.

"I'm coming. Give me a chance to put on some clothes." He ran and opened all the windows and turned on the fan. "Damn her," he mumbled.

She pounded again. "Open up, Lumas, open the door." He did.

She sniffed gas fumes, cringed, furrowed her brow, and immediately regretted the obvious stare on her face. She composed herself and spoke. "Where the hell have you been? I have been everywhere looking for you, you are avoiding me, the last person you should avoid, Lumas. I care so much for you."

That's all she had to say. He looked at the floor, did not want to make eye contact, embarrassed. His voice trembled. "I'm okay, well, I... I... I was asleep, I guess I accidentally left the stove on. I haven't seen you in a long time."

"You could say that, and you could also say you're avoiding me." She was careful but couldn't avoid an inflection of guilt when she answered. Frieda was anxious and appeared distraught. "I need your help. Can you get dressed?"

He wondered what she was up to. Frieda was smart. She smelled the gas, there was no way she couldn't. To him, this was obvious and planned. He was about to confront her.

She said, "Can you drive me somewhere? My car is shot."
"How did you get here?"
"Uber. Now you're stuck with me for a while. I'm late for an appointment, can you take me?"

He looked at her for a moment and relented. "Yeah, give me a minute," Lumas said with a sigh, starting to get dressed.

"Thanks, I need to go to Venice Beach. Can we go by way of the canyon? I always avoid the freeways."

She spoke nonstop but about nothing, just nonstop. Lumas was having an impossible time keeping up with her train of thoughts. Big oak trees covered the narrow winding road, causing an airy, cool, and comfortable ride. This early, there were very few cars or pedestrians, and only the occasional bicyclist trudging uphill. In the early sixties, the canyon was the retreat for the flower generation. Most of the homes were old and never renovated, and some still had fading peace signs or flowers painted on the doors. It was rustic, some would say beat up, but the canyon kept its charm. This was probably much to the dismay of developers, who longed to build boring condos, restaurants, and the redundant shops found in every mall. The old hippies had successfully held out all these years.

They turned on the Pacific Coast Highway and headed inland to Santa Monica to the outdoor shopping mall. There was a paucity of foot traffic now, mostly janitors, joggers, and laborers on the way to the restaurants opening for breakfast in a few hours. The walkway was centermost jampacked on both sides with restaurants, bars, clothing stores, and tourist shops. During the day, the area would bustle with families from middle America. Tourists wearing shorts and printed T-shirts strutted their sunburned legs as they strolled and gawked at the beach population.

But now it was quiet, the air brisk, and Frieda walked a quick pace with a purpose. She was obviously looking for someone, so Lumas just kept up and did not interrupt. She stopped occasionally, scanning the homeless sleeping in the corners on the cold pavement. Her gaze fixed on a mass of dirty tattered clothes stacked in a dark corner. Lumas looked closer and realized it was a blanket with tiny dirty hands sticking out of torn sleeves. The likeness reminded him of the pile of clothes he threw in the corner of his room. There was the soft look of a woman's eyes peeking out under a torn skull cap.

Frieda walked toward her and spoke, her voice cracked. "Hello, Mommy." Frieda sat and spoke with her lovingly, but the old lady just stared in response. Neither woman attempted to touch each other. The one-sided conversation went on for an hour. Lumas sat on a nearby bench and didn't interfere.

Frieda sat quietly on the way back. Her window was opened, and she tilted her head backward. The wind blew through her hair, her eyes were closed, and she appeared at peace.

"I am so sorry to see your mother here. How long has she been homeless?"

"For about ten years, but she's been gone much longer than that."

"What do you mean?"

"She just gave up trying to forgive herself long before living there. I don't know the whole story but there were demons, ghosts that haunted her since I was a child. She would clam up for days at a time and stop talking, eating, or bathing, but then she would have periods of being the most loving woman and mother. At night, I'd hear her screaming at them. They haunted her, but she never sought help, at least not professional help. Although the meds at that time probably would have turned her into a zombie. She was a smart person but never spoke to the universe, God, or whatever you call it. She never tried to be at peace, just succumbed to an existence of misery. If she thought she could get better she would have, that is the tragedy. Then she began to use heroin, crystal—whatever numbed her. Ghosts are never that powerful, unless you allow them to be, Lumas. Over time, her brain changed, remodeled into irreversible gray mush." Her voice softened. "She had choices. I go there to look into her eyes, but she never speaks, hasn't for years."

Lumas didn't understand the concept of *allowing* the ghosts to be powerful and struggled with the idea of choices. He thought the ghosts were all powerful and didn't feel as though he had much control over their strength.

"Frieda, I think psych illnesses are inherited or environmental. Counseling and medications are the only treatments."

"Don't you believe it," she replied, in an exasperated tone.

CHAPTER THIRTY-THREE

Dino and Lumas struggled to hold the vet still until his breathing became less labored. Jeremy stood motionless above them, bored.

Jeremy had ordered the patient to stand. The vet had congestive heart failure and was slow to answer and slow to move. Despite this, Jeremy taunted and berated him to move faster. "Can't you stand any faster? Your legs aren't broken."

Jeremy always started off the day torturing a vet. It was his way of exerting his power in front of the patients and the interns. This was the second patient who Dino and Lumas witnessed the cruelty that Jeremy inflicted on the vets, just to inflate his sick ego. Such cruel behavior would have been enough to fire him, but the complaints from nursing went to deaf ears when reviewed by Karlson.

The vet held the bed rail, trembling.

Jeremy raised his voice. "Get up. I don't have time for you to get your full benefits."

He didn't see the other ten veterans walk toward him from behind. Dino and Lumas did, however, and looked at each other, telepathically calculating an exit.

The vet's eyes rolled back in his head and he fell to the floor.

After Jeremy left, the big vet stepped forward and turned his attention to Guitano.

"Will he be all right?" he asked. "Yes, he's doing better."

He looked at Lumas after having sized up Dino.

"Doctor, can you explain to us why he did that again? Why does he hurt patients? We've seen him do this before."

Not so much a question as a demand. Both looked perplexed. "Not again?" Guitano asked him.

"Yes, he was here earlier today and did the same, but Corporal Higgins didn't have chest pains and breathing difficulty like this one. That was terrible to torture him like that. He has extremely poor cardiac output.

Lumas interrupted him. "You have a medical background and you know his history. Did you know him in…" Lumas caught himself. "I am sorry—that sounded very impersonal."

He didn't answer but turned his attention to the corporal, who was now calm but unconscious. Three vets walked toward the bed and lifted the sergeant up to the gurney after the nurses arrived.

The vet spoke, looking directly into Lumas's eyes. "He's going to the unit, correct?"

"Yes."

"Please keep a closer eye on him, especially when the other doctor is near the sergeant."

The tone of his voice implied it was more an order than a request. He turned and walked away, the other vets followed close behind.

When they left the ward, Dino turned to Lumas. "I was afraid that would escalate out of control."

Lumas stopped walking and looked hard at Dino. "It did. We were just threatened."

CHAPTER THIRTY-FOUR

Lumas woke to an atypical day for the city. It was fall. This time of year could be nippy but was not normally gray, cold, and depressing like San Francisco. Crawling out of a warm bed felt tortuous. He wanted to stay home under the covers with Frieda, but prior experience had taught him that hiding only made matters worse, he had to get to the hospital.

After the trip to see her mother, they began spending more time together. She kept him busy. Between hiking and yoga, she forced him to relax next to her and listen to lectures on mindfulness. They listened to the theories of Dyer, Tolle, the Dalai Lama, and other creative and courageous theologians, physicists, and philosophers. His head spun at times, but he felt good, not as lonely and frightened.

Dino was sitting at the computer terminal with Amin at his feet.

He turned but didn't have his usual good morning look. "What's up? You look pissed," Lumas observed.

"I have bad news and bad news for you, buddy," he said regretfully.

"Okay, what did I do wrong this time?" Lumas asked.

Dino turned back to the screen. "Nothing that I can find out yet. Last night that vet died, the one who Jeremy exacerbated his congestive heart failure."

Lumas's initial emotion was guilt. "Oh my god, no, the guy was doing well, what happened?"

Dino's voice cracked. "Someone lowered his dose of meds and it was on your call last night."

"Who?"

"According to the orders, you did, but I know better. You've been watching over that guy like he's your own son."

Despite Dino's support, Lumas's mind sped uncontrollably between self-reproach and acquittal, mostly the former. He tried to remember every hour of the night, the calls for antibiotics, pain medications, and sleepers, but he could not remember changing any of the corporal's medications. Irrational out-of-control thoughts bolted back and forth in his brain like thunder, his skull began to ache.

Dino sensed Lumas's emotions and turned to him. "Let's get to business, buddy, we have some sleuthing to do."

"What are you talking about?"

"Lumas, I know you didn't do it, and even though you're beating yourself mercilessly, you know it too. We both know who *did* do it, so we need to circle the wagons."

"How can we prove it?"

Dino turned back to the computer screen and typed in a few commands. "I'm printing all your orders from last night for starters, then calling the brilliant one."

"Who?" Lumas asked.

"Berger, of course. Let's put him to work finding the digital fingerprint, Jeremy's prints."

"I am not sure I want everyone to know about this."

Dino turned to Lumas. "Look, I know what's going through your mind right now, but you have to believe you did not kill that guy. Don't hit me, but stop feeling sorry for yourself, get angry, get even with that fucker. He killed a vet. He thinks he could do whatever he wants. He is a sociopath, Lumas. He wants us to know he did it and that he can do it again. He set you up. We have to stop him."

Lumas sat in the chair next to Dino. Amin sensed the tension in his demeanor and plopped his massive head on Lumas's lap.

"Why don't we go to Karlson? Maybe that would be a start."

"Because Karlson has blood on his hands also. He gave Jeremy orders to fuck you over from the beginning of the year. He does it every year, you were just a name in a hat, it could have been me or any other intern. The fucker has some reason but I've yet to figure out why. Look, you are a good doc. If you weren't, you'd have gotten canned a long time ago. Jeremy hasn't been successful booting you and Karlson's pissed at him for it. Jeremy doesn't have the balls to do this alone."

Lumas didn't believe he was just another name in a hat, a lifetime of self-reproach could not be dismissed by bad luck. His emotions swung from terror to apathy, indignation to despair. The terrified child in his subconscious wept uncontrollably. He deserved the inevitable.

"I can't believe Karlson and Jeremy would kill the guy," Lumas said despondently.

"It's not necessary to go there now; stay focused, buddy. Karlson's an accomplice. *Jeremy* is the murderer. They're both crapping in their pants as we speak. Jeremy fucked up. Killing the vet was not his intention. He wanted to cause enough damage to your credibility to have you gone, a myocardial infarction or really bad congestive heart failure and a transfer to the ICU would have sufficed, but he fucked-up, changing your orders too much, decreased the dosage too much and killed the guy. But Karlson and Jeremy are sick enough to write off this whole fuck-up as collateral damage, just another dirtball vet died of complications. In this case, your incompetent complication killing the vet."

Dino immediately knew he should not have said that, especially not now, and especially not to a guy like Lumas. He had to modulate his demeanor. He turned his attention to Amin and snapped his thumb. "Up, Amin."

The big shepherd jumped on Lumas's lap, knocking him out of the chair and flat on the floor. Amin began to slap his face with thick, sticky, smelly kisses. Lumas lay still for a second, stunned, then sluggishly turned his head to Dino and calmly spoke. "Ouch, that hurt. Dino, could you please ask T-Rex to kindly remove his one hundred pounds off my cracking chest wall? Please and thank you."

It had the desired effect.

"We have two sick narcissists who killed a guy and want to blame it on you. Now, can you please page Andy Berger?"

CHAPTER THIRTY-FIVE

"Can you do your magic and find out who wrote those orders?" Berger was staring at the screen.

"Of course, I need to log in using Jeremy's username and pass-word and that's it. I know it's in his phone contacts. I've seen him opening his phone to get it. I always thought it nutty he doesn't memorize it. Then it dawned on me; he has *all* our access passwords on his phone. Since all our passwords change every six months, he doesn't even try to memorize his own, much less keeping track of his targets' passwords."

Dino sat back and took a deep breath. "So now we need his phone also. Great, just great. If I had his password, I wouldn't need you."

"Yup, but you can't search his files dating back years for other interns he's fucked over in minutes," Berger shot back. "And you can't drop a virus that will destroy his ability to access the system by name, hospital ID, SS number, or any other way on earth for the foreseeable future. Also, once I get my hands on his phone, he's really screwed. Shall I elaborate?"

"No, he's not an idiot, at least not in that respect. We don't want him to suspect we know anything. Do you understand that? Nothing. Say it, Berger. This is not a video game. Jeremy is dangerous."

Dino had come to dislike Berger over the year and found him to be condescending and arrogant, with a propensity for quickly agreeing about medical issues in the groups, then berating his colleagues behind closed doors. He didn't trust him, but he needed his analytical brain now, so he just had to watch him closely.

"Okay, I didn't say I would do anything obvious. I mean nothing to make him suspect us."

That caught Dino's attention, but he chose to log it for the time being.

"So, how do we get his phone?" Berger asked Dino.

Lumas sat behind the two, listening, but couldn't fathom why they would plan a theft, and for him, nothing made much sense. And how did Dino know Karlson and Jeremy were firing residents yearly? Where did he get that information and was it accurate? Could Dino be wrong?

"Hey, I don't want anyone to get nailed for me," Lumas interjected.

Dino turned and looked at him. "Listen, we're not doing this just for you. We should find the other victims and expose Jeremy and Karlson. He's going to do this again and again. There's no telling how many years he's fired interns, conjuring up lies and harming patients. I can't imagine how devastating it is to get fired from an academic institution. There's nowhere to go, no one wants you, and you're committed to roaming the country, a nomad looking for a program and begging for a spot. And you can't practice medicine until you've completed your internship, which means at the soonest you're out for eighteen months. In the meantime, the MD isn't worth slop. And yes, we are doing it for you also. We don't know if Jeremy killed vets like this before. The university staff won't believe us, nor would they really want to know. Going higher up in the Veterans Affairs is probably a dead end also, although I don't know that for sure. But going to them exposes the risk of that information getting right back to

Karlson and we're screwed."

Lumas had difficulties with trust but not with Dino. "Okay, okay, I—" he began nervously.

"Come on, guys, we need a plan," Dino interrupted. "Lumas, go home. You're on call tomorrow, get some rest."

Before leaving the hospital, Lumas stopped at the lobby and sat in his dark corner again. It brought him a sense of solace, peace, and quiet, and a chance to decompress. He had called Frieda after the meeting and gave her all the details. She had been angry but not surprised.

"After work, come home. I will have dinner ready. We won't talk about the bosses during our time. Love you, Elliot," she said, in a calm and loving tone.

"Of course, I will see you then. Love you also."

She made him promise to call daily and more often if issues arrived.

As he sat in the darkness, he watched the traffic of administrators, clerical personnel, and doctors leaving. No one made eye contact with the vets uncomfortably sitting in old plastic chairs with metal legs, the kind of chairs most often found at garage sales. When the place was filled—which was all the time—folding metal chairs were brought up from storage. When those were used up, vets sat on the floor and propped their backs against the constrained wall space.

Most of them looked one step up from the homeless, the people not seen, living in cardboard boxes under the freeways. The men were dressed in clothes that should have been thrown away long ago: tattered stained pants and dirty torn shirts missing buttons. If the condition of a man's shoes could convey the condition of his soul, these men were waiting to die. They lost hope long ago. No one cared about the wretched. The right had disdain for their devotion to duty; the left used them as fodder for political gain.

"Can I share this step, Doc?" Lumas looked up to see Evans, the security guard, looming overhead.

"Sure, but it's pretty lonely in a dark corner. What's up? What did I do?"

Evans didn't respond but took a deep breath. "Why do you sit here so often, Doc? Always in a corner and always by yourself. It must be depressing to see the vets just vegetate in those plastic chairs for hours. Why don't you go home and relax, decompress?"

Lumas was surprised that the guard had been watching him for some time. "Can I ask you a question?" he responded.

"Sure."

"Why are you the only guard who doesn't carry mace or a stick? And you're the only guard I've ever seen give vets rides to the bus stop."

Evans thought for a second, then tossed it out of his head immediately. He didn't care, he'd long ago given up caring about what others thought of his out-of-the-ordinary behavior. Besides, he had no control of anyone's opinions anyway. "You're observant."

"So are you," Lumas shot back.

Evans didn't respond right away, choosing to compose his emotions before he spoke. He sighed. "I don't see myself ever hurting one of these guys. I think most of them have been beaten enough. If one of them gets out of control, frustrated, aggressive, or near violent, I treat them humanely and restrain myself from overreacting. Respect for these guys and self-discipline helps me sleep better at night. Can't blame them for being pawns in this mess, they're treated like slaves."

"So, you feel sorry for them."

"No, I didn't say that. Life owes them nothing."

It sounded cruel to Lumas, and Evans caught the look on his face. "Look, I am not saying they weren't given a huge obstacle to overcome but…" Evans stopped mid-sentence and reflected before continuing. "I read somewhere if you're losing your soul and you know it, you still have a soul to lose."

Lumas looked off in the distance as he took in the security guard's words. "You're not an ordinary security guard, are you?" Lumas commented.

Evans stood, walked down two steps, and turned before replying, "I just like to read a lot, Doc. See you around."

Lumas sat motionless, a bit stunned by the short interaction and wondered what had just occurred.

He gazed out into the hunched group of vets and noticed an older black man crouched against a corner wall. His legs were stretched out straight on the linoleum floor, arms crossed on his abdomen, and head slumped down to his chest, revealing matted kinky hair. Most of the vets slept in the lobby for hours, so no one took notice of the old, disheveled man not moving.

Lumas stared long enough to be certain he wasn't breathing before he slowly walked over and crouched down. The vet's parched eyes were half open, and the corners of his mouth had tiny cakes of white spit. He touched his hand, cold, there was no life left. An old, wrinkled man with a long gray beard and hair down to his shoulders wore farmer overalls and sat unemotionally next to the dead body.

Lumas turned and spoke softly. "I am Dr. Lumas. How long has he been dead?"

His beard was tobacco-stained yellow, and it was obvious from the echoing sound of his voice that he had no upper or lower teeth.

"All day."

"All day since when, please?"

"All day since all day, Doc. I got here at five this morning. He was here before me."

"Why didn't you tell someone?"

"Shit, Doc, nobody called my number."

CHAPTER THIRTY-SIX

Dino begged Jason to switch the call night with Jeremy. He was apprehensive but his dislike for Jeremy outweighed asking questions. He wished it was appropriately painful and said it. Dino kept a poker face.

The walls were cardboard thin, built quickly when the residency program opened. Each room had two military-style barracks beds, not much more than hammocks supported on metal bars. But the contractor was considerate enough to build small bathrooms with showers stalls.

They clocked the time Jeremy showered. He was consistent, as Dino had guessed both getting in and out, which didn't leave much time to break in, grab his phone, and download the SIM card data to Berger's phone.

Dino and Berger took up the next room, listening through the thin walls, impatiently waiting until they heard the shower door close, and the water turn on.

The key to unlock the door was universal. With the shower going, they were praying Jeremy couldn't hear them open the door, pull the phone from his white coat pocket, and lift the SIM card out. Berger slipped it into his phone and began syncing the data. It took less than a minute, and Jeremy was still showering.

Dino turned to leave but saw Berger jamming a chair against the doorknob to the bathroom. He grabbed his upper arm and pulled hard enough for him to whine. "What the fuck are you doing? We have to get out of here!" Dino hissed under his breath.

"No way. I have something planned for this asshole."

Dino had his hand under Berger's arm, lifting him. There was no time for this dangerous foolishness and unfortunately no time to stop him.

"He's going to know someone was here. What's wrong with you?" Dino had no idea what Berger was up to, but he didn't appreciate deviating from the original plan to get in and out undetected. He was pissed and pushed him hard toward the door.

Berger stopped and pressed numbers on his phone, refusing to move. "Wait a second..." he counted five seconds. "And now."

By this time, Dino was willing to deck him and make a run for it.

Berger spoke into the receiver. Dino couldn't make out the voice on the other side.

"Okay, we're finished. Call the operator and send security to the doctors' sleeping room, number one, basement."

The chair was still wedged against the door when security arrived, removed the chair, and banged on the door.

After Jeremy stopped screaming expletives and slammed the door on security, he threw the dilapidated wooden desk chair at the wall. It broke into pieces, and splintered wood flew like a bomb in all directions.

Jeremy sat at the foot of the bed for an hour, not moving a muscle. A sliver of spit dripped down the side of his mouth, his eyes were bloodshot, his heart raced, and his temples throbbed. He withdrew into a primal creature full of rage. There was nothing he wouldn't do now to destroy anyone who dared to question his autonomy and authority. Death was preferred to humiliation. He was more dangerous now, unpredictable, and volatile.

CHAPTER THIRTY-SEVEN

"Hey. Ganz called this morning and wants to talk to you." Lumas was suspicious. "What the hell did…"

Dino stopped him. "Can that. Ganz is a good guy, he cares. Just go meet him, see what he wants. Now, goodbye, buddy."

Amin escorted Lumas to the door.

When Lumas left, Dino leaned back, drew a deep breath, and whispered, "God, I hope this works."

"Hello, Lumas. How are you doing?"

Ganz sounded good. He was congenial and generally interested in Lumas's day-to-day clinical activities. Occasionally, he would ask about his personal life. Those questions usually stiffened the hairs on his spine, but Ganz was genuine and when he asked them, it didn't cause the same emotional response. Lumas wasn't threatened.

Ganz went on. "I've been speaking with the nurses on oncology. They are impressed with the way you cared for Mr. Otis."

"Thanks, but you talked me through it." The compliment made him uncomfortable.

"Nonetheless, you didn't leave his bedside and you experimented with all options to keep him comfortable. Take the compliment. Some of our colleagues would have written for Demerol and left. Otis would have suffered to death." Ganz paused. "I promised the nurses to work with you on the treatment of patients at end of life," Ganz continued. "You have the soul;

now you need the didactics. That crew knows talent and compassion, so they want to call you more often."

"Are you returning?" Lumas asked him.

"I think not. The time off has been good for my head. I've received calls from other institutions to come onboard, but I'll wait for a while. It's good to have friends, makes you realize the world doesn't revolve around medicine and certainly not at any one academic institution. Sometimes it's just not a good fit and has nothing to do with IQ or commitment, not everyone wants to be supercharged all the time or looking over their shoulder constantly. I don't think Hippocrates had this in mind. Docs need to step back a little and do some soul searching; we've lost our purpose as healers foremost. We're not supposed to be just academic knuckleheads. Meet me at the campus library after you finish tomorrow."

Click! Lumas only managed to utter the "o" in okay before Ganz hung up.

They met weekly. From the start, he didn't altogether buy into the concept of mentoring. Lumas knew he had skills and passion to be a good physician, but his insecurity overwhelmed him. But he felt with Ganz as a mentor and Frieda as a loving partner, he was improving his general outlook of life and medicine. Most important, he didn't feel so lonely. That huge black cloud that followed him every day, everywhere, finally vanished.

He knew he needed help, but the humiliation of psychotherapy was another hurdle to overcome. Shame and guilt were buried deeply, but with Frieda's encouragement, he began to meditate. He had hated life but not now, not with Frieda, Dino, and Ganz. He didn't forget about Amin either.

Lumas began to realize how much he hated his mother and

every person who had ever criticized him, who he vividly recalled even from childhood. Living with misery had become emotionally and physically overwhelming, and he felt like a prisoner. Survival depended on his ability to avoid conflicts, deny accolades, and become as invisible as humanly possible.

Ganz insisted they meet outside at the next meeting. He looked much healthier since leaving the VA Medical Center, thinner, and Lumas never smelled that stale pungent odor of cigarettes on his clothing. He'd lost weight, shaved, and generally looked happier.

"So, Lumas, let's walk and talk today. The shrinks say the more we exercise, the better we become at punching the demons out of our lives. They also expound on this with psychotherapy and medications at three hundred dollars an hour. How many people can afford that much money and balance that with a guesstimate of sixty percent of us needing counseling? It's no wonder we see high rates of alcoholism and prescription drug abuse in this country. And God knows how many people in jail could have benefitted from psychotherapy and antipsychotic meds before incarceration. I wish I had done it sooner. I suffered for a long time. I still have the demon days but at least now I am trying to tackle, not outrun, them. It's daily work, one day at a time. This business of medicine can be brutal. We are in a very demanding profession. The public expects perfection, and academia expects even more, with ghastly, unforgiving cruelty and punishment for mistakes. How many professions are the same? None. In the real world, docs have bullseyes on their backs. They are under constant scrutiny from Medicare, boards of medical quality assurance, insurance companies, and bloodsucking attorneys. They make a better income than professors, but at what cost? My guess is a hell of a lot of them are severely depressed and worse, most are working like hell to retire. Some make it, and some don't, Lumas. In the meantime, they're miserable."

Lumas wasn't sure where Ganz was headed.

"Academia is no picnic either, some of these chiefs of this and that are just mean. This place is filled with narcissists, lots of them have absolutely no interest in teaching. They want to publish and move up the ranks and they will steal and lie to do so. Researchers have bolts on their lab doors and never share data. There is no such thing as collaboration. God knows how many malignancies, cardiovascular accidents, or inherited disorders would have been cured if academicians behaved ethically and collaboratively. Don't think these profs don't make good money either, they're just experts at keeping it hidden. They rake in 'donations' from pharmaceutical and device industries, but they're under the radar."

Ganz raised both arms and wiggled his fingers, as if they were exclamation points.

"For instance, the new chief of orthopedics turned in docs from his division for accepting money from device companies. Turns out everyone higher up in administration knew this was happening for years, but they turned a blind eye because the division received some of that money. How's that for ethics? I'm sure his tenure here is limited. Hope he has an exit plan, because he'll never get another offer in a teaching institution again, ever. And it took some courage to do what he did. I am sure he felt totally isolated and rejected by his colleagues; he isn't a member of the good ol' boys club any longer." Ganz paused, took a breath, and continued. "I respect this guy.

"I understand he has his priorities in order. He spends a great deal of time with his family, leaves morning rounds early every day to take his kids to school, doesn't smoke, is a vegetarian, and exercises three times weekly. He's an educator, the students and house staff love him, and he's firm but fair. I did some checking on him, one can always learn by studying the habits of healthy people. You get where I'm going here, Lumas? What's important is what you believe of yourself, being blatantly honest, and not what others think of you, even those who try to force their opinions on you. A difficult way to think; very, very difficult if you're programmed to stay self-destructive. You must find your way through the bullshit, embrace and nurture it. It can be your passion for the sciences, teaching, family, or whatever. We all need to step back occasionally and reflect and be honest with ourselves. Or we become what others want us to become."

Ganz was becoming animated, flailing his arms in the air like he was a Baptist preacher. The VA was a few miles from the university hospital where the medical school was located. It was spring, and the street had a healthy stream of young women in shorts. Lumas found it difficult not to stare.

"I spent a lot of time trying to fit in and I failed. I am not a researcher. I can't pull in the grants or NIH money. The school wanted to retire me, and I gave them the ammunition to do it. I am only now working on my issues and the dumb shits gave me time to stop and be introspective. They think they punished me, ignorant sadists they are, but I got my life back. I lost a lot of time I can never recover, but my road to tranquility is out there and I am working hard to change my life."

With that, Ganz turned and began to cross the street. "See you next week. Don't leave me hanging, Lumas. Mentors and people who care are hard to find. Most people are trapped in their own hell."

CHAPTER THIRTY-EIGHT

Berger could not find Jeremy's password in the data, even though he had been trying for the last twenty-four hours. Nothing seemed to be going well—all the storage files were worthless, credit card numbers, online banking passwords, all worthless. He had managed to download a virus to corrupt his entire database after returning the empty SIM card to Jeremy's phone. Finding the hidden password was deadly serious. It would take Jeremy at least a week to recover his textbooks online and download the applications.

Berger's program corrupted all apps in the database and any new programs downloaded. The virus had a fuse attached and allowed downloading but self-destructed an application within twenty-four hours. That gave them time enough to find what they needed. The icing on the cake included reloading the virus every time Jeremy downloaded programs. Hence, Jeremy would literally have to change his name and other identifying information to use a smartphone soon. It was doable, but Jeremy had at least three months of hard work, not including time to find a debugging program good enough to pierce the firewall of the virus program.

Dino knew Lumas was on the verge of experiencing a bipolar swing, because he looked more withdrawn and anemic. Jeremy would eventually figure out that someone stole his phone and passwords and who. The two put Lumas to work covering their patients. He had to be kept busy, and patient care left little time to ruminate. Anyone in his position would panic. Jeremy had the deck stacked, years of honing his unethical and illegal skills plus Karlson watching his flank. In the interim, Jeremy framed Lumas for three lapses of care.

One for a delay responding to nursing in the intensive care unit. The nurses documented that he answered their calls within minutes, but Jeremy overruled them, claiming the patient suffered. But it was his word against the nurses, and it went nowhere.

Two others were more egregious accusations and difficult to disprove, but bogus, both complications of procedures resulting in infections. Both patients were in the intensive care unit. Antibiotics were started right after Lumas instituted minor procedures, inserting intravenous lines per protocol, but overwhelming sepsis killed both vets. The infectious disease specialist disagreed with Jeremy, but he persisted and filed an incident report, to be reviewed by Karlson.

Berger rotated shifts with Dino, sifting through contacts and the remaining storage programs. It took hours of work. Karlson was going to fire Lumas. But Jeremy had more ominous plans.

Dino fathomed all was lost, his feet stretched out on a table in the doctors' lounge. Berger was out, exhausted. His head lolled on the couch as he snored loudly. Amin whined at him.

After the break-in, Dino had shoved Berger forcefully enough through the door to tumble and roll on the ground. He had to restrain Amin from trouncing on him, that would have been bloody. He was livid and knew Jeremy would sooner than later realize he was the architect of the deed and all along protecting Lumas.

A text message clicked. "Follow the victims." Goddamn private number again. He had been receiving these cryptic messages for weeks, and they were driving him insane. *What the hell does that mean? Why doesn't he or she give something more tangible?*

He stood, walked to the door, and looked down both corridors, half thinking the person would be standing right there. Frustration funneled from exasperation to indignation. He began to type a curt message back, "Victims, what the hell does that-" then stopped.

"Fuck me." He walked down the dingy hallways.

The rooms came in two varieties. Some were built like barracks with eight beds lining the walls, which offered no privacy and nowhere to die without an audience. The other rooms were not much larger than closets without windows, one side of the bed flush against the dingy, dirty wall. They came equipped with tiny bathrooms without showers, small sinks, and barely enough space to sit on the toilets. In general, the remaining janitorial crew did their best to keep the facility as clean as possible, which was negligible.

He passed the room where the black vet died. Curiously, the vets were sitting in chairs huddled together in rapt attention. Dino couldn't see who was talking but could tell that it was coming from behind a curtain. One of the vets rubbernecked and looked at him. Dino felt the hairs of his spine prickling; he turned and walked away. He stopped at the Department of Medicine. On the wall were the group photographs of interns going back fifteen years to the inception of the residency program. Not much had changed over the years. Dino could sense the energy and enthusiasm from each class of interns. Casual clothing had replaced the traditional white coats and pants. The most obvious change was from white males to more females, minorities, and divergent ethnic groups. He fathomed this was a welcome change for medicine in general and especially in California, where ethnic groups comprised more than fifty percent of the population.

He recognized the young interns who were now their bosses, but one was missing. A young woman who looked Persian did not appear in the second or third year photographs. Dino never saw her before. He scanned more years, meticulously writing each intern's name and comparing it to second and third year residents. Each group was devoid of one physician from internship to residency. Each missing physician was a person of color.

"Victims," he repeated to himself. He ran back to the doctors' room and pushed the door open. Amin barked loudly. Berger jumped from the couch, his eyes glazed.

"What the fuck, Dino? I nearly peed myself!"

"I think I have it. The victims are the interns Jeremy fired from prior years. He probably logs them in his phone like trophies. I need to find the names of the interns he fired in the last few years. They'll be easier to contact."

"Victims, what victims? I thought we were looking for Jeremy's orders."

"No, and yes. We still need those corrupted orders, but I just found the names of Jeremy's hit list on the photographs outside the medical department."

"The missing interns are in the house staff pictures," Dino succinctly said.

"Call Jason. I think a lot of staff here will have a lot to explain eventually."

Berger spoke with a dejected demeanor, his shoulders slouched, and he fell into a chair.

"Jeremy does this every year, no one cares."

"Fear, what did you expect?" Dino snapped. "Good interns

don't just disappear, not without everyone knowing that person had issues prior to canning them. We work too closely to miss the obvious. No, they all knew that Jeremy fires an intern every year and the staff ignore it. No one wants to get involved. Welcome to medicine."

Then suddenly, something clicked in him. Dino looked Berger straight in the eyes as he walked toward him. Amin sat up, sensing the tension. Dino's face became flushed, his fists tightened, and his knuckles turned white.

"You knew! You knew it from the start of the year. Damn you. Why didn't YOU warn me? Why didn't you tell me this happens every year?"

"Whoa, I didn't say I knew anything concrete, but it makes no sense to fire an intern without provocation. It costs the program money. I know you thought about this also. There is some other financial incentive behind this; academic institutions love making millions. Fuck benevolence. One fact I know for sure is this is not systemwide: it's too dangerous. Whoever is benefiting from firing the interns must be pocketing some bucks, otherwise this makes no sense at all. Jeremy is a coward. He couldn't fire interns yearly without Karlson's oversight and approval. Put the pieces together, Dino. Don't be pissed at me. I knew people on campus who told me about the firings before I came here."

Dino took another step toward Berger. "Why didn't you tell me? Answer me, asshole. Maybe I could have gone to campus and alerted them. Maybe Lumas wouldn't be walking around with a bullseye on his ass the entire year. Did you ever think about that?"

"This is internship, Dino," Berger's voice quivered. "Everyone is on their own. It's survival of the best."

Dino was now outraged, and Amin was at his side, staring into Berger's eyes.

"Why did you help me get Jeremy's phone, Ber—" Dino stopped mid-sentence. "Oh, no, you've been in contact with Jeremy all along, haven't you, you son of a bitch? And that bullshit about locking him in the shower. Why did you do it?"

Berger took a step toward the door. "Jeremy told me I had to work closely with you guys, or else. After all I have done for him, he still treats me like dirt."

"You mean spy on us! You've been reporting to him from the start of the year!"

Dino walked toward him. Berger squealed. "I did what anyone else here would have done to survive. It was either Lumas or maybe me or you, Dino. I made a decision to protect myself."

Dino turned to Amin, then back to Berger. "Give me your phone, now," he demanded.

Berger complied.

"Is everything in here? And I mean *all* the fired interns' names and the corrupted orders? I'll know soon if you're lying to me."

"Yes… it won't happen any longer, Dino, but Jeremy will suspect something is wrong when I stop contacting him."

He walked closer to Berger until he was directly in his face. "Not my problem. Now get out."

Berger backed away. "Don't slug me again, please!"

"I won't," Dino answered, then turned to Amin. "Amin, teeth." The animal charged.

CHAPTER THIRTY-NINE

Jennens had to continue to cover up the murder of Betty. The VA pathologist was under his thumb, a simple call and threat, problem solved. Patrick's death was now a coroner's case. Jennens was contacted by the police after an autopsy revealed he was severely beaten and had a cocktail of drugs in his system, in addition to heroin, antidepressants, sedatives, and methamphetamines. Patrick was still wearing his VA ID tag when his body was discovered. The coroner labeled his death as suspicious and contacted Jennens to suggest an investigation, but the VA was under federal jurisdiction and couldn't demand one.

Jeremy had to force Lumas to either quit, fire him with enough cause, or just make him disappear. He enjoyed the thought of the latter. And Karlson needed to distance himself from Jennens. Jeremy was uncontrollable, zealous, and infected with loathing Lumas, whom he blamed for all his failures that year. Even if all their individual problems were solved - Tina was still missing with the recordings.

Jeremy thought of the how's and the repercussions of making Lumas disappear. He just wanted it over. His brain ruminated with rage, anything that would rid him of Lumas. He didn't sleep and skipped meals. At night, he'd wake in a sweat with his hands dripping with blood from grinding his fingernails into his palms, his bed soaked with sweat and urine. He shook uncontrollably.

In the cafeteria, he sat alone with his back to the other

residents, ignoring everyone. He looked as disheveled and pathetic as a vet. The only difference was the stethoscope hanging around his neck. He had an insane thirst for vengeance. He had to get back into Karlson's favor. He stepped up medical mishaps and complications on the veterans, blaming Lumas's negligence and incompetence on an insurmountable cascade of missed diagnoses and botched procedures.

He changed the call schedules on Lumas's pager, causing him to be absent without leave. The worst occurred when Jeremy switched a blood thinner on one of Lumas's patients with an active bleeding ulcer. The patient coughed and began to vomit voluminous amounts of bright red blood. He choked, kicked wildly, and screamed loudly enough that the adjoining ward of vets could hear his final "Oh my God, help me!" His eyes rolled back in his head, his chest fell, and he stopped breathing. Puddles of blood filled the intensive care unit, soaking the shoes of doctors and nurses, leaving a trail of red footprints in the ICU and out into the wards.

The younger nurses stood hypnotized, two ran to the head to vomit. The more seasoned staff began to gently clean the veteran's face and covered his body respectfully. Jeremy left the ICU without anyone noticing the smirk of gratification on his face. Lumas was becoming a liability to the other interns. He could sense their insecurities and fear in casual interactions and observed how their sentiments twisted from camaraderie to subservient selfishness.

Dino stepped up plans and contacted Ganz.

CHAPTER FORTY

Evans was reading but became continually distracted about Lumas. He was damaged, a victim, and Evans felt a pang of remorse for his plight but forced his brain away from destructive and nonproductive emotions of sympathy. Besides, the old birds gave him an assignment, a reading assignment. He was sure they wanted him to absorb something philosophical. Why him and who the hell were these guys? How did they seem to know him so well? These were the questions that ran through his mind. He felt like a puppet on a string. However, all in all it was somewhat consoling. Were they sending him instructions the entire time? He thought it couldn't be the case, as these were geriatric nice old guys enjoying retirement. But the last interaction gave him cause to question. Distractions, intelligence, chain of command, analytical rational reasoning, and every interaction with them left him perplexed and oddly with a sense of camaraderie. Everything he experienced, from the interaction with the nosy officer to the stepped-up surveillance of police at the park and subtle warnings, reinforced these feelings.

He took Ben's instructions and sat up nightly, plowing through the book Ben had given him—*A Better Human: The Stoic Heart, Mind, and Soul* by George J. Bradley. Not typical reading for Evans, but not out of his sphere of interest or ability to dissect. He thought how arrogant twentieth-century pundits were compared to philosophers twenty-five hundred years ago; there was no comparison.

Zeno's Stoicism captivated him the most. The ideal for a Stoic is to show complete equanimity with adversity; wisdom, justice, courage, and temperance.

The old guys must not have approved of the theatrics at the shooting range. How did they know? He contemplated on discipline and wrote down his thoughts:

Discipline is fundamental, a mindset and philosophy, keeping one in
Synchrony with whatever one is pursuing.
His mind was transfixed on Stoic lessons. Endurance of pain or hardship
Avoiding emotional extremes, not trying to change the world rather
Total acceptance of a harsh unforgiving world.
Life is it as it is, fundamentally humankind has not changed their nature,
Their propensity for fear and hatred, a species fate, by the gods, or the universe are destined for extinction and self-obliteration.

Evans thought of Ben and the others as mentors. But did he have a purpose for them also? Did they need an "Evans" also? Did the old guys need purpose? The phrase caught him in one of the Stoic's books. He didn't capture the implications then. Did pharaohs or emperors need dissidents who often disagreed with them? Yes, in fact, imperatively.

"Without a ruler to do it against, you can't make crooked straight."
—Seneca

"If you are distressed by anything external, the pain is not due to the thing itself, but to your estimate of it; and this you have the power to revoke at any moment."
—Marcus Aurelius

Maybe the old guys needed him as much as he needed their sensibility and mentorship.

Evans decided to set his mind to studying more philosophy. He knew his life consisted of contradictions and vicissitudes. But he was also aware of his gift of mental agility and temperament. He decided to calm his mind and think rationally. He was an inherently gifted rational individual.

Evans thought of the irony of modesty, ethics, and his ego. He was an assassin and one of the passages from Stoicism emphasized that not all moral corruptions are equally vicious. Did the early Stoics temper their anger and hatred all the time? No, that is impossible. No person errs in one degree of viciousness nor unremorsefully.

Do all Stoics ascribe to alter their future transgressions? Evans thought that made more sense. He was absorbing the concept like no other reading he had mulled over before. It gave him some peace and some hope that he could set his heart free of contemplating a life of solitude. He had lied to himself all these years, he needed human contact emotionally, physically, and psychologically. He was not created a murderer; he'd adopted it, the author and prisoner of his own destiny.

Evans finished the book that night. He did not completely understand why the old guys wanted him to read it. He'd already embarked on a course that he thought had purpose. However, he decided to reread it, dissect it, and study the philosophy of Stoicism for two reasons. First, it did cause him to reflect on his future, so called negative visualization, a Stoic philosophy. Someday he might fail an attempt to kill another degenerate and get killed himself. Was that his destiny? Had he ever pondered this destiny?

He did enjoy the company of the old guys and the people he'd met in the park, especially the group who invited him to join the volleyball team and the beer nights. They were a fun group to hang with. He caught himself thinking about a woman he'd spoken with each game. There was a sense of joy when he was with her, a strange sensation, something new and inexplicable.

Second, what if he were caught? He'd thought of that possibility. He would never spend the rest of his life behind bars, and he didn't want to be on the run if the police knew who they were looking for. No, if that occurred and he had no options, he'd go out *his* way. Maybe the old guys thought he was losing control after the target practice at the police officer. In retrospect, that was an asinine thing to do for many, many reasons, mostly he'd lost discipline and control for an egotistical, albeit humorous, minute. That was stupid, he'd never do it again. And now he knew the old guys had someone looking out for him.

He thought for a moment and decided what he'd do the following day. He knew where to find Lumas—in the corner stairwell as usual between four and six p.m., feeling sorry for himself. That morning he'd stopped at a bookstore to pick up another copy of *A Better Human*.

"Lumas, catch!" he called out, and tossed the book.

Lumas looked surprised. "What's this for? I mean thanks but—"

Evans cut him off. "I think you should read this book." He turned and walked away.

Lumas muttered, "Who the hell is this guy?"

CHAPTER FORTY-ONE

Dear Grandparents,

Another sleepless night, ghosts again. But I fought the desire to drive around the city looking for distractions. I have someone in my life who loves me, at least I believe she does, but the emptiness I feel can still be insurmountable and uncontrollable sometimes. I realize changing one's imprisonment with their subconscious and the psychologically destructive force takes real work, and recognizing the triggers are critically important.

At times I cannot see through the depression and hatred I feel and motivate myself to attack the pain and take back my life. Intellectually, I understand how my childhood affected my depression, but I know with time I will develop more emotional strength.

I believe Frieda is my guiding light, not my savior, my soul mate. She understands me and we have much in common. I know I am falling deeply in love with her.

Elliot

Lumas perused through the book Evans had tossed him. In retrospect, it was more an order to read it than casually persuasive. After a few chapters, he faded into a deep sleep.

He was seeing an apparition of an old man sitting at a solid oak table under a fading candle. He sat hunched forward, scribbling on parched linen paper, absorbed in his thoughts. His mind was buried and focused, he wrote quickly before the squib emptied. The power of his mind sprinted before the ink faded, creating a race of sorts, taunting his brilliant intellect to write his meditations before it mused and faded like a whisk of wind scattering petals off a blossoming flower, a race with his subconsciousness that forced discipline and wisdom while he pondered his destiny.

He didn't recognize the old man, but his clothing was that worn by men and women many millennia past. When he finished scrolling, he sat back and took a deep breath. The morning dawn was shining through the curtains. He coveted this time of the day, he could focus, absorb and envision his space in the natural order of the universe. It was a gift, but exhausted him and created intense loneliness, nonetheless.

His meditations were his only solace and created a sense of peace poised against the hectic distractions of consciousness he loathed. He stretched and faced Lumas, peering directly into his eyes. Lumas was sure the man was in the room, not an apparition, a vision. The old man's frail form faded away slowly, but he smiled at Lumas, then turned to look at the sunset, now shining through the entrance to his tent.

CHAPTER FORTY-TWO

Jennens pushed Jeremy hard. He fell to the floor and crashed against the opposite wall. Karlson stood up behind his desk but didn't move.

"Two murders!" Jennens screamed. "Along with a slew of so-called complications resulting in deaths. Morbid deaths," he scoffed at them. "Do you idiots think I'm stupid? Do you know how many complaints I've received from nursing? Too many to bury." Jennens was screaming as he tossed the paperwork of nurses' complaints at Karlson. "I told you before that nothing goes on here, nothing that I don't know about. I own this place. I have people everywhere."

Karlson interrupted Jennens's tirade, his voice shook. "You can't accuse us, we're not murderers."

"Shut the fuck up, you pompous dick," Jennens shot back. "One or both of you have been stupidly overzealous and killed vets and you're both too dense to realize there are people out there smarter than the two of you Neanderthals. There have been more morbid deaths this year than in the last five."

Jeremy stood up unconcernedly, brushed off his clothes, and casually spoke. "So what? It makes the case for Lumas being the psychopath more tangible."

Jennens's jaw dropped. He looked at Jeremy, stunned. Karlson fell to his chair.

Jennens spoke with his lips pursed in anger. "You killed all those vets, the cardiac arrest patient, the bleeder, and engineered all those complications yourself."

Jeremy sat and casually crossed his legs. "The complications resulting in the deaths, yes. I engineered those to look like Lumas fucked up. I didn't kill Patrick, and I don't know who beat the shit out of him. That was someone else's doings. Irrespective of Patrick, we have enough of the other complications and the oncology woman's death to give up Lumas. However, I see no reason we can't implicate him in everything. Lumas sticks out like the likely murderer. He has a string of medical complications leading to three deaths and now the murder of Patrick, perfect. You know, Jennens, I had a complaint filled out for Patrick to sign alleging Lumas slugged him, then tipped over his bed, and nearly killed him. But Patrick disappeared by the next morning."

"Let me get this straight. Lumas gets into an altercation with Patrick, drugs him with sedatives—the ones only you idiots prescribe—then walks through skid row, buys heroin, and kills him, without bothering to remove his hospital tags. Does Lumas look like a resident of skid row or that he'd have the balls to buy heroin on a street corner? Are you mentally retarded? I already received a call from the coroner questioning the psych drugs in him. They're not as stupid as you; they'll want answers eventually."

"So, tell them you're in the process of investigating but it's still internal, a federal jurisdiction."

Jennens scrutinized Jeremy's face. "You idiot. I don't want to have to tell them anything. I've been under the radar for years till you two created this mess."

Karlson stared at Jeremy in utter surprise, his jaw hung open, and Jennens's face turned bright red. "Jeremy, you killed vets without my permission. That's unacceptable," Karlson said.

"What? What did you just say?" Jennens screamed.

"Unacceptable! Unacceptable!" Jennens was livid. He turned his back to Jeremy and crossed the room around Karlson's desk, facing him. "You're criticizing him, not for murder, but for not asking your permission first?"

Karlson responded in his most commanding tone. "Well, of course, Jeremy takes orders from me only."

"Let me explain," Jeremy interrupted. "As of now, I know every- thing. From the murder of Betty and, yes, I have something on the drunk pathologist also, the idiot came to me for help. The irony of that, hysterical," he laughed inaptly. "I know how Lumas supposedly stole drugs and caused the questionable deaths, but in reality didn't. Which translates into you're a sloppy chief of medicine, Karlson. Oh, sorry, Dr. Karlson. I can sign a bogus death certificate, or not, and I can force your drunk, addicted pathologist to cough up the truth, Jennens. Or I can do nothing, go on vacation, and read about the drama at the VA. The arrest of the CEO, Lumas, and maybe you Karlson, although you're useful for my career. I'll give you more thought."

Jeremy stood and walked out.

Jennens spoke in a flat resigned tone. "What the hell have you created, Karlson?"

CHAPTER FORTY-THREE

Tina was still alive. Evans broke the code first. With unlimited access to the emails, Evans and Dino followed any out-of-the-ordinary messages. He noticed a series of numbers and letters that kept appearing at the end of what appeared to be official hospital bulletins. Then Evans noticed the odd grid on the message board that changed daily. Simple tap codes, a way to encode messages with a grid by using two numbers. One set for the down row using a five-by-five grid of letters representing all the letters of the Latin alphabet, except that the letter "C" replaced "K." The second designated the column.

Vietnam prisoners tapped on the floor or pipes to communicate by tap codes using this simple formula.

Everyone thought the odd taps at exactly seven a.m. were the faulty intercom system booting up. Tina was sending instructions to the hospitalized vets and other staff. Evans began to decipher the codes daily. Most were instructions to avoid medical procedures unless it was life or death. Next was encouragement that the plans were on schedule, stay alert and don't give up. The taps always ended with: "you are not alone."

Evans sent the code to Dino without a return address. Evans knew the administrative assistants arrived at seven and Jennens at ten, so he changed the grid at nine, hopefully by that time everyone had received the message except Jennens. Jennens was not a fool though; he would eventually decipher the emails and find the grids.

CHAPTER FORTY-FOUR

Evans casually walked toward the old guys. Ben saw him coming the second he stepped out of his car. No one spoke as the chess pieces moved across the board. Ben studied each of the men's faces as candidly as possible, no one acknowledged him for a full ten minutes.

Ben spoke first. "Have you been reading, Evans?"

Ben's tone was determinative. Evans temporarily lost the color in his face, his heart pounded.

"Well, go on, educate us old guys. Incidentally, the cops are still over there playing basketball, idiots. Well, I shouldn't be too hard on them now that they think we're hiding something. They think they're protecting and serving us."

The other guys chuckled.

"We specialize in staying under the radar, Mr. Evans. You compromised that," Ben went on.

"Well, speak, my man, sorry I keep interrupting you."

Now Evans knew the police officer at the range had reported the shots fired at her.

Evans composed himself. The old guys still moved the chess pieces without looking up. Evans spoke. "Practice misfortune, perception, perspective, and balance; take a view from above; meditate on mortality, is it in your control or not; journal; practice negative visualization; love everything that happens."

Ben stopped him. "Did you read the part about anger and passion?"

"I don't remember that section."

"Oh, yes, you're right. That's from *Meditations*." Ben continued. "Sins committed out of desire are worse than the ones committed out of anger. Are you an angry man, a victim, or a survivor, Mr. Evans?" Ben and the group were either really pissed at him—presumably because of the target practice at the cop—or they were questioning his honesty, virtuousness, or both. Either way, he was extremely uncomfortable, clearly aware they knew much more about Evans than he was willing to acknowledge about himself.

After what felt like an eternity, all the old men disregarded their chess games and looked at him intently.

Evans took in a deep breath. "I expect men who commit sins for pleasure and anger and continue are expected. But to expect them to ignore me or those I covet is arrogant."

The others looked down at their chess boards again saying nothing.

Only Ben continued to eye Evans. "Well-spoken, Mr. Evans, even if you bastardized Plato a bit."

One of the men spoke softly without taking his eyes off the chess board. "Philosophy major morphs into philosopher."

The others smirked at one another.

Ben looked down at the chess pieces again and took his eyes off Evans. "Remember, the nearer a man comes to a calm mind, the closer he is to strength."

Ben made a chess move, the man across from him grimaced. "We need to talk more about our little group here, Mr. Evans."

Evans's shoulders dropped. He could feel his muscles relaxing and calmly spoke. "If you choose to, but I already know, and I understand why you gave me the book." He went on. "Pilots in Vietnam shot down, then kept at POW camps."

"So, you read the book."

Evans continued. "Every one of you survived on one another, depended on one another. I don't claim to understand more."

The group continued to ignore Evans, however he knew each one was processing every word he uttered. "What I don't understand is why me? Why did you choose me? I was damaged from birth."

Ben took a deep breath. "That's destiny, Mr. Evans, destiny. You can say we found each other."

Evans spoke. "Tina and the old guy she meets with at the hospital are your people, right?"

Ben shrugged.

The next morning, Evans left a coded message on the board before the administrative assistants arrived.

"Tina, contact me. You decide where and when. Ben sent me."

CHAPTER FORTY-FIVE

Dino was deep into documentation when Evans walked into the lounge. He startled him initially, then recognized the security guard. Amin sat up, stared momentarily at the guard, twisted his huge frame with his tail bent, wagging timidly between his legs, lowered his head, and hopped onto Evans's chest. Dino had never seen Amin act so friendly, especially not to a stranger. Amin's weight jumping into Evans's arms didn't budge his muscular frame.

Initially awestruck, Dino said, "Who the hell are you? I've never seen him do that before."

Amin licked Evans's face, while Evans scratched the dog's head, then propped him softly on the floor.

"My name is Evans. I smashed the window and pulled him out of the car when we found the dead vet some time ago. You remember now?"

"Yes, you grabbed me before I hit the ground. I remember too clearly seeing that vet with his head nearly blown off," Dino recalled, shuddering at the memory.

Evans sat down. Amin parked his head in his lap. "Seems Amin remembers you pretty well."

Evans didn't immediately respond. "It was an ugly sight, Dr. Guitano, very sad."

Dino spoke cautiously not knowing what the guard wanted. "If I didn't say it at the time, thanks for catching me."

Evans didn't respond or make eye contact and kept

scratching Amin's head.

Dino thought it would be stupid to ask the big guard what he could do for him. He could sense he didn't need much from anyone.

"Have you been sending me the emails?" Dino asked.

"No."

"But you know everything that's been going on here, the money, the deaths, why did you get inv—"

Evans curtly interrupted him. "I know it all."

It was obvious that Evans was allowing Dino to consider the next question carefully.

Dino finally asked, "What do you want me to do?"

"Go to the nursing director tomorrow and have her put in a request for all the medication door locks to be changed by the end of the day."

Dino sat back wondering what the big guard would tell him to do next. This was more an order than a request.

"She won't ask questions, and she'll handle the repercussions."

Dino didn't question it. The guard was shrewd, intelligent, and precarious.

"What else?"

"Create an atmosphere of paranoia among your colleagues again. They've gotten too sure of themselves, indifferent, and dangerously apathetic. Your friend is going to suffer."

"How do I…"

Evans stood up. Dino knew what was coming next.

"I am sure you'll figure out some way, but it better be soon, or I'll be back. Don't expect a pat on the back, something should have been done sooner."

Dino felt a chill down his spine. His initial reaction was to say something in defense of his prior efforts, but the door closed behind Evans's swift departure before he had the chance.

"Shit."

Amin had followed Evans to the door and whined. Dino turned his chair toward him. "Come here."

The big shepherd sat where he was instead and occasionally looked toward the door.

"Traitor," Dino said.

The next morning, he did as instructed. The director didn't ask any questions but turned and walked away. By the end of the day, all the locks were changed. None of the doctors had access to medications without her approval.

Jeremy was shunned, like a spoiled child when he protested. Dino put out the word that Jeremy had given up on firing Lumas and was more out of control than in the prior ten months. Everyone should watch their backs, keep a close eye on Jeremy, and assume they are the next target. No one questioned Dino, he took special pleasure telling Berger, emphasizing that no one was safe, especially not him. Jeremy would assume he was not telling him everything, especially *who* convinced the director to change the locks. It didn't come from Karlson or any of the other staff. No one really cared who controlled the drug cabinets except Jeremy.

The environment changed almost overnight. Interns' demeanors veered from relief and satisfaction that the year was coming to an end to anxiety and dread. No more idle bantering in the break rooms, changing call schedules, or camaraderie that forced them to work in collaboration and be able to successfully complete the physically and psychologically miserable year.

All that changed, it was palpable and obvious to the nurses as well. They were supportive but scanners were back up. Interns documented procedures emphasizing negative complications and contacted one another whenever Jeremy arrived in the morning and also his movements throughout the hospital.

Jeremy felt like a caged, starved animal. He knew he was under constant surveillance. He was crippled, but the morbidity rate was down.

CHAPTER FORTY-SIX

"Hello, Doc."

Lumas was initially startled, until he saw that it was the old man in the tacky overalls.

"Can I take this spot here?" he asked. "Sure."

"Thanks," the old vet gave him a toothless smile. They both faced the lobby.

"Doc, you look beaten up, like dried dog shit." They both laughed.

"Is that right?" Lumas responded. "Would you care for a stick of gum, or can I treat you to a steak?"

The old guy smacked his chops and laughed loudly. "Lost them in the war in a POW camp, VC beat the shit out of me, hanged me upside down and knocked all the teeth out of my mouth. Can I bend your ear for a while, Doc? You got a little time, please?"

Lumas nodded.

"Kicking the shit out of me was nothing compared to what happened to some of those guys down there," the old vet went on, as he pointed down at the waiting room. "We did a lot of praying but the one thing that got us through was changing our attitudes, becoming more rational human beings. Sounds impossible, but it was true. There was always something we could learn and teach the new guys, something to give them hope and let them know they were not alone, such as visualizing the worst-case scenario. That seemed to at least defuse some of the fear of what was to come," he said.

Lumas gave no response. He knew of the treatments inflicted on the vets in POW camps during the war. He'd read about it and occasionally vets gave him their stories. All were starved and beaten and confined in dark, damp, rat-infested cubicles. Others were inflicted with more creative forms of torture, the ropes, from what he gathered, were the worst. Tight ropes were wrapped around their necks, hands, and ankles, then the vet was forced to kneel. The ropes were tightened such that any movement would cause the noose to tighten and strangle the guy. POWs were left in the ropes for days, some died, others were subjected to repeated days of torture between interrogations.

The old guy spoke. "Those men suffered and most abandoned hope. A little philosophical, Doc, but we had a purpose. We were officers and had a chain of command, even in prison. We devised ways of communicating between the walls, shared food, took care of the sick and dying, even had an occasional laugh. Men would share stories about their cheating girlfriends or first sexual encounters—that created the most humor. We'd have to laugh quietly so the guards wouldn't indiscriminately beat someone. Even when that happened, we'd clean up the vet and begin again."

The man took a breath and went on. "We had names for the guards like Sadistic Sam, Wart Face, Gimp, and Shit Face. It's what kept us alive, Doc, looking at life as fate and defusing the future possibilities of failure, no matter what was in store for us from day to day. Losing hope was the real killer. Forgiving them relieved us of anger, another killer. If we hated every day, we ate up our souls and our ability to control what we could control and what we couldn't. However, we had no control over day-to-day events, but we could control how we processed them. After that, vets would return to the cell with a whole different attitude, although I didn't laugh much when those fuckers knocked out my teeth. But I never gave up hope, and I came to visualize worst-case and best-case scenarios. The VC wanted to strip us of all hope, but we adapted, they failed."

Lumas knew the old vet had him in mind; he was a smart old bird. His outward appearance hid the mind of an intelligent and screwed maneuverer. However, he was clueless as to why he would speak with him and what the old guy was up to. The last month had become almost surreal.

"How long were you a prisoner?" Lumas asked.

"Was flying an F-4 Phantom II, shot down about a klick over Hanoi in 1965, released March 1973."

Lumas held a straight face for a long minute, then spoke. "I couldn't do the same, I know that."

"I heard that so many times, Doc, but it's not true. Look how far you've gotten."

"It's not like being a prisoner in a POW camp," Lumas argued.

The vet chuckled. "Torture comes in all different forms and lasts for different durations. I did seven years. Some people have a lifetime of torture. Think about Mandela. The guy spent over twenty years behind bars and got out with a smile, determination, and a vision for his country. There was no hatred in his heart; he stressed reconciliation. I can name you a hundred more Mandelas."

Lumas looked at the old guy. "I don't know your name."

The old guy stood. "You reading the book the security guard gave you yet, Doc?"

Lumas tried to avoid showing his shock, but the old guy caught it. "Don't worry. Just keep up the studies, the medical journals can wait temporarily. You have some other issues to work on."

He took a few steps down and turned. "Don't panic. Someone will be in touch."

CHAPTER FORTY-SEVEN

"I won't do it." Lumas was vehement.

Dino and Ganz arrived in the doctors' lounge early, well before the change of intern shifts, and waited for Lumas to arrive.

"I thought you were both on my side?" Lumas immediately caught his destructive reasoning; his brain was starting to boot up and open the insecurity files. "What's all the mystery?" he went on. "Jeremy is locked in his office every day, and I haven't been blamed for anything lately. Why should I go back to becoming a target again?"

Dino spoke first. "This is just the quiet before the storm, Lumas. They are setting you up by making you think it's all over. I had to scare the other interns, created a little smoke, and blinded Jeremy for a while. But he isn't finished, he's just recalculating his next move. Don't let your guard down yet."

Lumas was getting irate. "I don't want to go back to that dark place. I've wasted enough of my life. I have felt sorry for myself and

I've acted out. Both of you have seen me at my worst. I was neither honest with myself nor did I behave like a physician. I craved attention in all the wrong places to dangerous extremes. I will not abandon the work I've done."

"You have to do this, or you're gone from the program or worse," Ganz said.

"What does worse mean, what can be worse?" Lumas asked in exasperation.

Ganz answered slowly and looked at Lumas dead-on, which sent a shiver down his spine. "Worse means you can lose your purpose. Just walk through those doors downstairs or down the street. You've seen the vets camped out on the street right in front of the gates, sleeping on the sidewalks, standing at the corners begging for food. They did not start out life like that. They had families, friends, and comrades, but then something traumatic occurred, whether it was the war or injuries or PTSD, and they didn't have the tools or the help to find their purpose again. This led to a loss of socialization, loneliness, feelings of abandonment, drug use, and just like that, they are lost. The ones talking to themselves are booted now, they are gone. You could be one of them."

Lumas was irate. "That's a horrible thing to say, Dr. Ganz."

Ganz ignored him and kept going. "Karlson wants to fire you from the program, but Jeremy wants to destroy you, mentally and emotionally. A few weeks of therapy is no match for his upcoming plans. You are no match for him, not yet. We don't want you to think you're out there by yourself, you're not. You'll have us all the time watching your back, and there is someone else, but we have yet to understand why he's involved."

"You mean the security guard."

"Yes, and we think he's not alone."

"This is like a goddamn soap opera, and I'm the protagonist," Lumas said, punctuated with an exasperated and despondent sigh. He stood and said, "I'm going home." He walked out.

Lumas was still upset by the time he drove home. He called Frieda and asked her to spend the evening, and maybe the night, with him. By now, he shared many of the deepest, most painful life events. But he also knew he could sabotage their relationship if he didn't focus on his emotional health; he had to do the work.

The book Evans gave him was thrown on his bed. He was psycho- logically and physically fatigued, disgusted with life and his inability to find some semblance of solitude. He knew he must gather the strength and stop searching for love in alleyways or live miserably forever and just die. He grabbed the book and flipped through the introduction. For the next two hours, he read the twenty-five hundred-year-old letters from Greek and Roman philosophers. These were men who wrote for posterity. Human nature hadn't changed one bit. Fear, depression, deprivation, anger, and regret—Lumas could remember so many times he'd experienced each one, painfully.

He knew he'd suffered as a child and had a healthy dose of PTSD. His subconscious collided with unhealthy thoughts, so often paralyzing his productive rational behaviors, he dubbed himself the gold medalist of procrastinators. But here were letters written to future generations, describing the emotional torture the brain can inflict. Most important, and if he was willing to do the work, they also provided the way out.

He read and for the first time in years visualized the subject matter and the authors, including Seneca, Marcus Aurelius, Epictetus, Plato, Zeno, and more contemporary authors.

"Life is divided into three periods—that which has been, that which is, that which will be. Of these the present time is short, the future is doubtful, the past is certain. For the last is the one over which Fortune has lost control, is the one which cannot be brought back under any man's power. But men who are engrossed lose this; for they have no time to look back upon the past, and even if they should have, it is not pleasant to recall something they must view with regret."

—Seneca

"There is a limit to the time assigned to you, and if you don't use it to free yourself it will be gone and will never return."
—Marcus Aurelius

"Your ability to control your thoughts—treat it with respect. It's all that protects your mind from false perceptions—false to your nature, and that of all rational beings."
—Marcus Aurelius

"How long are you going to wait before you demand the best for yourself and in no instance bypass the discrimination of reason? You have been given the principles that you ought to endorse, and you have endorsed them. What kind of teacher, then, are you still waiting for in order to refer your self-improvement to him? You are no longer a boy, but a full- grown man. If you are careless and lazy now and keep putting things off and always deferring the day after which you will attend to yourself, you will not notice that you are making no progress, but you will live and die as someone quite ordinary."
—Epictetus

"Self-criticism is consistently associated with less motivation and worse self-control. It is also one of the single biggest predictors of depression, which drains both 'I will' power and 'I want' power. In contrast, self-compassion—being supportive and kind to yourself, especially in the face of stress and failure—is associated with more motivation and better self-control."
—Kelly McGonigal

Lumas searched the internet for more tenets from the Greco-Roman philosophers and current Stoics. For the first time in years, he felt a sense of relief and compassion. The Greek philosopher, Epictetus, provided a list of categories of control. We can control our opinions, desires, aversions, and actions. We cannot control the body, property, reputation, and offices.

Lumas reasoned that his frustration with life was because he was powerless over controlling other people's attitude and opinions of himself, his reputation. His insecurity controlled his thoughts and interactions. This made him bend in any direction that would produce conflicting emotional thoughts, most often destructive.

Either way, he couldn't control how people judged him, whether they perceived him to be a good person, an unhealthy person, or were indifferent toward him. That tormented his frail subconscious. A mind can be a vicious, inhumane torturer. He had to at least partially control how and why his thoughts produced such massive rushes of pandemonium and mayhem. Maybe that was why Ganz thought he could lose it, due to the lack of control over his rational thoughts.

What Dino and Ganz were asking was dangerous for his recovery. His thoughts raced through different scenarios that could bring about the same outcome without compromising his work. Should he trust them? What was in this for them? Did Dino just want to protect his career and Ganz regain his academic position? What if their plan failed?

He was both their savior and their Achilles' heel. He had trusted them before, but now his mind raced toward thoughts he knew were destructive and events that would be out of his control. He caught himself from going to that familiar destructive default zone where he was trying to control events. If he abandoned reasoning, events thereafter were chaotic. Control was still an illusion and existentially impossible.

CHAPTER FORTY-EIGHT

It didn't take long for Jennens to notice the odd crossword puzzle on the messaging board and unscramble the code. It was in his nature to stay alert to anything odd occurring within the VA. He sat in his office and tried to figure a way to lure Tina out into the open. He needed those recordings, or he'd spend the rest of his life locked up for embezzling from the government, conspiracy to hide medical errors with Karlson, and framing the deeds on Lumas.

Once caught, the investigation would include interviewing his pundits, all the idiots who worked in his office and had lied or skimmed the budget for favors, gifts, or kickbacks. Idiots, all idiots. How to lure Tina out would not be difficult since he had the code. How to eliminate her for good was the issue. At that point, the recordings were moot. She probably hid them where no one could find them, including the old man. He surmised she was savvy enough to produce the evidence at exactly the right time.

Jeremy was a borderline psychopath and couldn't be trusted. Jennens didn't want to kill Tina himself, he'd never killed anyone and except for a bullet to her head, he'd probably screw it up. Then there was the fact that her body needed to disappear for good, the deed needed to be done to look like she had committed suicide, the only reasonable solution.

Most people never give any clue beforehand to their plans to end their lives. They just go about their business and disappear for a few days until someone gets suspicious. No notes, no explanations. It would all fall into place, maybe better than originally planned. Karlson and Jeremy were on their own. The idiots would never implicate each other, or they'd spend the rest of their precious careers behind bars. It was a perfect fluke.

The only person he could possibly coerce into killing Tina was Evans. The man hated him, but everyone had a price and a history. Evans could snap his neck with one hand if he pissed him off. He needed something failsafe to threaten him, something flawless. He buried the thought in the back of his mind for processing, something would materialize. In the meantime, he would pull his application and dissect it. He also followed Evans a couple of times weekly. That was simple. All the guards wore tracking cell phones at the VA, within a radius of five miles. Jennens had access and began logging Evans's itinerary daily.

CHAPTER FORTY-NINE

Lumas spoke openly and honestly to Frieda.

"Are you going to do this?" she asked him. "It's dangerous, Lumas. Anything can happen, you're not an actor, you can't just walk back into the hospital and act like a paranoid schizophrenic. You can't fake being a dangerous doctor. They ask too much of you, it's not fair. There must be another way."

He interrupted her. "Maybe, but I have to trust them, that's almost impossible for me with my history, but—"

"But what Lumas?" Frieda abruptly asked.

"I have to trust someone. I've been nothing but a drifting ship all my life."

Frieda maintained a straight face. The last thing she wanted to do now was acknowledge that comment.

"Dino may have his grants to worry about and Ganz wants back in eventually," he went on. "But for now, I have to trust them irrespective of their own motivations. Listen Frieda, Dino has lived the life of Riley, money, family, career, and position. He was born with a silver spoon in his mouth but at least he doesn't behave as if he's entitled. He's not condescending, critical, or demeaning. Ganz has entirely changed; he is more like me than Dino. I can learn a lot about how to dig myself out of the gutter from him. I want to—no, that's incorrect—I *have* to emulate him to change and forgive myself of all the harm I've done to myself and others."

Frieda's demeanor changed. "Is this why I haven't heard

from you more consistently?" she asked.

"Yes, I don't want to lose you, Frieda. The days, almost all of them are struggles, struggles just to get myself out of bed, much less be responsible for my behavior with you in my life. I love you very much."

Frieda flushed, her eyes began to tear. She reached for Lumas's hand and spoke as if she were giving her heart to the person she could love forever. "You are too hard on yourself. You must forgive yourself from the past and live in the present. I know it sounds easy for me to say, but it wasn't easy growing up in a home with such emptiness. I think having a rotten start in life is devastating, but it can be overcome, not that I am always successful. But I've learned everyone has demons and everyone can either attack them or not but only if they become conscious of all the dirty little tricks our brain plays. Our brain is cruel and unforgiving, but only if we allow it."

Lumas tried to interrupt. She stopped him, part of his reasoning abilities would hinge on listening first and calming his brain second. Frieda went on. "Not everyone thinks about you all the time, although pain makes it feel like it. Everyone has their own baggage. So, rule one is don't take everything so personally, build a wall; thick-skinned people are the happiest people. You, me, and everyone must develop inner strength. Call it selfishness or protecting your sanity, whatever, this place, this time, I mean *life* is a daily wrestling match with insanity. Most thoughts that enter our minds are camouflaged with an assassin close behind. Nature, God, whatever, put us here, dropped a bomb in our heads. You give up and it takes everything—your happiness, self-control, honesty, self-esteem, joy, everything—and you end up like my mother."

Lumas was embarrassed. He was uneasy with Frieda

speaking about something he should have grasped long ago. And it was all in the books he was plowing through on Stoicism. His ego was getting the better of him. He knew it and forced his brain to stop playing the game of who's in charge.

"I've been reading this book," Freida went on. "No, more like devouring it, and visualizing the material and the authors. The philosophers have helped me more than behavioral therapy, and believe me I have spent a lot of years, time, and money on therapy. Wisdom and experience, that's why it's made a difference. These men and women lived through the same brain games three thousand years ago, nothing has changed. When you dissect their writings, they're giving us a prescription to healthier minds, either as results of internal or external causes. It takes a lot of practice but it's doable, Lumas."

Lumas stopped her. "What's the title of the book and how did you come across it?" he asked.

"*A Better Human*, but I've been reading Seneca and Epictetus also. It was in my locker after the end of a shift at the beginning of the year and I have no idea who put it there."

"This is weird, Frieda."

"Why?"

"It's the same book a security guard gave me—rather threw at me. He told me rather aggressively to read it, like it was nonnegotiable. Do you have any idea who put that book there?"

"None."

"Have you ever had a conversation with a guard here, a big guy, muscular, kind of stands out from the other guards? The guy looks intimidating and always hangs around the vets in the lobby."

Frieda thought for a minute. "No, but I am usually in such a hurry I don't notice things like you do."

"I didn't notice him; he noticed me. Approached me while I was huddled in the corner in the lobby."

Frieda spoke with a dazed look on her face. "Why do you hang out there?"

Lumas smiled and smirked. "Duh." Frieda got it.

"Who interviewed you for the position here?" Lumas asked.

"The same person who interviews all the new grads, the director of nurses."

"Tell me about her."

"She was tough, not what I thought the interview would be like. She took me through the usual questions about my application, experience, and goals—stuff like that I'd expected. Then she started to ask about my family. Were any of my parents in the medical field? Where did they live? Were they divorced? Was there a family history of depression? All the questions she wasn't supposed to ask. Those question threw me off completely, what was I going to tell her?"

Frieda choked up for a second.

"I told her the truth, I blurted it out and told her the truth. My mom is a homeless schizophrenic. I knew nothing about my father, he abandoned us when I was young, and I have no siblings. At that point, I thought I was history. But she pushed me more. I was going to leave, but each time she stopped me and I kept blurting out my story." Frieda went on, recalling a line of questioning from her interview. "Do I ever see my mother? How do I feel about her? Am I angry at her? Have I ever tried to contact my father? Lots of personal questions. I kept trying to read her face. Was she generally interested in my history, which I share with few people, or was she simply a bitch that got off prying into someone's personal business? But I couldn't read her, she was stone-faced the entire interview, it was traumatic, but a few days later, I received a letter that I was hired."

"When did the book show up?"

"Maybe a week later, not long afterward."

"Did you suspect she gave you the book?" Lumas asked. "No, I just thought someone accidentally left it in my locker."

"What do you think now?"

She didn't answer for a minute. "What's going on at this place, Lumas?"

"I really don't know yet. For now, I am going to follow directions." The next morning, he called Dino. "I'll do it with one exception, I won't stop the therapy."

"Are you sure you can do this?" Dino replied. "Do I have much of a choice?"

"No, and after this we can't be seen together, not with Frieda or Ganz either."

"How long do I have to be in purgatory?"

Dino didn't answer right away. "Dunno," then hung up.

CHAPTER FIFTY

Dear Grandparents,

This is the last I will be writing you. I will journal, but it's time for me to move my thought to the present, not dwell on the past. The letters to you were cathartic, but I wasn't attempting to focus on the now. I guess that's part of PTSD. I internalized my hurt and selfishly thought, rather convinced myself, I was the only man on the battlefield. That's ego.

I am slowly learning to accept those challenges, even welcome them, and rationally grow by the experiences, whether I fail or not. If I fail, then I win. If I lose, I win.

Goodbye, I love you,

Elliot.

CHAPTER FIFTY-ONE

Evans found the letter on his rocking chair on the porch. He hadn't received any letters for nearly a month. It didn't bother him, he had other projects he'd created himself.

"What the fuck is this?" he exclaimed out loud. It read, "Evans, first, you're being followed."

Underneath were three pictures of a blue Mini Cooper. He hadn't noticed the car, that itself was odd. Evans had a keen sense of discerning the unusual. His car was not in the photographs, which meant he was being tracked. Only the hospital cell phones were accessible to track him. He thought for a minute and left it on.

The letter continued. "Second, contact the kid's friend, Dino, tomorrow. Ask him what he needs from you now." The letter ended abruptly there. That was it—orders.

Dino was in the charting room at midnight when Evans walked in. He said nothing to Dino. Amin walked to Evans and dropped his snout on his lap.

Dino spoke while looking at the big shepherd. "My dog is conflicted. He's somewhere between Benedict Arnold and Groucho Marx, both brilliant and a traitor."

"Don't worry about that."

That was the last comment he wanted to hear from the big security guard.

Evans scratched Amin's head and spoke. "I've been told you need something, what is it?"

Dino looked at him. "I don't know what you're talking about."

"Think hard. I don't have all day. What are you doing on the computer at this time?" Evans pointed at the computer.

Dino shrugged his shoulders and spoke dejectedly. "I need to get into someone's account, and I can't hack it by myself."

"And you need the chart information for what reason?" Evans demanded.

"Dr. Lumas is a friend—"

"You're wasting my time," Evans interrupted.

"I have to get into the system of our boss to protect him," Dino said, speaking fast.

"Who can break in?" "Dr. Berger."

Evans stood and walked out.

Dino took a deep breath and leaned back in the chair, he was still squirming.

Within a minute, Evans forcefully pushed open the door to the charting room. He hurriedly walked toward Amin. Dino jumped to his feet, he felt like he was going to pee on himself.

"Dr. Guitano, there are no accolades here, you did what you were supposed to do."

Evans dropped to one knee, scratched Amin's head, and pulled out a bag of burned bacon. He said nothing to Dino, turned, and left. Outside in the hallway, he smirked. He enjoyed taunting Dino.

CHAPTER FIFTY-TWO

The next day Berger was sitting in the front seat of his car with a Smith & Wesson handgun pushed to the back of his head. His assailant was applying just enough pressure to hurt him and maintain his attention. Evans had lowered the front and rearview mirrors and crouched low behind Berger's seat. It was dark again and he never forgot the first beating he took under similar conditions. Since then, he'd demanded a guard walk him to his car. Unfortunately, on that particular night, no one showed up. He was parked far from the exit again under those low parking lot lights that were worthless.

Tired of waiting for an escort, he sprinted to his car, jumped in, and took a deep breath.

"Hello, Doctor."

Berger began to turn around.

"You turn, I will put a bullet through your head." He shook and mumbled incoherently.

"It's okay, I won't kill you as long as you do exactly as I tell you."

Evans's voice lowered to a hardly audible grim gab. He tossed a computer tablet in Berger's lap.

"Tap into the EMR and log in under your boss's username and password, and hurry," he commanded.

"Okay, just don't shoot me. Don't shoot me. I'm a good doctor. I was just following orders."

"Type and talk. What were your instructions? From whom,

why, and how did they choose Lumas?"

Berger stopped typing. "How, how, I don't..." he stuttered. "Did I say stop typing? Hurry up, my arm is getting tired holding this gun to your pathetic head." Berger struck the last key hard.

"Now copy and paste the password and username in a file marked with your name and move it to the desktop."

He protested and received a solid thump to his temple. "Do it now, get out the car, and keep your eyes looking away from me."

Berger did as he was told. For a solid five minutes, they stood without moving, neither uttering a word. In the distance, Berger could see a car approaching, it flashed lights and pulled up next to him.

The driver spoke. "Hello, are you Dr. Berger?" a dark-skinned man with a heavy Kenyan accent asked with a smile.

He looked behind him, his assailant was gone. "Yes, but I didn't call for an Uber."

"The guy said you'd say that. Come on in. He told me it's a surprise." The driver opened his door and politely pointed to the back seat. He could tell the man was taller than six feet and hugely muscular. "I was told not to tell you where I'm taking you but that your itinerary—I love that word, makes me feel smart and educated—everything has been taken care of, and I'm to make absolutely sure you get there promptly. I'm responsible for you. You have a good friend there. He said I'm supposed to take a few pictures of you when we arrive and text them to him. That guy really wants to make sure he surprises you, probably going to pull out those pictures when you guys are old friends."

Berger was terrified when they pulled up at the airport. The driver jumped out and grabbed one small carryon suitcase.

"Let us go, Doctor. I have our tickets. I'm supposed to check us in." Berger's face curled. "Uhh, we? Where are *we* going?"

The man smiled a broad set of white teeth. "I told you, it's a surprise; you ask too many questions, man."

The big African looked at him with deadly disdain. Berger shook. The man's demeanor abruptly changed. He looked into Berger's eyes, his facial features changed in a heartbeat. His brow furrowed, eyelids opened widely, and his smile disappeared. His expression was grotesquely serious.

"I think your guest is watching us, just to make sure all goes as planned."

They checked in. The man had Berger's passport and treated him like a dignitary. The man told him not to speak.

"But suppose someone asks me a question."

"You're a mute, Doctor. I do all the speaking for you."

The Kenyan never left his side; warned him not to speak to anyone. When they arrived at the gate, Berger saw the sign behind the counter. Three stops and twenty-five hours later, they touched down in the Democratic Republic of the Congo.

After the long flight, the two men deplaned. The man kept Berger's passport while going through customs, translating in French that his friend was a deaf mute, then escorted him to a restroom. He shredded Berger's passport and tossed the wad into a toilet. He told Berger to empty his pockets.

"You have no money, no passport, no return flight, and a shirt and a pair of pants in the suitcase. Eventually the DRC government will ask a lot of questions and someone will want to know why you left the country in a hurry with nothing but a one-way ticket," he informed him. "The nearest American embassy is two hundred kilometers away. I am to tell you that if you're lucky enough to get home, he'll find you."

CHAPTER FIFTY-THREE

Lumas thought of leaving the program. After talking with Frieda, Dino, and Ganz, he realized he was all alone again. No one could do anything to avoid whatever Jeremy and Karlson had in mind; no one knew. That's what his mind kept bouncing around. All he knew was that they needed him gone. His mind began to shuffle between mania and depression. Besides, all those homeless souls who stand all day and talk to the telephone poles didn't start out life that way. Something uncontrollable took their souls and minds. He was terrified.

Death was a peaceful thought, living as a failure was the worst. He thought about leaving the states, maybe Frieda would follow him, maybe not. In fact, anywhere he fled, he knew rationally there was nowhere to hide. At least he was still processing semi rationally.

He sat, lonely, desperate, and pensive. Why did nature convey a vicious intellect on humans, capable of incomprehensible moral and ethical vicissitudes? Animals have a purpose and kill to survive. Humans have yet to develop purpose, except aggressiveness. As a species, humans lack humanity.

Lumas tossed his books and found Seneca's *Letters from a Stoic*.

He began to read a page that fell open easily.

1. Do you suppose that you alone have had this experience? Are you surprised, as if it were a novelty, that after such long

travel and so many changes of scene you have not been able to shake off the gloom and heaviness of your mind? You need a change of soul rather than a change of climate. Though you may cross vast spaces of sea, and though, as our Vergil remarks, Lands and cities are left astern, your faults will follow you whithersoever you travel.

2. Socrates made the same remark to one who complained; he said: "Why do you wonder that globe-trotting does not help you, seeing that you always take yourself with you? The reason which set you wandering is ever at your heels." What pleasure is there in seeing new lands? Or in surveying cities and spots of interest? All your bustle is useless. Do you ask why such flight does not help you? It is because you flee along with yourself. You must lay aside the burdens of the mind; until you do this, no place will satisfy you.

Reflect that your present behavior is like that of the prophetess whom Vergil describes: she is excited and goaded into fury, and contains within herself much inspiration that is not her own: The priestess raves, if haply she may shake The great god from her heart. You wander hither and yon, to rid yourself of the burden that rests upon you, though it becomes more troublesome by reason of your very restlessness, just as in a ship the cargo when stationary makes no trouble, but when it shifts to this side or that, it causes the vessel to heel more quickly in the direction where it has settled. Anything you do tells against you, and you hurt yourself by your very unrest; for you are shaking up a sick man.

3. That trouble once removed, all change of scene will become pleasant; though you may be driven to the uttermost ends of the earth, in whatever corner of a savage land you may find yourself, that place, however forbidding, will be to you a

hospitable abode. The person you are matters more than the place to which you go; for that reason we should not make the mind a bondsman to any one place. Live in this belief: "I am not born for any one corner of the universe; this whole world is my country."

4. If you saw this fact clearly, you would not be surprised at getting no benefit from the fresh scenes to which you roam each time through weariness of the old scenes. For the first would have pleased you in each case, had you believed it wholly yours. As it is, however, you are not journeying; you are drifting and being driven, only exchanging one place for another, although that which you seek,—to live well,—is found everywhere.

Can there be any spot so full of confusion as the Forum? Yet you can live quietly even there, if necessary. Of course, if one were allowed to make one's own arrangements, I should flee far from the very sight and neighborhood of the Forum. For just as pestilential places assail even the strongest constitution, so there are some places which are also unwholesome for a healthy mind which is not yet quite sound, though recovering from its ailment.

5. I disagree with those who strike out into the midst of the billows and, welcoming a stormy existence, wrestle daily in hardihood of soul with life's problems. The wise man will endure all that, but will not choose it; he will prefer to be at peace rather than at war. It helps little to have cast out your own faults if you must quarrel with those of others.

6. Says one: "There were thirty tyrants surrounding Socrates, and yet they could not break his spirit," but what does it matter how many masters a man has? "Slavery" has no plural; and he who has scorned it is free,—no matter amid how large a mob of over-lords he stands.

7. It is time to stop, but not before I have paid duty. "The knowledge of sin is the beginning of salvation." This saying of

Epicurus seems to me to be a noble one. For he who does not know that he has sinned does not desire correction; you must discover yourself in the wrong before you can reform yourself.

8. Some boast of their faults. Do you think that the man has any thought of mending his ways who counts over his vices as if they were virtues? Therefore, as far as possible, prove yourself guilty, hunt up charges against yourself; play the part, first of accuser, then of judge, last of intercessor. At times be harsh with yourself. Farewell.

—Seneca

CHAPTER FIFTY-FOUR

"It's too dangerous to use the board any longer."

The nursing director was so upfront and curt she bordered on rude. Evans pictured her as hard-ass ex-military, no-nonsense, to the point, and even a tad bitter. After all, unlike today, women were delegated to either clerical or medical units during the Vietnam War. Evans thought that ironic. Men usually made tough decisions based on testosterone levels. Women, with few exceptions, were much more rational.

For the most part, men were intimidated by intelligent, strong women. They forced small men with selfish agendas to realize their insecurities, consequently their only choice was to subjugate women to substandard menial tasks or to lie about their bright futures. The ladder being the path of least resistance, men being men.

Evans caught his mind drifting into the past, his childhood and how viciously his father beat his mother. Between the violence, he criticized her for being born. He successfully cheated her into believing she was expendable, trivial, worthless, and deserved his constant bantering. The only peace Evans ever remembered as a child was smashing his head with the bat and the three blessed days of peace and quiet as his father recuperated in the hospital. Evans took the opportunity to steal his revolver and leave the holster in plain sight in the man's recliner chair.

After returning home, Evans stood next to the chair as his father threw open the front door. He was going to beat and torture

Evans till he passed out from exhaustion. The man seethed with anger and enjoyed the thought of the beatings. Maybe with his belt buckle first, then a tree branch, fireplace poker, chicken wire, and then lock him in the hall closet. He'd make excuses to the school that Evans had run away to his grandparents' home in Chicago and probably wouldn't return. Instead, the man lost all the color in his face seeing the empty holster.

"Where's my gun, boy?" he asked in a venomous tone. "Where's my gun, boy?" he repeated. "I'm going to beat the shit out of you if you don't give it to me right now."

The boy spoke calmly, which both startled and angered his father more. "Do you want the bullets first?"

The man lunged at Evans, his mother screamed. Evans was too young to hold the revolver with one hand. He was, however, strong enough to pull the weapon from the back of his pants and point, balancing the handle with one hand and the barrel with the other.

His father froze. "You gonna shoot me, boy? Yah can't even pull the trig…"

Evans squeezed the handle as tightly as he could. The bullet struck just below and to the side of the man's testicles. A blotch of blood poured out of the hole and ran down the man's pants.

He howled in pain and grabbed his balls. He righted himself and attempted to grab the gun. Evans squeezed off two more shots, which blew holes into the opposite side of his crotch, missing his testicle by inches. The man dropped to the floor screaming, squeezing his inner thighs. Evans's ears hurt, for an instant all he heard was a loud whistling. The sound of the shot from the long-barrel .38 special reverberated throughout the house.

His mother screamed again, shouting at him. "Evans, don't

kill your father."

"He ain't my father. I don't have a father."

Evans turned to her. "Go pack a bag for him. he's leaving for good." The man looked up, eyes wide, bulging, and bloodshot.

Evans took a step forward. "You ever coming back here?" The man's face contorted into a grotesque mask of rage. "I said, you ever coming back here?"

He didn't answer.

Evans stepped back and pulled hard on the hammer of the gun, locking it in place. He wasn't shaking nor did his facial expression expose any remorse or fear. Evans began to squeeze off the last shot, this time to the head.

He felt a thud to his shoulder that floored him. He looked up, his mother was standing over him, tears flooding her eyes.

The man was still groaning and uttered words in pain. "Shoot him, kill him, or I will."

His mother took the gun from Evans's hand, turned, pointed, and let off two rapid shots. One directly through the neck and the other through his right eye. The man's body seized for a second, then he was gone.

She turned to Evans. "Go pack some clothes, baby."

She stepped in front of him as he walked down the hallway blocking his way.

"Who is this coming from?" he asked. He immediately regretted that question. She kept stone-faced for an uncomfortable few seconds, which made Evans feel even more like he had lost some valuable points with her.

"I'll let that question pass and try to forget you asked." She walked away.

Evans didn't move. His mind raced back and forth, uselessly recalling the events that led him there. Not just his physical presence at the VA but to a certain mental state. Up until five months ago, he'd remained under the radar intentionally, or so he had thought. Now he was embroiled in a stratagem and took orders from people he was barely familiar with, for reasons that confounded him.

CHAPTER FIFTY-FIVE

"Success is not final. Failure is not final. It is the courage to continue that counts."
—Sir Winston Churchill

Lumas had given his word to Ganz and Dino, trusting they were thinking about his well-being first and not their own personal agendas. If he let his mind wander too far and did not catch himself, he would spiral into an abyss of self-denigration and critical assertions.

The Stoics would be proud of him, except Aurelius who would cast it out as expected. He would continue to practice Stoic ideas of ethics, humility, honesty, control, and what was out of his control. He continued seeing the psychiatrist, abstaining from alcohol, and sharing his most intimate feelings and thoughts with Frieda, and that was terrifying. He was exposing his innermost insecurities and emotional catastrophes, however, he knew he had little choice but to trust her. His emotional strength depended on it as well as his rational thoughts, even his very existence.

He added an hour each morning to journaling in addition to meditating, studying, and forcing his hand, writing like a Stoic. He came to realize it was a healthy habit and the thoughts flowed, although at times he rambled ad nauseam and frequently bastardized *Meditations* by Aurelius, depending on his mood. He didn't think of this as theft or plagiarizing but adapting and modifying for himself. Besides, Aurelius had no intention of publishing his meditations. He expected them to be destroyed, so rationally he wouldn't mind Lumas's snatch and run attitude.

"Take the shortest route, the one that nature planned—to speak and act in the healthiest way. Do that, and be free of pain and stress, free of all calculation and pretension."
—Marcus Aurelius

Lumas journaled, "I wake up early each day, before my cohorts. I am learning, albeit with difficulty, about nature and feeling my soul and its inherent simplicity, quirkiness, and cruelty with or without interrogations. Afterward, I prepare myself for war." Lumas found it therapeutic to put his own brand of sarcastic spin on philosophy.

His ruse would begin that day. He took his time getting dressed in a dingy, wrinkled, battered white coat with fading blood splattered around the circumference of the coat. Then he put on his dirtiest tennis shoes with mismatched socks. He didn't brush his teeth or comb his hair.

He walked into morning rounds intentionally late, entering the forward door, so everyone could get a good glance. Jeremy was cross-examining one of the interns and stopped for a full minute and stared at Lumas as he took a front-row seat.

He looked at Lumas. "You're late. Why?"

"I didn't know I was late. What time is it, Jeremy?" Lumas said in response.

Jeremy fumed, how dare he answer with a question. "It's not my responsibility to tell you the time or remind you of your responsibility to attend meetings on time. And furthermore, you look like a pig."

Lumas ran both his hands through his hair, making it spike like a punk rocker. "How do I look now?"

There was silence in the room. No one ever ridiculed Jeremy, especially not in front of an audience.

Jeremy was temporarily stunned at Lumas's insolence and disrespect. The two locked eyes.

"You can continue now, Jeremy," Lumas said. Someone in the back of the room chuckled.

"I want to see you in my office in an hour," Jeremy fumed. "Sorry. I can't make it in an hour. I'll leave a message when I'm available. Or I'll have my people call your people."

Jeremy could feel the blood rushing to his head. "You're in so much fucking trouble," he said.

"I said, I'm sorry, or maybe I didn't… sorry," Lumas responded, his voice dripping with sarcasm. "Come on, Jeremy," Lumas went on. "You can't fire an intern for messy hair, asking a question, or being late to morning rounds."

More interns and residents laughed.

Jeremy punched the speaker's stand and walked off the podium, slamming the door behind.

Lumas turned to the room full of doctors. "Well, what are you looking at?"

That stunned the room. It was out of character for Lumas to act so erratically. And further it wasn't like him to dismiss his colleagues so rudely.

He walked out.

Dino sat in the back of the small auditorium and felt a huge sense of remorse, guilt, and empathy wash over him. He had asked Lumas to do the impossible—completely isolate himself from the staff and the other interns. He was all too convincing, now everyone would avoid him. Jeremy would revert to his primal behavior but be crueler. But there was no other way to protect Lumas, even if he was unaware of it.

Jeremy had already tried to overdose him and sabotage his work during the entire year. He wasn't going to give up, especially not now. Lumas feigned he was psychologically unstable and was easy pickings. Dino and Ganz were calculating, but to make this work they had to rely on Lumas following through if he could. But Jeremy fed on chaos. Without order, there was only confusion and the mob-like behavior would become the norm.

A nuclear explosion is chaos and disrupts the natural order of the universe. Oppenheimer knew this and hypothesized the bomb might have caused the destruction of Earth by creating pandemonium on the nuclear level. There was no order in the mind of a psychopath like Jeremy. He was not clever. Dino's only recourse was creating more chaos, stoking the fire in an already sick mind, hopefully keeping him muddled as long as possible.

Then there was the big intimidating guard. Ganz and Lumas had no idea of his agenda nor who else was lurking around with a plan.

The basic tenet now was every person for themselves. Watch your back, pandemonium and fear was apparent everywhere among the interns. Watch Lumas closely, especially when directly in contact with patients or when doing procedures. No one wanted the mortality rate to climb again. Interns could lose positions at prestigious residency programs, if the mortality rate crept higher. Staff would be under the microscope for incompetent oversight. And Karlson could be demoted and endure an audit for quality of care from the university. Everyone knew what was at stake. Interns huddled in corners, realizing now they had two psychologically unstable physicians to keep a close eye on.

When Jeremy entered his office, he slammed the door and threw a book against the wall. He called Karlson. "We have a problem."

Karlson dreaded speaking to Jeremy. Not only had he failed firing Lumas but he'd killed one vet, maybe more. There were probably many more questionable deaths if the university audited the mortality rate. Jeremy was controllable in the past, not now.

Karlson could not see that changing in the foreseeable future.

Jeremy recounted morning rounds. Karlson listened. At the end of Jeremy's ranting he said, "So, what's the problem?"

Jeremy was stunned for a second. He expected Karlson to start screaming at him despite their last interaction when he threatened both Karlson and Jennens. "The problem is he's not the same. He's not stable, not terrified of me. He made me look like a fool."

Karlson spoke calmly. "It's perfect, Jeremy. Look, I can't fire him. The university has a policy of psych evaluations and committee meetings for interns with psychiatric problems. That would delay plans past the end of the year. And they may not vote to fire him, but instead give him a long leave of absence, and force him to see a shrink, to medicate and monitor him. Now you have a clean opportunity to make him disappear forever."

"How?"

"Push him over the edge. You've done it before." With that, Karlson hung up.

Eventually, Jeremy would have formulated a plan, a final solution to fire Lumas. He would not be made a buffoon and demeaned as this class had done. Whatever it took to force Lumas out, he was going to do. It didn't matter how brutal the deed or the collateral damage, Jeremy was going to destroy Lumas. He wanted him dead, first psychologically, then physically, icing on the cake.

But death would come last. He'd rather see him suffer a slow painful end of life. He wanted Lumas to die detesting his existence, to suffer like the vets that camp out on the streets every evening, foraging for food in trash cans and begging for handouts. Lumas, Dino, and Ganz had intentionally moved up the time clock. Jeremy now had only one month before the internship ended.

CHAPTER FIFTY-SIX

Lumas left the hospital late that day, intentionally. He spent twice the amount of time examining patients and charting.

Often repeating the same questions and seeing the same patient four or five times.

One of the patients complained to nursing to find him another physician. "There's something wrong with that doctor," the patient had said. "It's crazy enough around here, then you guys send me a nutcase." Another patient refused to let him draw blood after seeing his hands shake. He was seen walking the hallways talking to himself, to the fire extinguisher, or even to the paintings on the walls. At lunch, he sat in the corner table alone and conversed ostentatiously having a bitter disagreement with the invisible visitor sitting across from him. He stood angrily and barged out, seemingly having lost all his patience. The nurses avoided him, the clerical staff complained to their bosses, and even the janitors complained when he took one of their mops and began cleaning the floors in their break room. Some of the doctors asked if he needed to sleep or offered to cover for him and take a call day off. He never responded to the offers but walked away and began conversing with his ghostly nemesis. The consensus was that he had to be watched closely or everyone was at risk.

Dino shadowed him, hoping to give encouraging words of support until Lumas screamed at him and called him the gestapo. After a while, Dino began to worry that Lumas wasn't pretending at all.

He called Ganz. "I'm really worried. He's either really good at faking it or he really is gone."

"My god, what have we done?" Ganz responded.

Lumas closed the door to his condo and took a deep breath. "Fuck me."

He took a long shower, but decided not to shave, then sat in the tub and meditated for twenty minutes. Before he relaxed with some reading, he called Frieda.

She decided not to ask the ridiculous question. She listened to the stories of Lumas's behavior all day long. At one point she found she couldn't listen any longer and locked herself in the restroom and shed tears until her shoulders and neck became stiff.

"Can I come over? I need to hold you," she spoke lovingly.

"Yes, I need you now also."

He opened *Meditations*.

"It's unfortunate that this has happened.

No. It's fortunate that this has happened, and I've remained unharmed by it—not shattered by the present or frightened of the future. It could have happened to anyone. But not everyone could have remained unharmed by it. Why treat the one as a misfortune rather than the other as fortunate? Can you really call something a misfortune that doesn't violate human nature? Or do you think something that's not against nature will violate it? But you know what its will is. Does what happened keep you from acting with justice, generosity, self-control, sanity, prudence, honesty, humility, straightforwardness, and all other qualities that allow a person's name to fulfill itself?

So remember this principle when something threatens to cause you pain: the thing itself was no misfortune at all; to endure it and prevail is great good fortune."

—Marcus Aurelius

CHAPTER FIFTY-SEVEN

Jennens texted Evans. "Meet me in the cafeteria at nine." Evans knew what Jennens wanted; the meeting wasn't to discuss hospital security. And Jennens needed something from him also.

"Why meet here?" Evans was abrupt with Jennens, he never trusted him. But Jennens hadn't become the administrative CEO of one of the largest VA Medical Centers in the country without cunning, patience, and preparation. He also had the instinct to smell trouble. Evans decided to keep his mouth shut and let Jennens talk. Besides, oftentimes corrupt people loved to share, veneration for their cleverness. He also suspected it was one of Jennens's cronies who was trailing him.

Jennens answered in a sarcastic tone. "Why? Why? That is hysterical. You disdain me, Evans. Nothing would give you more pleasure than gouging out my eyes. But I need you and crowded, noisy places are the best places to meet."

He pointed around the room. "People can't hear us above their own bumbling."

"So, what do you want?"

Jennens leaned back. "Not so fast, first things first. I have been doing some background checking. You don't exist, you're a ghost. According to all the databases, you are the invisible man before coming here. Don't know how you faked the paperwork, and I really don't care, but my guess is you have good reasons and contacts. I can find out, you know that. I just decided to stop, let's say out of respect. Keeping myself out of your business unless I need to. But you're a smart guy. I know we can work together. I can make it very profitable for you."

Jennens took a deep breath and tried to read Evans's facial expression. He couldn't.

"What... do... you... want, Jennens?" he asked, aggressively drawing out the words.

Jennens lost his smugness and composure. "I want to get the recordings from Tina."

"I don't know where to find her."

"I do," Jennens said smugly.

That caught Evans's attention. Tina hadn't responded to any of the coded messages Evans left for her. Jennens wanted those recordings. Whatever she recorded was a threat to Jennens, that much was obvious. He also guessed Tina had something on the two docs who frequented his office and maybe a lot of other nefarious goings-on recorded.

"So, you think she's just going to give them to me?" Evans asked, his tone suddenly turning sarcastic.

"I suspect you can be persuasive, Evans. But, no, I want you to bring her to me. Here's the address where you can find her." He slipped a piece of paper across the table. "She's been living with one of the clerical personnel. There's a group of them from the same Army regiment here. A bunch of bitches."

Jennens did his homework better than Evans. Besides, he had an office full of staff who took their orders from Jennens seriously.

Evans said, "She must have copies."

"I don't care if she does. I suspect Tina wouldn't hand them to anyone except the person she's living with now. They are long-term friends from the service. From the little I know about her, I know that Tina would not want to put anyone else at risk."

"What do you mean 'at risk,' Jennens?" He didn't answer.

Evans was getting annoyed. He said, "You're being naïve. I think she wants the world to know."

"I'll take my chances." Jennens began to stand. "Sit down, Jennens."

Jennens's face flushed.

"I will do this, but I have two, no three nonnegotiable requirements. One—money, fifty thousand. Two—the passwords to all the physicians' cell phones, including staff. And three—after I finish, never contact me again."

Jennens became noticeably uncomfortable. "Why do you want the—"

"None of your business," Evans interrupted.

Evans leaned forward with his face nearly touching Jennens. "How persuasive am I, Jennens?" he asked.

A chill went through Jennens. He looked around, expecting someone to notice the odd exchange. "Okay," he said. He stood and left fuming. If one thing were for certain, Evans would never threaten him again.

Jennens left the passwords on Evans's desk in the security office under a pile of papers. He texted him that evening. "Bring her to me within a week. I'll give you instructions when you have her."

The next morning, Evans opened the door to the doctors' lounge, startling Dino.

He jumped to his feet. "I did as you asked, I mean I did as you told me, sir."

Evans was amused at the response but didn't let on. Amin jumped to his chest, his big snout inches away from Evans's face, and began to lick his nose. Evans grabbed him under both shoulders, one quick lift and Amin was in his arms. Evans held him like a puppy with one arm and scratched his neck with the other. Amin's tongue hung out the side of his mouth. Dino was amazed at how easily Evans elevated the big shepherd.

"Excuse me, sir, but I've never seen Amin do that before." Evans didn't regard the half-statement, half-question.

"Here." He pulled the paperwork out of his back pocket. "Those are all the passwords for the entire physician staff. I figured one wouldn't get you much. Whatever's going on here is more complicated than one person's design."

Dino took them.

"How long will it take you to get the information you need?"

"Not long now."

"You don't have help any longer?"

"I never really had help. The other doctor was working for—"

"I know that he's not around any longer." Evans didn't look up but kept scratching Amin.

Dino didn't want to know more but couldn't help but ask. His voice shook. "Dr. Berger left a message for me and the director of the program that he needed to leave immediately, something about a family emergency..." Dino's voice trailed off questioningly.

"I know."

That was it? Dino thought, shrugging in dismay at Evans's concise and uninformative response. "I will never ask a question again in my life when something in my head says stop."

Evans stopped scratching Amin and looked at Dino threateningly. "That's a good habit to have, Doctor."

Dino could have peed himself.

Evans gently let Amin down and walked out of the door. He enjoyed scaring the crap out of Dino again and walked down the hallway smirking again.

CHAPTER FIFTY-EIGHT

Lumas woke earlier the following day and every day afterward to read books on philosophy, both contemporary works and those written thousands of years ago. He was particularly impressed by the quotes from Epictetus and Thoreau, who wrote enormously similar words, despite being written at such distant times.

"If someone handed your body over to a passerby, you would be annoyed. Aren't you ashamed that you hand over your mind to anyone around, for it to be upset and confused if the person insults you?"
—Epictetus, *Enchiridion*

"Public opinion is a weak tyrant compared with our own private opinion. What a man thinks of himself, that it is which determines, or rather indicates, his fate."
—Henry David Thoreau

He realized philosophers were healers of the mind, therefore the body. He began to understand if he truly wanted to change, it would be to study philosophy. Psychotherapy and antidepressant medications would only dull the pain. Intellectually, he understood the damage and still carried the scars. But he needed the prescription for how to effect meaningful changes. The writings of the Greco-Roman philosophers and those who followed them provided the answers, which started with realizing and abandoning shame.

"It is circumstances which show men what they are. Therefore when a difficulty falls upon you, remember that God, like the trainer of wrestlers, has matched you with a rough young man. 'For what purpose?' you may say. Why, that you may become an Olympic conqueror; but it is not accomplished without sweat."

—Epictetus, *Discourses*

"You must live in the present, launch yourself on every wave, find your eternity in each moment. Fools stand on their island of opportunities and look toward another land. There is no other land; there is no other life but this."

—Henry David Thoreau

"If you now neglect things and are lazy and are always making delay after delay and set one day after another as the day for paying attention to yourself, then without realizing it you will make no progress but will end up a non-philosopher all through life and death. So, decide now that you are worthy of living as a full-grown man who is making progress, and make everything that seems best to be a law that you cannot go against. And if you meet with any hardship or anything pleasant or reputable or disreputable, then remember that the contest is now… and you cannot put things off anymore and that your progress is made or destroyed by a single day and a single action."

—Epictetus, *Enchiridion*

He decided he must stop drinking and roaming and bring an end to any activity that left him feeling disreputable, as Epictetus wrote. And he kept his promise to Dino and Ganz and continued the ruse. Besides, if they were correct, he had no choice. Jeremy was reenergized to demean him to quit or die.

He downloaded the quotes of Marcus Aurelius to his phone

so he could easily refer to them whenever need be. They were better than the Bible. He reread a couple that felt particularly relevant at that moment in time:

"The best revenge is to be unlike him who performed the injury."
—Marcus Aurelius

CHAPTER FIFTY-NINE

Dino downloaded years of notes from Jeremy's phone. They read like the psychopathic rantings of a serial killer. He detailed the circumstances and the names of the four interns he had forced out of the program. Each was a minority physician. He wrote about how he chose each intern and their ethnicities. He had an ability to spot their insecurities, emotional and psychological temperaments, and vulnerabilities. He was patient, calculating, and focused until he pounced on the unsuspecting rookies and destroyed their enthusiasm and confidence.

Jeremy wrote about the pleasure it gave him torturing each one, especially the women. The most important information he'd gathered after plowing through two hundred notes was the end of the year mortality and morbidity conferences. Jeremy had used that day to castigate and demean the intern in front of the entire staff. Then he and Karlson would escort the person to his or her office and ask the intern to voluntarily resign.

Jeremy was always successful. By the time the year was ending, the young physicians embraced the thought of an end to the physical and psychological torture.

CHAPTER SIXTY

Evans' back ached from the three hours he spent curled up behind the passenger seat. By the time he heard footsteps approaching the car, his feet were numb. Tina opened the trunk and threw in something that was heavy enough to make a loud thud. Evans figured it was a suitcase. She came around and slid into the car.

Before she started the engine, Evans sat up. "So, you're the infamous Tina."

Tina responded with an impressive amount of composure, looking at the rearview mirror. "And you're Evans. What took you so long to find me?"

"You hide your tracks well, but not well enough for Jennens to never find you."

Tina shrugged. "It was just a matter of time. He's neither ignorant nor a fool. That's why he sent you, isn't it? Are you here to kill me or take me back to him? I'd guess the latter, he doesn't trust you either."

"He doesn't trust anyone." Evans had a twang of sarcasm in his voice.

"That's true, but he's terrified of you. You realize, he can't let you go, like that," Tina said, snapping her fingers for emphasis. "When he decides, you'll disappear. You're a loose cannon, everyone mixed up in this has something to lose, except you. Unless, of course, you have something to hide, and he's threatened you…" she prodded.

"He did," Evans quickly supplied.

"Oh, so the man has a sordid past," Tina shot back sarcastically.

Neither spoke for a moment, neither intimidated the other. Evans realized what she was doing.

"Is she behind me?" he asked, already knowing the answer.

"Yup," she confirmed.

Evans looked over his shoulder into the barrel of a .38 special revolver. The gun held steady, dead in the middle of his face.

"Now what, Tina?"

"Are you armed?"

"Nope."

She opened her window and gestured to the person behind. Tina began to talk as the other person got in and sat next to Evans, gun in hand.

"Okay, so you don't have a gun. I doubted it anyway, but it does pay to be careful."

The other person was Tina's age, although unlike her, she was bitter and sweet. She caused Evans some concern. It was probably this one who orchestrated distracting him till she crept up behind hm. She kept both eyes fixed on him and continued to point the pistol. He looked at her and eased back in the seat.

"I suppose I can't convince you to put that down or give it to Tina?" he asked. "She can still shoot me if I do anything to piss you off."

"Nope." Tina turned to face Evans.

"So, you don't have a gun?" she asked him. "You wouldn't lie to us, would you? That would be a problem."

The other woman ran her hand down his chest and thighs, as Tina continued her line of questioning. "And you're not really Jeremy's crony, are you, Evans?"

She pulled him forward and checked the seat behind him. "And you're not here to kill me, are you? More like really curious… right?"

She looked at her friend while the other woman simultaneously checked his ankles, hips, and slowly his inner thighs to the groin and squeezed.

Evans looked at her hard. "You know that hurts a bit. Are you finished yet?"

The woman gave a final squeeze between finished and yet. "Nope," the woman answered.

"So, who are you, Evans?" she asked. "None of your business."

"Born nowhere, grew up nowhere, educated nowhere. Application to VA security job, total fabrication. You cover your tracks well, but not well enough for Jennens to find out you really don't exist. Which brings up the question as to how you passed the background check."

Tina let out an exasperating sigh. "You're not going to tell us anything, are you?"

"Nope!"

"Well, if we don't know who you are or why you work with Jennens, where do we go from here?"

"You play chess?" Evans asked.

CHAPTER SIXTY-ONE

"At dawn, when you have trouble getting out of bed, tell yourself: 'I have to go to work—as a human being. What do I have to complain of, if I'm going to do what I was born for—the things I was brought into the world to do? Or is this what I was created for? To huddle under the blankets and stay warm?' So you were born to feel 'nice'? Instead of doing things and experiencing them? Don't you see the plants, the birds, the ants and spiders and bees going about their individual tasks, putting the world in order, as best they can? And you're not willing to do your job as a human being? Why aren't you running to do what your nature demands? You don't love yourself enough. Or you'd love your nature too, and what it demands of you."

—Marcus Aurelius, *Meditations*

Lumas had to peel himself out of bed. He picked up *Meditations* and imagined how Aurelius felt every morning when he had to contend with thousands of Jeremys, daily. Except the usual way—kill him. Irrespective, he found some fleeting comfort realizing human emotions, conflict, irrational behaviors, selfishness, and anger were out of his control.

Only the way his mind collected and processed the thoughts was important. The feeling of control is only attained by constant practicing. That was curious to him, because he found the more he practiced and felt he was examining his life in perspective rather than emotionally, the more a heightened sense of loneliness tended to settle in on him.

Recalling a lecture he found on YouTube about Aurelius's life gave him more insight. A philosopher historian from NYU postulated the emperor died a lonely man having the life of a Stoic sage. Lumas wasn't comparing, not realistically, but striving to live a virtuous life resulted in noticing the flaws of his colleagues and that was both dangerous and arrogant.

Irrespective, he could control the inclination easier by reminding himself of the question: who was he to judge another human being? He even felt a twang of pity for Jeremy but decided to leave that for a higher power. He should only judge his own behavior and be the captain of his own ship.

Judgments are what contributed to his lifelong feeling of loss of purpose. Associations with those who had judged his character based on others' yardsticks. He thought what a pity it was, how much time he'd lost torturing his fragile psychological well-being. He also thought of how much work there was to do, how much to gain to enjoy his life with its challenges. Human beings thrive on adversity after all, and every adversity is an opportunity. Lumas had enough of suffering to death.

"Suffering arises from trying to control what is uncontrollable, or from neglecting what is within our power."
—Epictetus

Lumas drove into the parking lot, late for morning rounds, intentionally. Before walking through the lobby, he crumpled his white coat and walked into a puddle of muddy water splashing his slacks, all the while constantly bantering to himself. He feigned the perfect schizophrenic. He walked into the conference room, slamming the door. All the physicians shuddered; it was going to be another day of babysitting Lumas.

Despite Jeremy assigning him to do high-risk procedures, the other interns would have to step up and do the procedures them- selves. This made Jeremy seethe, but there was very little he could do against an entire group of interns who were obviously protecting their own asses. Jeremy also encountered resistance from the other attending physicians who also didn't want to see morbidity rates increase toward the end of the year. That would only highlight the fact they were not doing their jobs.

Morbidity rates should drop throughout the year as interns developed their skills. Besides, it was becoming clear to many that Jeremy was out of control, having failed firing Lumas thus far. By this time in prior years, the deed was guaranteed.

Lumas walked to the front of the room and began wiping the chair repeatedly, took off his dirty coat and dropped it on the floor. The presentation was another case of a young man with emphysema and alcoholism. Two of the most common diagnoses seen at the VA, all VAs. A large percentage suffered from effects of psychological trauma returning from Vietnam, Korea, Desert Shield, and Desert Storm. The VA resisted recognizing PTSD. The Pentagon covertly took the position that unquestionable devotion produced trauma, and these men and women probably had prior undiagnosed psychological issues.

At least the presenter was good to gawk at, mid-thirties, with long beautiful legs and great tits. No one thought much as he sketched her figure on a notepad. As she presented, Lumas spoke to someone invisible in the next chair, and everyone tried to ignore him.

When she finished, Jeremy took the podium. "The end of this year's mortality and morbidity conference is scheduled for next week," he spoke impatiently. "I'll be presenting the case and I will pick the interns to discuss the differential diagnosis."

Lumas raised his hand and flapped it like the wings of a bird. "What do you want, Lumas?"

"I volunteer."

It took Jeremy by surprise, he'd thought he'd lost the element of surprise, but this was even better. It was his intention to nail Lumas, then fire him right afterward. The hell with the potential complications of firing a psychologically ill intern, that was an administrative matter. His response would be quality of care and protection of the veterans. Everything else was up to Karlson to clean up.

Jeremy still thought of the ways to push Lumas over the edge to end his life but that was much more complicated. He might have to settle for him taking up residence in a tent city somewhere. The reality of that defeat was a bitter pill to swallow.

"Anyone else want to volunteer with Lumas before I pick one of you?"

Dino put up his hand.

A hand rose in the back. It was Timothy Simon. He never volunteered for anything, he was the invisible man.

Jeremy hesitated. "Okay, you and Lumas—" he began, looking at Simon.

"No. I refuse if you pick me to participate," Simon interrupted.

"You can't refuse. I run this program." Another hand went up.

"I refuse also."

Another hand. "I refuse also."

Jeremy's face turned beet red. "None of you can refuse!" he exclaimed, growing flustered.

The event unfolding was a brazen act. Interns faced expulsion if they refused to participate in any clinical activities, including presentations.

"I refuse."

"I refuse."

"I refuse."

"I refuse."

Everyone in the room raised their hands and refused. Jeremy was cornered—he couldn't fire everyone. The last person he wanted with Lumas was Dino.

Dino raised his hand again. "I volunteer."

Jeremy stormed off the podium, turned at the door, and shouted. "You two motherfuc—" then caught himself, "better be prepared," he challenged.

Dino called Lumas that evening. "How did you know he'd come at you then?" Dino asked.

"I didn't, but I had to take the chance and push him to give it up. He would have never otherwise, and I wouldn't have known I was in the oven till the very last second. Now we have some time to find out how he's coming at me."

"You sound like a sleuth; what's happened to you?" Dino began, but stopped himself, "I didn't mean that."

"No problem," Lumas replied collectedly, not missing a beat. "How did you get the interns to refuse, especially Simon?"

"I didn't," Lumas responded despondently. "That just figures."

They both laughed.

CHAPTER SIXTY-TWO

"You want dinner?" Tina asked.

The three walked back to the house.

"Sorry about the gun, Evans," Tina's friend apologized.

"First time I've had a gun pointed at my face. At least it was you and not some kid stealing my wallet."

She smiled.

"Well, I'm not sorry seeing you grimace in pain getting your groin squeezed," Tina spoke flippantly.

He ignored her.

After a moment of processing, they all laughed.

"So, where do we go from here, Evans?" Tina spoke before Evans could say anything. "I figure Jennens will retire and disappear in two weeks when the interns graduate. The VA will be chaotic as the new class arrives. Karlson will take his extended posh vacation, but not before he takes care of your friend Dr. Lumas. Jeremy will continue to kill veterans. Two criminals gone, one physician's career ruined, and the place remains the same. Jennens probably paid off his staff and recommended one of his cronies to his position. God knows how much money he's stolen."

Tina's friend looked at Evans. "What's with you and Lumas? Why are you helping to protect him?"

"I'm not. Well, I guess I am. He reminds me of someone I knew a few years ago. The guy is drowning, lonely. I gave him a book I thought might help."

Evans was speaking to them like old friends. He felt comfortable. In general, he was a loner but knew loners do not do so well in the long run. However, getting to know the old guys and the park-goers seemed to have made a difference in his attitude toward being more social. He had come to like Lumas, Dino, and Ben. He enjoyed intimidating Dino, just for the fun of seeing his reactions and his envy when Amin charmed him. He wondered if these two women really knew his past and what their reaction would be.

The other woman introduced herself. "I am Michelle. It's nice to meet you. I am Tina's partner." She shook his hand, gripping it tightly to make a statement. "What book did you give Lumas?"

"*Meditations*."

"Marcus Aurelius," Tina quickly responded.

Evans said, "Yes, for some reason, that book gave me some peace during my bad times."

The women exchanged looks.

Tina spoke as she unlocked the front door. "Evans, I suspect you have quite a history. The old guys must have done some checking on you; they don't trust just anyone. They took you under their wings, they're teachers, you should listen to them. They have lots of experience."

Evans stuttered for a second and spoke. "I… uhh… okay, now, I am completely confused. Everyone knows about me. I was recruited by the old guys, essentially without my knowledge. I thought I was fairly good at being under the radar, but I guess not. You two know I have been keeping track of Lumas, Dino, Jeremy, and that I hate the guy. You probably know I live alone, my daily routines, and…"

He trailed off, waiting for her to answer.

Michelle spoke first. "Listen, we are just careful. We're not interested in things like sexuality or hobbies, although the shooting range incident was pretty, let's say, stupid."

"You saw the whole thing and reported back to Ben?" Evans gathered.

"Yup."

"We also know about your childhood history," she went on. "That you lived from trash can to trash can, what your mother did for you, and a lot more. We are thorough," she assured him.

"Who are we?" Evans interjected. "Who's running this operation and what's the purpose?"

"We are retired veterans, fortunate enough not to be hospitalized in a VA Medical Center," Tina answered. "Over the years we've seen the fuckups, but that is not the main problem that's inherent in training programs, however, not to the extent it's covered up there. It is the corruption and lack of respect for the vets. They're treated like concentration camp internees, not survivors. They're coerced into thinking the VA will always take care of them, then wait months for an appointment, and more months for procedures. A lot of veterans die waiting. If they are hospitalized, they're housed in bunkers like boot camp with little-to-no privacy. The place looks lovely from the freeway but walk in and it's an armpit. It's a training program, so the vets are subject to what would be routine procedures. But because the attendings are trying to spend the least amount of time here, oversight sucks. Consequently, morbidity and mortality rates are high, higher than Karlson reports to the main campus. It's a travesty for the vets. They were lied to, in so far as the extent they would be taken care of after discharge, after all their devotion and duty to their country. There could be a sign outside the lobby 'Arbeit Macht Frei'—'Work Sets You Free.' Work and devotion left millions of veterans prisoners of an indifferent monolithic cesspool."

"So, to answer your question," she went on. "We are almost the entire staff, less the idiots in Jennens's office. And Ben and company are in charge. The farmer is our contact person, Colonel Sheen, USMC."

Evans took a deep breath. "Military intelligence, you were both in military intelligence, right?" A moment of silence passed.

"Yes, are we that obvious? Never mind, don't answer that."

"You're a smart guy, Evans."

He hesitated for a moment. "Not everyone can point a gun and not have second thoughts about pulling the trigger."

"She would have killed you, just don't know where we would have dumped your body."

"Who killed a woman on oncology a few months back?"

"Why are you asking us?"

"I think you can trust me."

Tina looked at Michelle, and after a few seconds she spoke. "I killed her, but I rather think of her death as painless and dignified," Tina admitted. "Well, more like put her out of her misery. We called her Major Betty; she was a smart lady and had a lovely soul. She asked us to do the deed for her. She made us promise." Her eyes swelled with tears.

"The VA hasn't caught up with the rest of the world. They let people suffer to death. Betty gave us an order, no questions asked, we follow orders."

"You sound like you're still in the service."

"We don't don the suit, but we will always be loyal to one another."

"Did you have to get permission from the farmer?"

"Enough questions, Evans, or I'll shoot you myself,"

Michelle interrupted. "You can see Tina is getting emotional."

Evans changed the subject. "I have to get back to Jennens. Here's what I have in mind."

Later, Evans walked up his front doorsteps and saw the white envelope partially sticking out the bottom. He scanned it and cringed.

CHAPTER SIXTY-THREE

"I'm gone in two weeks," Jennens declared.

Jennens was seated in Karlson's office with Jeremy.

"Where are you going?" Jeremy asked.

"None of your business!" Jennens screamed at Jeremy.

"If it wasn't for you, I wouldn't have changed my itinerary, just know that, Jeremy. I want to get as far away from you as possible before you kill another vet."

He turned to Karlson. "You think you can keep this psycho under control for two weeks?"

"Jeremy has enough to do till our last conference. He did what he had to do."

Jeremy said nothing but the thought of killing Jennens crossed his mind.

Karlson stood. "When do I get my money?"

"We can meet the day I leave. Two weeks, the day of your last grand rounds, when you castigate Lumas. I already wrote my resignation letter. The remainder of the money will be transferred to your account the next pay period—two weeks."

"And…"

"I'll meet on Lumas day."

"You'll get your money," he assured Karlson. Jennens stood and walked toward the door.

Karlson grabbed his arm. "What about the recordings?"

"Oh, yeah, I'll have them soon. Let go of my arm, now." Jeremy stood up after Jennens left.

Karlson spoke in a condescending tone. "Don't go anywhere, are you prepared for the conference?"

"Yes."

"Tell me."

"No."

Karlson was stunned, Jeremy had never spoken to him like this. "Just be there, Karlson."

Karlson's mind raced, Jeremy was uncontrollable. "Jeremy, you'll be in charge while I'm gone."

"I am already in charge of the residency program."

"No, I mean interim chief."

Jeremy looked at him hard. Karlson had him now, power was more important to Jeremy than money. Being chief would keep Jeremy's nefarious activities under control. He was too high profile to kill anyone, and his responsibilities would keep him on campus two to three days a week. That stroked Jeremy's ego. Karlson didn't want to read about a psychopath caught killing patients while he was away. Not that he cared about the vets dying, but it would spoil his vacation—the dean would immediately call him back. When he returned, he'd deal with Jeremy.

"You'd do that for me, the interim chief?"

"Sure, you've always been loyal. I always had you in mind to replace me."

"What about you?"

"Maybe the main campus, maybe retirement, emeritus professor. But I'll have to spend some time here before I leave." Karlson had no intention of leaving. "Now tell me about the conference."

Jeremy sat again. "In short, I picked the case. One of his, of course, relatively straightforward till I—"

Karlson interrupted him. He didn't want to know details, too risky. "You don't have to tell me more. Where do I come in?"

"I am going to destroy him."

"You fire him in front of the entire medical staff. Hopefully, he'll jump off a bridge. He has no idea what's coming. I doctored the chart perfectly."

"Excellent."

CHAPTER SIXTY-FOUR

Dino was at the computer, monitoring Jeremy's cell phone usage over the last week. He had received another email from the unknown sender, telling him to start now, as if he didn't know who it was, the security guard. He didn't know how much he knew, only he had given him the order to step up the pressure on the interns.

Whatever that did coincided with the end of the year, and he surmised Jeremy was going to attempt to use the last conference to nail Lumas. He knew he had little choice but to assume he was correct. And he didn't want the big security guard to visit him again. Dino's mind raced for a second. He leaned back and took a deep breath.

Evans threw the door open and walked directly toward Dino. Dino stood and backed up, hitting the wall behind him. "What, what, what! I did everything you asked."

Amin stood and walked toward Evans. He lunged, but instead of crushing Evans's face with his massive jowls, he licked his face and began to jump repeatedly and whining loudly, as if he were still a pup.

Evans ignored the dog. "Come here, Doctor. Sit down."

Dino didn't move. "What did you do to my dog? He's mush now."

Evans didn't acknowledge the comment but scratched Amin's head. "Come, sit down."

Dino did as he said. "Now, go to calendar."

Dino opened Jeremy's calendar.

"Go to the date of your next conference."

Dino read the date and the log. He read the words, 'Lumas is dead.' "Is he planning to kill Lumas?"

"You know him better than me. I only know he's done it before." Dino questioned the inference. "How do you know that for sure?"

Evans ignored the question. "What's he going to do?" Evans asked instead. "When and where?"

"His last entry tonight is in the S Note," Dino answered. "It took me a long time to figure that out."

Evans grunted. "Get to the point," he barked. "Sorry I was temporarily patting my own back."

"Don't. That should be expected of you, aren't you his friend and associate, you and his girlfriend?"

Dino wondered how this guy knew so much about Lumas. Maybe he knew that much about all of them. "Okay, the numbers at the bottom of this page were written today, it's an electronic medical record number."

"And…"

"Jeremy will change Lumas's orders, rather create another set of orders. No paper trail or computer trail from Jeremy, just Lumas. He quickly changes back to the original orders after his bogus meds are dispensed."

"Why didn't Lumas figure this out when patients began to have complications or died?"

"The program is antiquated, it doesn't change the orders in patients' electronic medical records immediately. And, as a boss, he can change orders and not sign on to the chart, so no electronic medical record trail at least not immediately. If Lumas did check it was probably too late and orders were changed back to his originals, again by Jeremy. The pharmacy staff do not override physicians' orders, they have no time to review all the orders in the hospital— cutbacks. And Jeremy knows the system and when to enter the orders, always during the busiest time of the day. The dosages would be the most difficult to track, pharmacy wouldn't know the patient's age, weight or diagnosis before releasing medications. The system is years behind newer programs, the VA won't spring for a new one, so this system does nothing to lessen medical errors."

Evans asked, "So, why not check the pharmacy records?"

"Can't take that chance. Interns are not allowed in the pharmacy. If I screw around down there, the chief pharmacist, who's a real asshole, will report me to Jeremy. Then we're really screwed—he'll cover his tracks, and we're back to square one. If I could have had the help of Berger, who would never want to see me again after I ordered Amin to maul him, just if I could trust him, he could have broken into the system and..." he rambled.

Evans cut him off. "You won't see him again; he's busy learning another language."

Dino bit his tongue. He did not want to know what that meant. Evans went on. "So, you need the password for the pharmacy, right?"

"Yes."

Evans stood, walked toward the door, and turned. "Don't screw this up, Doc. Be well prepared, I don't want any screw-ups, you understand?"

Evans stared into his eyes.

Dino had a chill down his spine, his face turned beet red. "Yeah. I mean yes, sir."

"I'll have the password for you tomorrow." Evans left, walking with purpose.

Dino turned to Amin. "You are worthless."

The next morning, Dino found an envelope taped to the door of the lounge. His name was neatly typed on the front. Inside, he found the password and one sentence. "You won't see that pharmacist again. He left the country to learn another language."

Before going to bed, Evans wondered why he was doing all this for Lumas, Tina, and the vets. But he felt good about it, he felt like a human being.

CHAPTER SIXTY-FIVE

Lumas journaled daily. As suggested by Stoics, he wrote about what he accomplished that day and how he would improve his next day. Afterward, he wrote as the thoughts flowed through his mind. He never planned sharing what he wrote.

He journaled about his ego, his insecurities, or his anger issues, but his pain was not unique to just him. These were difficult to scroll through. They hurt, but now he listened to his heart, which always spoke to him compassionately and with wisdom. Shame was most difficult to journal and challenging. Shame returned his brain to all the negativity he subjected himself to attempting to distract the pain.

Self-deprecation leaves a festering wound; philosophy was somehow able to guide him to forgive himself.

"You will give yourself relief if you do every act of your life as if it were the last, laying aside all carelessness and passionate aversions from the commands of reason, and all hypocrisy and self-love and discontent with the portion which has been given to you."
—Marcus Aurelius

"Dig within. Within is the wellspring of Good; and it is always ready to bubble up, if you just dig."
—Marcus Aurelius

It was all a test. Nature and his heart conspired to awaken his destiny by testing and challenging him. It was all a test. The thought gave him comfort, because he felt stronger and he didn't feel lonely any longer. Not the kind of loneliness when you lose a friend or a family member, but losing purpose in life, losing his soul.

If he listened to his heart and had the courage to continue, fall, and get up, listen and learn again and again, all his fears would disappear. Nothing again would surprise him or cause him to stray from his destiny. He understood it was all a test in his life and how inadvertently he persevered. He never understood what god-like entity guided him throughout his life, but he chose not to despair and listen to his heart and soul perpetually. He was healthier; he was a Stoic.

CHAPTER SIXTY-SIX

Evans picked up the receiver. "Security."

"It's Dino Guitano."

"Yes, I know who you are."

Dino felt another cold streak down his spine. "I am sorry to bother you, the password you gave me for the pharmacy has all the information I needed, thank you."

"And…"

"And I need your help again."

Dino waited for an answer, it felt like a lifetime of silence until Evans answered.

"And that is…?" Before Dino could recover and answer, Evans stopped him. "I want to know the date and time you plan on releasing what you've uncovered."

Dino sighed. "That's just it. We need to plan this together. It's the only time to really get Jeremy for good."

"No, I am working with you to help Lumas, but my fish are bigger. However, I will be there at your conference."

"Thanks, that's all I needed to know."

"You're right," Evans responded, then hung up.

Dino spoke to Amin. "I wish he wouldn't do that."

Amin cocked his head, his big eyes stared into Dino's as if to say, "You don't know the half of it."

CHAPTER SIXTY-SEVEN

An unintended benefit of the password that Evans gave Dino was that Jeremy had collected the passwords of almost every administrative employee and medical staff member over the years. He and Tina surmised he did this as necessary by rummaging through one email at a time and so on without any staff knowing the difference. Over the years, Jeremy insulated himself from suspicious deaths, medical errors, and missing medications with a simple threat from an unknown sender to physicians, pharmacists, and nurses. Evans was not computer savvy enough to sift through the files in Jennens's computer, but his cronies were stupid enough to create files on their desktops, cataloging transfers of monies from department accounts to Jennens.

Thereafter, Jennens would create budgetary changes, cutbacks, and disseminate to directors of the divisions, who would complain. But Jennens shrugged his shoulders and suggested writing

Washington. He was just following orders. When directors did contact Washington, they were ignored; the last issue the VA wanted was oversight committees auditing any of the VAs. That could produce a rippling effect and so on. If that happened, worthless top-heavy administrative staff would be exposed, and the quality of care given to the veterans finally uncovered.

Veterans Affairs would have much to explain, so the orders to ignore budgetary complaints came right from the top. From

Washington down to the local level, everyone benefitted from their cushy VA jobs. And veterans were left with a crumbling, incompetent, and corrupt healthcare delivery system. Medical care was less affected, although still substandard, since the VA training program was partially funded by the university.

Naïve graduates from prestigious medical schools vied for spots because of the academic environment, proximity to the main campus, acceptance to fellowship programs, and the perk of living in a wealthy posh community. Salaries at this VA were higher than the national average because of the higher cost of living. But the money that was supposed to go to new technology, lecturers, upgrades in equipment, and generally anything that improved the overall academic environment was siphoned off. Jennens and Karlson had sat on a cash cow for years. Evans met with Tina twice daily, sifting through emails and desktops, cataloging the transfers and communications between Jennens's staff.

Tina sighed and spoke. "These people working for Jennens are idiots. Everything is here, transfers, account numbers, even vacation plans. Jennens must not know his people are stupid. They think they can go on forever and no one would suspect otherwise."

Evans leaned back and took a deep breath. "Something's missing."

She looked at Evans. "What? It's all here, we have enough to go after him anytime."

"Not really, what's not here is who is Jennens paying off up the chain of command? If we don't know that, everything can be buried. No one wants this out there, not from here to Washington. We'll be crushed, servers will go down everywhere in the country. We need help. The year is ending for the new doctors and from what Larry, Moe, and Curly Joe have planned, two disappearing and one, God knows what he's up to, we will have lost our window."

Tina took a deep breath. "But I still have the recordings."

Evans turned and looked at her hard. "Yes, that's why Jennens has to get rid of you and the recordings."

Tina's expression didn't change, she looked hardened. "Hmm, I didn't think he had the balls to kill me."

"He does," Evans said.

Tina was composed. She whispered. "Control what you can control, know yourself and your enemy. 'Let your plans be dark and impenetrable as night, and when you move, fall like a thunderbolt.'"

"*The Art of War*," Evans said with a nod. "I know that book."

"I don't like surprises," Tina said. "We need to force him to move and at the same time not let him know we're orchestrating everything, otherwise, well, you know the otherwise, I'm dead. You have any brilliant ideas?"

Evans turned and stared at the computer screen. "Crumbs, or I can just kill all three of them," Evans suggested.

"I don't know if I wanted to know that," Tina responded flatly, a bewildered look on her face.

"Crumbs," Evans repeated.

CHAPTER SIXTY-EIGHT

One Week before End-of-the-Year Conference

Evans spoke casually, almost congenially to Jennens. "She was where you told me to find her, 5107 Hillberry Drive in Simi Valley. She has a significant other she lives with, but Tina is out of town till next week."

"How do you know all this?"

He was suspicious, but Evans seemed to have a talent for the unexpected. He didn't answer Jennens.

"Can you bring her to me?"

"I could, forcibly, but there's another way."

Jennens was out of his comfort zone. He needed Evans, he was dangerous, but he had little choice.

"Okay, tell me."

"I did some checking on Tina. She won't just give you the recordings. How were you planning to convince her otherwise?" Evans asked.

"You."

Evans knew that was coming.

"You're the bogeyman, Evans. We spoke about this before. You do this and I'll forget all about you."

"Not good enough, I want the file."

"What file... I don't..."

Evans stopped him. "You want my help or not?"

Jennens weighed his options and decided it was best not to lie to Evans. "Okay. I'll give you everything I have, the entire file."

"No."

"What do you mean no?"

Evans raised his voice and feigned an angry tone. "No, I want a hard drive."

Jennens knew now that Evans knew much more than he'd ever let on. The man was cunning and intelligent. But he had little choice except to negotiate.

"What do you want with my computer? I said I'd destroy the file."

"You really think I believe you, Jennens? Don't take me for a fool."

"What's preventing me from copying the files for insurance?"

"If I suspect you did that, you're dead." Evans took a second to compose himself.

"I need my computer."

"Download everything. I will be there at ten a.m. to pick up all your files."

Jennens was copying a second set of files he'd selectively down- loaded for Evans. He left one file for Evans and copied another for himself. He would take the chance Evans wouldn't know the difference and there was no way he'd leave himself exposed for blackmail in the future. The files he would give him were filled with nonincriminating junk. Besides, he figured Evans didn't know anything about his back-door accounting. It would take years to decipher where the money came from, even if he had all the files.

Evans walked into the large office. Jennens's private space was in the back. A large wall-sized window separated him from the other accounting personnel. The shades were closed.

Evans unceremoniously walked over and stood in front of his desk. Jennens looked up and smirked. "Here," and shoved a stack of CDs at him.

Evans walked toward the window and opened the shutters. Jennens stood. "What are you doing?"

Evans walked out of the office toward a male busily typing. He pulled the chair out from under the clerk, dropping him to the floor, then reached down and disconnected the computer, lifting it under his arm.

Jennens ran out of his office as the clerk stood and attempted to grab the device back.

Evans grabbed the man by his shirt collar and looked at Jennens, who suddenly stopped. Evans gave the man a shove, which caused him to fall over his chair and tumble backwards, landing hard on the floor. He moaned and rolled back and forth. Evans walked out.

Jennens screamed at the limp body rolling in pain. "What the fuck was on that computer?"

Evans had previously downloaded every file from Jennens's computer, eliminating the junk. He already had the files from the idiot clerk. Taking the computer was simply to put Jennens on notice, to make sure he would not try anything extraordinarily stupid.

CHAPTER SIXTY-NINE

Evans sat in the park, all the old guys were there. They listened with purpose. As Evans outlined his plans for Jeremy, Jennens, and Karlson, the men said nothing.

Ben spoke first. "Okay, that takes care of the battle, what about the war?"

Evans pulled out the CDs. "I did my best to eliminate the junk that Jennens left for distraction. I think he didn't have enough time to erase all the dirt. If you have someone dig through the files, quickly, we have him and anyone else he's been paying off."

"We have friends who can handle it," Ben assured.

Evans thought how ridiculous he must have sounded. Of course, they had people everywhere.

"And we know it's time sensitive." Ben went on. "You've received a letter."

Ben chose his words carefully. "I have difficulty with it."

"Go on."

"I'd rather all three."

"We have plans for the other two; we need them," Ben said with authority.

Evans let it go and passed the disk to Ben. The men looked down at their chess pieces, signaling to Evans he was excused.

CHAPTER SEVENTY

Jeremy sat at his computer and rifled through Lumas's cases. Only two were in the intensive care unit, one of which would probably die in the next few days. There were numerous consultants working on the other sick vet, someone would notice a dosage change or medication error and change the orders, other than Lumas. Jeremy needed a case that was straightforward, one that Lumas handled alone and looked like irresponsible and incompetent care that led to a patient death or near death. Jeremy would, of course, save the patient's life in the end. His backup plan was simple, if a case didn't materialize, he'd just transfer care of another patient to Lumas, someone too late to save.

Dino was closely following Jeremy, scrolling through charts at the same time, but he had to be constantly on the alert to monitor Jeremy's use of the hospital records. Jeremy could make the changes at any time, so it required constant review of Jeremy's logging in and checking any changes he made to Lumas's orders. Jeremy would have to make a subtle but lethal change in orders or ventilator settings. He could also sabotage procedures—there were any number of ways to kill a veteran.

Dino needed help, he left and stood in front of the class pictures and wrote the names of the interns who didn't graduate from the program over the last four years: Doctors Bhar, Thompson, Starks, and Lin. Their contact information was still in the database. He thought it was worth a try and called Dr. Starks's number first.

"Hello?"

"Dr. Starks, this is Dr. Guitano at the VA." Starks didn't say anything in response.

Dino surmised the call would initially be traumatic and immediately evoke a torrent of emotions. He waited and said nothing.

"Why are you calling me?" Starks asked.

"I know this call is a shock, but I know what Jeremy has done to you and other physicians."

"Don't call me that, I'm not a physician, I was thrown out of the program."

Dino cringed, his heart skipped a beat, he became nauseous. "I know, I know everything, and I found out who set you up."

"Dr. Guitano, everyone knew who set me up, no one did anything to stop Jeremy or Karlson."

Guitano took a deep breath. "I can help you get back into the program, but I really need your help."

"No."

Dino's brain began clicking. He had to convince Dr. Starks that he was sincere, and he could help him to recover his life. He had an idea. "Dr. Starks, may I send you a text in about ten minutes?"

Dino called Evans. "Do you investigate all the suicides in the hospital?" he asked.

"I do a preliminary investigation, interviews and pictures mostly. The rest is done at a level above the local hospitals. That usually means nothing is done. The rate of suicides overwhelms the staffing power to do anything like an adequate investigation. What do you want?"

Starks opened the text message. "Oh my god."

The body of an old man hung from the handle of a Hoyer

lift. His neck was stretched grotesquely, his face dusky blue. A thick red wire cut off the blood supply to his head resulting in one eye bulging out of the socket, the other hanging over his left cheek by threads of thin veins. Both hands, frozen in rigor mortis, were clutching the noose.

He ran to the toilet and vomited.

When he composed himself, he called Dino. "Jeremy, my God, I didn't think he would go that far. The poor guy must have criticized him openly. I guess Jeremy made it look like suicide."

"Yes."

"What can I—"

Dino interrupted. "Meet me at this address," telling Starks the location.

"No, not before I contact Bhar and Thompson, they'll want to help."

"What about Lin?"

"Jeff jumped off the Colorado Street Bridge last year."

CHAPTER SEVENTY-ONE

Evans, Tina, and Michelle were working to get Jennens. Dino, Ganz, Thompson, Bhar, and Starks were after Karlson and Jeremy. Ben and company emailed them when they found anything useful. It all began with greed, corruption, and a lack of ethics and morality. And worse, eventually, it led to the deaths of otherwise innocent men and women.

Evans and the crew were making better progress than Dino's group. But Ben and the older men found bank accounts, transfer vouchers, and, most important, the recipients of Jennens's bribes. They had resources that stunned Evans and had collected all this information in forty-eight hours, plowing through hundreds of files. Their network of highly skilled individuals must have been enormous. They collected the data; it was up to Evans to use it when he thought the timing was right. Dino and company shared shifts and monitored Jeremy's emails, texts, and electronic pharmacy orders around the clock.

Evans had a long talk with Tina and her companion. Neither were enthusiastic about his plans for them but neither argued.

Dino and Evans guessed Jennens would do his deadly deed in the evening or early in the morning, avoiding the frenzy of physicians checking new lab results or new orders from the nighttime physician. The conference was only two days away.

CHAPTER SEVENTY-TWO

When the phone rang at ten p.m., Dino was groggy but perked up when he heard Starks's voice. "Jeremy is online doing a lot of research on a patient in the ICU. I think it's the case he was looking for and it's Lumas's patient."

"Tell me."

"Straightforward as you thought. It's a forty-five-year-old guy with an uncomplicated heart attack. Vitals are stable, no signs of heart failure, straightforward. But he has runs of cardiac arrhythmias and is on meds for it. Looks like he's dependent on the drip till his heart is more stable."

Dino sighed, rubbing a hand over his forehead. "One more item we uncovered."

"What's that?"

"Jeremy is not very creative. We were all fired in the same way. Last day of the program, all the patients were in the intensive care unit and all deaths were medication errors. Supposedly, all of us picked up the wrong medication from the cabinet and killed the patient."

"Didn't the pharmacy or the attendings do a case review?"

"No, there was a different attending each year, none of them made any inquiries, including the pharmacy. All those deaths were just covered up and we took the hit for them."

"What are you—"

Starks interrupted him. "You don't get it; all the attending professors know Jeremy is killing patients and no one is saying a thing."

Dino went silent.

"Are you still there, Dino?"

"I can't believe it."

"Believe it, no one will stand up to Jeremy and Karlson. The two of them probably have something on everyone, from funding grants, affairs with staff, promotions, corrupting data, gifts from pharmaceutical companies, etc. Don't be so surprised. Anyone here could have turned in Jeremy for the morbidity he's caused the vets over the years, but they chose to ignore the obvious. There is a culture of silence and fear."

If Starks was right, Dino was in way over his head. He made himself a cup of coffee, paced back and forth, and then called Evans. "I–I–I," he stuttered. "I think I am way out of my league. I've had former interns, interns who were fired by the chief of staff…"

"Karlson," Evans supplied. "How did you know?"

"Go on."

"Everything, everything having to do with unexpected deaths was done on purpose, the staff, all of them are in on this."

Silence, then Dino heard Evans take a deep breath. "You don't know the half of it, but you and your associates are doing a good job of snooping."

"Wait a second, you knew all this before. You've been following our searches every day."

"Not every day, that wasn't necessary. I just tapped into the files you created daily."

"But those files have passwords, how did you do that?"

Evans's tone became curt. Dino was afraid he'd pissed him off, maybe by insinuating that Evans couldn't break into files so easily.

"That's enough questions and answers. Have all your incriminating charts ready to present at your conference, rounds, whatever you nerds call it. Don't screw it up, let me repeat myself: Be prepared. What time does it begin and end?"

"This Friday from five until six-thirty p.m., the entire staff are required to attend."

"Okay, after your conference, I assume Jeremy and his boss will probably want to leave soon, along with probably a lot of the other physicians. Don't hesitate to leave yourself, no explanations, and don't engage in conversations or get trapped in explaining anything, just leave."

"Then what?"

"Then nothing, go home," Evans answered sarcastically.

Dino was afraid of Evans. He gulped and fell backwards on his bed. "I'm dead."

CHAPTER SEVENTY-THREE

Evans called Jennens.

"I have Tina's girlfriend."

"Where is Tina?"

"She'll give you the recordings for the safe return of her significant other."

"Did the girlfriend resist?"

"Yes."

Jennens's text screen flashed open. A woman was smashed into a car trunk, bound and gagged. Her eyes were swollen shut, lower lip splayed open, cut through and through, and her clothes were covered in blood. She appeared unconscious.

"Did you kill her?"

"Not yet."

"So, we're doing an exchange."

"Yes."

"What assurance do I have that Tina will give me all the recordings?"

"I know where her mother and father live."

"Well done, Evans."

"Don't patronize me, Jennens. I'd just as well off you too."

Jennens said nothing after his attempt between sarcasm and being condescending backfired.

"I'll contact you when and where tomorrow but for now plan on afternoon." Evans hung up.

CHAPTER SEVENTY-FOUR

Lumas was having an argument with the wall. He screamed obscenities, spit, and kicked, until people came out of their offices and stared. Upon seeing the crowd gather, he turned and ran down the service stairwell and strode into the ICU.

He caught everyone's attention by announcing his entrance, loudly. "Lumas is here."

Even Dino was surprised, but he kept his distance. He had his occasional concerns that all the borderline behavior was invented, but he couldn't be entirely sure. He hadn't spoken with Lumas in a week. Jeremy would think even his best friend had abandoned him. As quick as his outburst began, he stopped, took a chair at the desk and stared at his patient.

Howard Freedman, aged sixty-four, suffered a myocardial infarction, was on an amiodarone drip, stable, and scheduled for an electrical cardioversion tomorrow morning. All routine. Afterward, he'd be transferred out of the unit to cardiac rehab. Lumas was responsible for running the procedure scheduled at four p.m. Jeremy insisted Lumas was in charge, no excuses.

After an uncomfortable fifteen minutes, one of the nurses approached him. "Dr. Lumas, can I get you anything?"

"Yes," he answered, not making eye contact with her. "I need, I need..." he began to quote Marcus Aurelius as he stared off into space. "How I die is my decision. How I depart is my intention. My life is mine, so is my death. How I depart is my tension."

He stood and walked out.

The nurse felt a coldness throughout her body. She had no idea what he had been mumbling about, only the word death stuck in her mind. She reported what Lumas had said to the nursing director. "Thank you," the director turned and walked away. She closed her office door and called Frieda. She spoke in a most serious and cold intonation, purposefully. "This is Margaret O'Grady, nursing director. I am afraid Dr. Lumas has had a psychological meltdown of some sort. Maybe you can check on him later today. I don't know much more, but it seems serious."

Without giving Frieda time to speak, she hung up. Frieda wasn't surprised.

CHAPTER SEVENTY-FIVE

Lumas walked around the large outside parking area, feeling only half alive. He was lost in both time and space. While everyone was thinking he was playing the part of a decompensated schizophrenic, he was dying a little more every day. The days sucked the remaining psychological strength he had remaining.

How dare they ask him to sink further into the darkness of Dante's hell? He had no strength to continue and began to contemplate ending his life. He gazed up at the highest floor of the hospital. The sun reflected brightly off the windows into his eyes. He looked away, but large black circles temporarily blinded his vision.

"Dr. Lumas, are you all right?"

Lumas couldn't see the man's face but his voice was familiar. "It's Evans."

Lumas turned, the big security guard was in his face. "You look a bit disoriented. Here, get into the car."

"No, I'll be okay, thanks."

Evans grabbed him under his right shoulder and pushed him toward the car door.

"Evans, what are you doing? I said I'm okay."

A woman's voice spoke from inside the car. "Dr. Lumas, we know you're okay. Evans is a bit rough, but we mean you no harm. Can you please get in the car? It's important."

Lumas was still partially blinded, but the woman's voice was consoling. "Elliot, it's okay. Get in the car."

Lumas's face filled with surprise. "Frieda?" he asked.

"Yes, it's me."

His vision cleared, without saying anything more, he opened the door and slipped halfway in.

"Hey, this is my car, how the hell did you get my car?"

Evans spoke. "No one screws with a security guard breaking into a car. You really don't take care of your ride, Doc. The transmission slips, you have an oil leak, the tires are bald, and the back seat looks like a shithole."

Lumas looked at Evans in dismay. "The obvious question then is why did you steal it?"

Evans parodied him. Frieda was silent.

Tina tapped Evans on the shoulder. "Let's go."

The car sputtered off with all three flopping back and forth till the clutch engaged.

"Piece-of-shit car," Evans mumbled.

Evans drove the car directly into Tina's garage. The three got out of the car and walked into a spacious living room with the fireplace blazing. The walls were filled with photographs of stout soldiers with uniforms from the Vietnam War and vintage signed Civil War photographs taken by Mathew Brady. Lumas was amazed. An attractive red-headed woman stood and rounded the couch and extended her hand.

"I am Michelle, Tina's significant other. Welcome."

"Thank you. The photos are amazing."

"Ahh, yes they are, the Civil War photographs tell the story of Brady's passion to leave a legacy of the most horrible war in history. He captured the fear and despair in the eyes of the soldiers and families they left behind."

Lumas looked at her surprised. "These are originals…"

"Is that a question or a statement, Doctor?"

"I have volumes of books on the Civil War, it's kind of a passion of mine in an eerie way. No one photographed the horrors of war like Brady. These are originals," Lumas confirmed.

"Bravo, Doctor," she commended.

"Why am I here? Why is Frieda here?" Lumas asked, still staring at the photos.

"We're going to stop you from killing a vet tomorrow."

Lumas was numb. "I never killed any—"

She interrupted him. "We know that. Thanks to your friends at the VA, we found out in time. There's a lot more. Let's have dinner; we'll tell you everything."

Lumas listened to the events of morbid and avoidable complications, deaths, and murder since Jeremy arrived at the VA four years ago. There was no way to prove anything until Tina was lucky enough to be in the right place at the right time when all three—Jennens, Jeremy, and Karlson—boasted about their exploits and she recorded their conversation. Michelle emphasized that the VA was filled with patriots working in different departments, doing everything from clerical to janitorial.

"There were some things we had to do that were heartbreaking. The patient, Betty, who was dying on oncology, we helped her die."

Lumas looked around the table. Evans was the only one staring him in the eyes.

"And we had to eliminate Patrick before he killed you; he would have."

"So, what am I here for? I am totally confused. Where do I fit into all this?"

"Well, Frieda, you may want to hold your friend's hand now." She did.

"Tonight, you're going to have a terrible accident and end up in the hospital."

"What the hell—"

Evans caught him mid-sentence. "Don't worry. You won't end up a quadriplegic. It will just consist of some bumps, scrapes, and the destruction of your car."

"My car!" Lumas protested. "What am I am supposed to do for transportation?"

Michelle smiled at him. "You won't need a car for a while. Lovely Frieda has taken care of that."

Michelle winked at Frieda.

Tina curtly interrupted. "Okay, then folks, let's get going."

"Wait, don't I have anything to say about this?"

Evans rounded the table, put his arm around Lumas's shoulders. "If you do this, you'll save a lot of lives, now let's go," he said.

Evans and Lumas drove his car with the three women following into one of the canyons from the valley to the Pacific Coast Highway.

Compared to the others, that canyon had a paucity of cement blocks between cars and a three-thousand-foot vertical drop to a dry creek bed. There were at least thirty collisions a year and sixty percent resulted in severe injuries.

It was dark, as Evans passed one of two tunnels and made a sharp turn, skidding to a stop just a few feet away from the steep drop. Lumas took a deep breath.

"Don't worry, you're safe, for now," Evans said. "That's not funny, Evans," Lumas hissed.

"I wasn't trying to make a joke. Get out and hurry." Lumas dropped his right foot on the ground, just as the car lunged forward and careened over the cliff.

"What the hell, Evans? You could have killed me!" Evans smirked at him.

The second car pulled up quickly before any other cars were looping around the switchbacks. Evans and Lumas jumped in. Michelle drove down the hill and turned off onto a long narrow road without streetlights.

"So now what?" Lumas asked.

Michelle turned to Frieda. "You come with us."

She took a flashlight from her purse and the three women left the car and disappeared into the underbrush. Lumas looked at Evans. The man was an imposing figure, if not a downright terrifying man—all muscle, brains, and business.

"Did they have to pee that badly?"

"I dunno, let's get out. I wanna stretch."

Lumas followed Evans as he investigated the brush as if he were seriously focusing on something down below. Lumas leaned over to get a better look.

"Sorry, Doc."

"What?"

With an effortless push, Lumas went tumbling head over heels through dead brush and small boulders.

"Uhh, ow, uhh, uhh, uhh, ehh, ehh, shit, shit!"

Some fifty feet below, he ceased falling with a thumping plop and rolled over in pain. He moaned loudly and heard footsteps approaching. He attempted to stand and run, thinking it was Evans approaching to finish him off. Someone pointed a flashlight in his eyes.

"Oh, Lumas, my babe, are you okay?" Frieda asked.

Lumas was still gasping for air. "No. Why did Evans do that? Is he coming back? Does my arm look broken? Shit, I hurt like hell. Let's get out of here before he returns."

"I'm right behind you, Doc."

Lumas let out a yelp. "Stay away from me."

He backed up and bumped into Michelle and Tina.

"Did you break anything, Doc?" Michelle asked in a caring tone. "No, I don't think so, but keep Evans away from me."

He turned to Evans, but he was gone, then back to the women. A millisecond later, Michelle slugged him in the nose. Lumas fell to the ground in excruciating pain. He felt the warm ooze drip down his nostril and down the side of his face. His head was spinning. He was on both knees in a fetal position, drooling blood.

Tina raised his head.

"Don't fucking hit me again. Woman or no woman, I am going to kick the crap out of both of you."

"No, I think you look convincing enough now."

"For what?"

"Driving off the cliff, rather veering off the road to avoid a drunk driver, and agile enough to jump out. Congratulations. Now, let's drop you back at the launch site."

"That is not funny at all."

Evans called the highway patrol after dropping Lumas off at the crash site. He declined to identify himself and left with the women. After questioning him about the details of the crash and near-death experience, the officer took a breathalyzer test and cleared the paramedics to transport him to the nearest local hospital. After a standard series of labs and X-rays and Lumas's persistent complaints of back and neck pain, he was scheduled for a twenty-four-hour period of observation.

CHAPTER SEVENTY-SIX

The last conference of the year was scheduled at five p.m. Jeremy ordered a ten-cc syringe vial of Dilantin and carefully replaced the label from Dilaudid to Dilantin. The patient was to have an intravenous line placed in the interior jugular vein and Dilaudid would be used for simple sedation. It was an easy procedure done in less than fifteen minutes. Jeremy insisted Lumas do the procedure. Starks monitored the drug distribution from the pharmacy all night long and saw Jeremy ordered Dilantin and Dilaudid. Switching the drugs would cause a lethal cardiac arrhythmia and sudden death.

After that, Jeremy could invent any contrived complication to pin on Lumas.

"Dino, this is Starks. Jeremy just substituted medications. Come down. I'll show you how he's going to frame Lumas."

Dino was about to hang up the phone when he heard Starks's comment. "Whoa, what's going on here?"

The computer screen was flashing on and off. Then one final plop and an Excel program appeared. On the vertical column were lists of clinical instructors and dates. Horizontal columns listed drugs and dosages, and the far right vertical column listed interns. The data was scrolling so fast it was impossible for Starks to read names with absolute certainty.

"Dino, get down here fast, please."

Starks looked hypnotized when Dino entered the lounge, still transfixed on the screen.

He nudged Starks's shoulder.

"Someone is downloading all the pharmacy distributions for years."

"Why would the pharmacists do that?"

"I don't think they know they're being hacked."

"Then why is it on your screen?"

"My guess is the hacker has been following our progress, he or she wants us to know it now."

"Can you print?"

"No."

"Screenshot?"

"No."

Dino dropped into a chair.

"Do you think someone here is doing this?"

"Nope, too sophisticated."

Starks looked at Dino.

"Whatever is happening is bigger than Jeremy, Karlson, Lumas, all of us, the hospital, maybe even the university."

CHAPTER SEVENTY-SEVEN

Jeremy sat in his office waiting for the code blue. At four-thirty, the operator sounded the alarm and announced, "Code Blue, ICU bed 10." He casually walked to the service stairwell next to his office headed for the ICU floor. He grabbed the handle but became distracted by a white coat crumpled in the corner stairwell. He picked it up. Lumas's name badge and stethoscope dangled from the dirty lab coat.

Jeremy smiled. "Gotcha, Lumas."

Jeremy approached Dino. "What are you doing here? Lumas was supposed to do the procedure."

"I was told he was here earlier, but I didn't see him. We went ahead and gave him a shot of Dilaudid and his heart stopped, we couldn't resuscitate him."

"Who is we?"

"The director of nurses was helping me."

The curtains were closed around the hospital bed. Jeremy walked there and pulled the curtains back like he expected to find Lumas hiding. The man's face was uncovered. Before Jeremy arrived, the director of nurses had cornered Dino.

"Don't ask questions, help me cover this guy. He died this morning, so I kept him here. And change his patient ID tag before your boss arrives. Stop staring at me and move it. What the hell made you think you could fool Jeremy into thinking a sleeping vet is a dead vet?"

"I was hoping to distract him."

She looked at him like he was an imbecile.

The director of nurses walked toward Jeremy and pulled the curtain out of his hands.

"Can we have a little respect, please?"

Jeremy barked at Dino, faking indignation. "Show me the medication vials."

Dino pushed the procedure tray toward Jeremy. Without hesitation, he picked out the Dilaudid vial and began picking at the label until it tore off and "Dilantin 100mg IV injectable" could be clearly read.

"I can't believe Lumas would kill someone," Dino said, sounding alarmed.

Jeremy pointed at the director of nurses. "You, call the VA guard. Don't move anything."

Evans walked into the ICU fifteen minutes later.

Jeremy spoke authoritatively. "I am in charge here. One of the doctors killed a patient this morning. I found his white coat in the stairwell. His name is Lumas."

"Is that all you have, Doctor? How do you know it was him? What's your proof?"

Jeremy became irritated. "Don't question me."

Evans pretended conciliation. "Okay, no more questions. Get out so I can start my investigation."

"Investigation? What's to investigate, look at this." Jeremy picked up the partially sealed vial of Dilantin and poked it at Evans's face. "This is what killed that guy over there. Dr. Lumas did this. I have proof."

Evans let him go on, he acted interested.

"Yes, proof, I have been tracking his prescribing practices all year. He's a psychopath; he's killed other patients."

"Why didn't you report this sooner if you were so sure?"

"I'm planning to expose him tonight in front of the entire staff, others will come forward and say the same. Up until today we all suspected it was Lumas killing patients, but now I have proof. It's time to say it to his face, in front of everyone, he can't cover his ass in front of the entire staff."

"Doctor, since when are you the judge and jury?" Evans was needling him more. He wanted to make sure Jeremy would have no second thoughts about his big show tonight. Pissing him off would bend his ego even more, if that was at all possible.

Jeremy stepped away from the big man.

Evans's tone softened. "Before I call the feds, can I go to your lecture tonight and see the evidence for myself?"

Dino picked up what Evans was doing and stepped forward. "Neither of you are the judge and jury." He raised his voice. "Call off the conference, Jeremy. It's no place to make accusations."

"No, and shut up." Evans turned to Dino. "I want to hear what you have on this guy, Lumas, I'll record it. If you're right the feds will be... well, we'll see, won't we?"

Evans gave Jeremy a cryptic grin. Jeremy turned and walked out. Jennens called Evans at four p.m.

"Where is she and where are the recordings?"

"I'm going to drop her off at parking lot two in the back of the old research buildings at six, spot sixty-one. It will be dark then. I've taken care of the other woman. Give her the location I'll text you; her girlfriend's in the trunk. Don't be late."

Evans went to his office and texted Karlson from Jennens's number. By now, he had the ability to text anyone using someone else's cell number. Whatever additional help he required came from the old guys.

Jennens (CEO) to Karlson (COS): "Meet me at lot two, 5:45, spot 61. Don't be late or I'll leave."

CHAPTER SEVENTY-EIGHT

Thompson had his feet stretched out on the computer table when Dino walked in with Amin. The big canine sat next to him and begged for head scratches.

"Why aren't you digging for more pharmacy dirt? The conference starts in an hour. We need—"

"I know, I know. It should be here very soon."

"We don't know each other well but, do you have a drug problem?

What are you talking about?"

Starks was a tall Afro-American man who seemed unusually calm. There was no anger in the man's emotional or physical demeanor, he was calm and focused.

Dino didn't understand why Thompson wasn't a psychological wreck. "How can you be so calm?" Dino asked.

"Hmm, where can I start? I needed to understand what good I could make of what then seemed like the end of my life. I learned it wasn't; life still putters along and there was no way I was going to feel sorry for myself in the time I had left of my life. No one could take that from me, no one. I traveled a lot and found a world filled with people who are happy and content with little or nothing. Communal, social people who enjoyed life without the accolades and avarice. It was hard, Dino, don't want to make this sound simple. It was really hard and required lots of work."

He reached out to pet Amin and continued. "Losing the position two years ago and finding an alternative purpose was my destiny, adversity might have damaged my dignity and self-esteem, but I found purpose again. After all, life without adversity was an emperor's life." Lumas recalled a TED Talk that greatly perplexed him. An Afro-American wrongly incarcerated for thirty years was finally acquitted. When freed and asked about his experience of being wrongly jailed, he answered, "It was a grand experience, a grand experience."

Dino was losing patience. His way of handling adversity was to attack and conquer. He advanced toward Thompson and raised his voice. "Okay, do we just sit here and wait while Jeremy skewers Lumas?"

Amin had been lying in the corner with his eyes at half-mast. When Dino raised his voice, the dog sat and fixed his eyes on them both.

Thompson chuckled and dropped his legs.

"Don't laugh. We have to stop that maniac and Karlson." Dino was panicking and becoming aggressive. Again, he raised his voice. "I am getting back on the computer if you don't." Dino walked toward Thompson's computer.

Amin sprang to his feet and lunged at Dino's back, gripping a mouthful of his white lab coat. Dino fell backward and took a hard thud on the linoleum. Dino writhed in pain, the fall knocked the wind out of his lungs. Amin sat next to Dino, then lay his muscular body over his chest, further restricting Dino's ability to catch his breath.

"Amin, what the fuck?" he gasped.

Thompson interrupted. "Animals are intuitive like that. He sensed no anger coming from me, just you. You weren't threatened by me in any way. Small dogs would whine and cry, your monster was just cooling you off. You should give him a big scratch on his head."

Dino rolled over and looked at Amin. "I'm going to make a carpet of you one day." He stood. "Sorry, really sorry."

"No problem."

"Look, someone has been following everything that's happening right up until this very moment. The cryptic texts you've received, the big man who materialized from nowhere, even the deaths, there is some purpose here."

"Purpose, is there some purpose to murder?" Thompson asked, careful not to raise his voice. "We're not expected to understand everything, Dino, but that doesn't mean we shouldn't help to stop it."

The screen lit up. It was the Excel spreadsheet again but this time with much less data.

They both studied it for five minutes without speaking.

Dino spoke with a tone somewhere between sadness and disappointment. "I had no idea it was this many vets."

Thompson said, "And look at the pharmacy orders. The prescribing doctors, there are so many staff members who changed meds, dosages, or intervals. This means the morbidity rate is much higher than reported. Jeremy is the most egregious. He killed patients. The other docs were, *are,* covering their mistakes. How could this have been missed?"

"It wasn't missed. It was covered over, buried, probably ordered by Karlson. High morbidity rates would ruin his promotion to the main campus."

"Why didn't the pharmacy director report these?" Thompson asked.

"Probably brought it to Karlson's attention, and he ordered Jeremy to threaten the director with something, who knows what."

"So, let's go after the director."

Dino took a deep breath. "Not necessary and not possible. Number one, we have all the information we need from this spread-sheet and number two, the pharmacy director is out of the country learning another language."

Thompson looked at Dino with a sarcastic frown. "So why send this to us? Whoever hacked and organized the data could have just as well sent this to the feds."

"Because for better or worse, we are right in the middle of this. Some of our colleagues, people we trust, are probably on this list. We need only to find their ID numbers. But I have no intention of doing it. Once we nail Jeremy for killing vets, along with firing you and the other interns, the rest of this goes to the Department of Justice. Then all hell breaks loose, and we are witnesses. Either way, we're screwed." Thompson spoke so softly Dino could barely hear what he said. "The present moment is *all you need*. It's enough. Good or bad. Scary or exciting. A man must live in the present and face it with courage.

Starting today."

"You sound like Lumas," Dino commented.

CHAPTER SEVENTY-NINE

Lumas had lots of time in the hospital to read. The early morning before shift change was dead. The night nurses were charting, the air filled with the sound of their pens softly scratching at paper. Patients were still sleeping, and dawn was just an hour away.

He closed the door.

Frieda was sound asleep in the pullout chair. Today was D-Day. But he was clueless to the plans, whether they were organized plans or if the whole lot was just winging it, attempting to catch Jeremy and Karlson in lies.

Before Evans and the two women left the hospital, Evans said to him, "Stay here." Not so much a request as an order.

He had to occupy his mind and opened *Meditations* to read on his cell phone.

"People try to get away from it all—to the country, to the beach, to the mountains… Which is idiotic: you can get away from it anytime you like. By going within. Nowhere you can go is more peaceful—more free of interruptions—than your own soul.

"Ignoring what goes on in other people's souls—no one ever came to grief that way. But if you won't keep track of what your own soul's doing, how can you not be unhappy?

"To shrug it all off and wipe it clean—every annoyance and distraction—and reach utter stillness.

"The things you think about determine the quality of your mind. Your soul takes on the color of your thoughts.

"When jarred, unavoidably, by circumstances, revert at once to yourself, and don't lose the rhythm more than you can help. You'll have a better grasp of the harmony if you keep on going back to it.

"You have to assemble your life yourself—action by action. And be satisfied if one achieves one's goal, as far as one can. No one can keep that from happening."

"How do you feel?" Frieda asked.

Lumas looked at Frieda, she was truly a beautiful woman - Middle Eastern, with gorgeous, tanned features and golden hair, a firecracker, provocative and intelligent. What Lumas really appreciated about her was her honesty. She loved life, despite the heartbreak of her mother's psychological health. She also had a hearty laugh, from deep down. Lumas laughed.

"My nose is broken, and I have two black eyes. I'm black and blue from head to toe, and I think my incisors are loose. I can't feel my face because I'm too swollen and the facial nerves are protesting by occasionally shocking me with excruciating neuropathic pain. I think some thorns are stuck in my hair, all my hair from head to groin, and I think something bit me on the ass."

Frieda began to laugh and covered her mouth with both hands. "You're all going to purgatory for a while."

He tried to smile, but then became serious. "What's going on, Frieda? I mean, why all the theatrics? Why is Evans involved with the residency program and who were the ninja sisters?"

"I wish I knew. All I was told was we were to stay here and expect a video call in about an hour. And specifically, to stay here till that call comes through. He emphasized the call would be coming from Dino, and he depended on you being right in this hospital room to answer it."

"But the conference is beginning in half an hour," Lumas

began, but the pain from speaking made him grab his jaw. "OWWWW! Goddammit, that woman has a powerful slug."

"Lie down. I'll rub your back, uhh legs, uhh shoulders, uhh never mind. I think that would torture you more. Maybe I can massage your palms."

They both laughed.

"Very funny," Lumas managed to get out, between painful gasps.

"Big baby," Freida whispered.

"What did you say?"

"Nothing."

Karlson sat at the front of the room as was customary for the chiefs of staff. He was surrounded by the other chiefs from all the other medical divisions. All the staff were required to attend the last conference of the year. The new chief residents and the list of grants awarded to individual divisions announced.

Jeremy was responsible for reviewing the yearly mortality and morbidity statistics and for figuring out ways to improve the data and highlight the program as one of the best. There were five other programs at different hospitals, all supervised from the main campus. The room was full, standing room only. No one noticed the three former interns sitting together in the middle of the room.

He stepped to the podium. "Good evening, everyone. Welcome to the last conference of the year."

Coming from him, this caused silence at a time when interns would normally yelp for joy.

Jeremy didn't look up. Unembarrassed and not caring either way, he proceeded to thank Karlson for his dedication to the program and mentioned his upcoming sabbatical. "Dr. Karlson has offered me the position of acting chief in his absence. I have graciously accepted."

No one applauded. Karlson knew where this was going and decided to make his exit earlier than planned by Jeremy.

"May I interrupt you, Jeremy?"

Jeremy looked up at Karlson and gave him a suspicious gaze. "Yes, uhh, yes, of course."

Karlson took the position next to Jeremy who didn't move, nudging shoulders with his boss like they were old friends. "Well, it's been a wonderful year. I will return in six months to clean my desk and hand over the reins to Jeremy. You can't get rid of me that fast, Jeremy."

No one thought his humor was anything but pathetic.

Karlson continued, "I have a plane to catch shortly and my wife will kill me if I'm late. So maybe we can announce the morbidity and mortality data first. The university will be impressed with the dedication to medical excellence this class has shown."

Jeremy stepped up. "Of course. Our stats rival the other programs, making our program number one in the system."

Karlson and Jeremy expected applause, none came, the audience continued to remain silent. Karlson caught a few staff eyeing him with profound disdain. Jeremy looked around the room, finally noticing the three former interns. The staff turned to look at what caught Jeremy's attention so much that his face turned red and his hands began to shake.

"Well, go on, Jeremy. I have a plane to catch."

Jeremy composed himself but didn't take his eyes off the three. "I have an announcement to make. One of our interns will not graduate, and I am afraid his actions will be reported to the university and the authorities. I know all of you have tried to cover for Lumas, that's commendable, but reckless. Many patients were hurt, and I am afraid some may have died due to negligence."

Someone protested from the back of the room. It was Ganz. "That is totally wrong of you to make such a suggestion. Any claim of misdoings should have been brought to the attention of university counsel first. You have no right to make such an assumption."

"I have only lately found out the truth, and I have decided to announce it now to warn all of you to cooperate with the investigation. Further, if you see Lumas in the hospital, you are ordered to call security. This morning a vet was killed by Lumas, so first, we need to protect the vets, that is why it's important to announce this now."

Ganz spoke again. "You said a crime occurred this morning, is that correct?"

"I saw the order written by Lumas yesterday morning to substitute medications that resulted in the death."

"You have no right to make unfounded accusations," Ganz screamed.

"I have a responsibility to protect the veterans. Now, everyone will be on the lookout for him when and if he's stupid enough to return. If he hadn't been so protected throughout the year, I would have stopped the deaths earlier."

Ganz walked toward the front of the room. Karlson knew he had to make an exit soon. "When did the drugs get switched, Jeremy? When did the pharmacy dispense it?"

"At exactly six a.m. today and his ID number was on the order. But who are you to question me?"

Dino was in the back of the room at the audiovisual equipment. Evans sat next to him. The screen on the stage dropped. Jeremy and Karlson turned. Lumas's battered face came into view.

"Lumas, this is Dino. Can you hear me?"

The audience gasped to see Lumas's face. He was barely identifiable.

"Where are you?"

"At Saint John's Health Center in the city."

"How long have you been hospitalized?"

"Three long days now."

"What happened to you?"

"A drunk driver ran me off the road in the canyon, almost killed me."

"Is there a police report?"

"Yes."

Karlson pushed at the screen, angered enough to think Lumas would fall. He grabbed Jeremy by the arm. "You idiot," then stood and walked toward the back exit.

Evans diffidently moved his chair closer to the door, blocking Karlson's exit.

Over the speakers, voices were clearly speaking. Jeremy, Jennens, and Karlson could be heard negotiating plans for exchanging VA monies and disappearing after firing Lumas. One planned a sabbatical, and one planned to retire. Jeremy's voice could be heard clearly admitting he hung the old vet. The audience was transfixed by what they heard.

Dino turned off the recording and opened the Excel spreadsheet, displaying it on the screen, while Jeremy and Karlson watched angrily. Karlson was trying to push Evans out of his way until Amin trounced over toward Karlson's groin and flashed his white canines.

"Here we have the list of drugs, dates ordered and released by the pharmacy, and the ID numbers of the interns for the last four years. On the surface, it all looks very straightforward to us. To experts, who know how to go deeper into the hard drive, all the data you see has been corrupted. Orders were written by those doctors, appropriate orders."

He pointed at the three physicians sitting together and Lumas.

He flashed another Excel program onto the screen. "Here you see the changes made by physician 6755 and after the meds were released by the pharmacy the original physician's ID was replaced again. After all the jostling, the changes look just like the original physician wrote orders that killed or severely endangered the patients."

Someone asked a question from the back of the room. "Why didn't the pharmacy clarify physician 6755 making blatant medication errors?"

"Simple. Jeremy knows everyone's ID numbers, he never used his number to make the changes, only the target interns. No one would have known the difference if the pharmacy computer wasn't hacked and analyzed. Jeremy and Dr. Karlson have been doing this for years."

Karlson grabbed the doorknob. Amin lunged but Evans grabbed his collar. He looked at his watch. "You can go now."

Karlson texted Jennens. "I am on my way, have the money ready." Evans texted Jennens. "Tina will be there in twenty minutes.

Don't screw with me, Jennens." Then he sent another text. "Karlson and Jennens on the way, ready here in ten."

Karlson picked up the pace to his office. He could explain his way out of anything. His ego and years of experience lying and maneuvering his way to the top gave him an edge on Jeremy. He had a plan, but first he wanted his money.

CHAPTER EIGHTY

Jennens drove Evans's VA security cruiser, which he'd stolen earlier. He was not going to have to look over his shoulder for the rest of his life. Evans had an invisible past and the feds would be most interested in interrogating him first. He parked in the darkness of the old, dilapidated brick buildings. All the parking lights were out of order, it was pitch black, but he could still discern the silhouette of someone. The area was empty, he started the engine, turned on the high beam headlights, and began to creep forward.

Jennens pushed the accelerator to the floor, the rear wheels burned rubber, and the car raced forward. Thirty feet, twenty, fifteen, when he was just about to slam into the person, the headlights shined on the terrified face of Karlson, who waved too late.

Jennens was shocked when he saw the horrified look in Karlson's eyes. He hit the brakes, but the old cement, littered with pea-sized pebbles, didn't stop the momentum. Karlson took the brunt of the blow to his chest. His upper body arched down by the centripetal force, sent his head crashing into the hood.

Jennens hit the brakes simultaneously spinning the car in a semicircle. It catapulted Karlson's limp lifeless body, which careened on the cement, rolling numerous times to a stop. Jennens was still screaming when the cruiser slammed into a pile of cement blocks. He hit the steering wheel and window hard, knocking him unconscious. Tina and Michelle walked out from behind the dark building.

They looked at Karlson first.

"Dead, really dead," Michelle said.

Tina pointed at the cruiser. "What about him?"

"Probable concussion, chest contusions, small stuff."

"Dislocate his shoulders, so he can't open the car door. Then open all the suitcases, especially the briefcase, and throw everything in and around the car, including the recordings."

Tina turned her back as Michelle ripped both rotator cuffs, pulling the humeral head out of the socket. It gave them both the jitters hearing the snap and seeing Jennens's body jerk in excruciating pain. He groaned loudly. Tina covered his mouth until he passed out again. Michelle looked at Tina. "Two down, one to go, that's the deal. Text Evans to call the feds now, and let's get out of here. Evans has this thing for the docs; he'll finish his business tonight. After that, no one knows his plans."

CHAPTER EIGHTY-ONE

Ganz walked toward the front of the packed auditorium. Lumas's face was still on the screen, but now Frieda was next to him.

"Dino, can you explain the final column with ID numbers?"

He hesitated. "Yes, those are the attending instructors' numbers." Some of the professors squirmed.

"Are we to assume some members of the teaching staff knew orders were corrupted and didn't report it?"

"Yes. I have the names of those professors, the dates orders were cosigned by them, and the intern on the case. There were different professors involved with the coverup, some here now, but the same interns were targeted. They are the three people sitting in the middle seats." Dino named each one.

Ganz looked around the room. "Oh my god, has medicine come to this? Do we destroy lives and kill patients? When did we forget the Hippocratic Oath, or were they just empty words? What has occurred here will always be remembered as a repugnant disgrace on our profession."

Jeremy's face turned ashen. He headed for the door, but Evans grabbed his arm and cuffed him to the outside of the room.

"Fuck you, uncuff me!" he demanded.

He pulled and kicked at the door, then felt the presence of someone behind him. The hallway was filled with patients, nurses, clerical staff, the old man with overalls, and Ben and company. No one spoke. Jeremy continued to pull at the cuffs and screamed expletives at the gathered crowd.

Lumas spoke on the screen. "Dino, I have something to say to everyone in the room. First, I harbor no anger in my heart. And second, I can only live in the present and forget the past and not deceive myself that the future may not repeat itself. This is a quote from *Meditations*. "To expect a bad person not to harm others is like expecting fig trees not to secrete juice, babies not to cry, horses not to neigh—the inevitable not to happen. What else could they do—with that sort of character?"

Lumas went on. "Philosophy has become my religion. It has guided me to be a better person and especially not waste my life in fear and anger. Life goes by very fast. I have decided to leave the program, I've graduated, so I may come back one day. But for now, Frieda and I are leaving to work on ourselves, otherwise what kind of physician will I become? As for Jeremy, I do not want blood on my hands, whatever becomes of him is out of my control. The other physicians in this room must decide among themselves what honesty and virtue remains."

Lumas's face disappeared from the screen.

The room emptied, the patients and staff slowly left. No one said anything to Jeremy, who was still pulling at his cuffs.